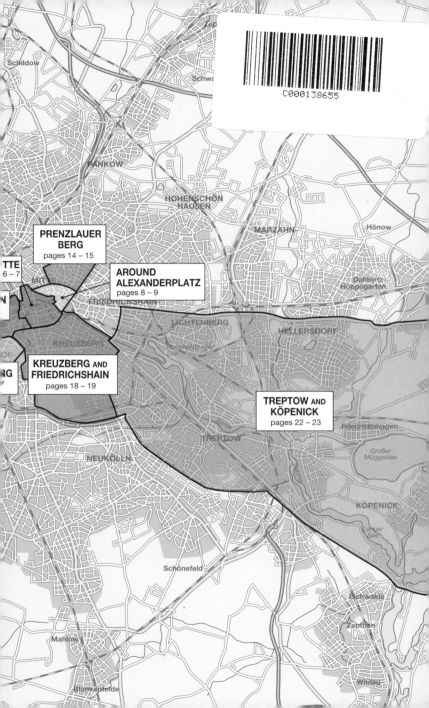

INSIGHT GUIDES

BERLIN
smart guide

APA PUBLICATIONS **L**
Part of the Langenscheidt Publishing Group

Contents

Areas

Below: the iconic East German car: the Trabant.

A–Z

Left: the Berlin Sculpture.

Atlas

Below: in Karl Friedrich Schinkel's graceful square, Gendarmenmarkt.

Berlin

More than any other major European city, Berlin still bears the scars of the last 100 years. The new Berlin does not hide its ghosts. Instead, they live among the bold architecture and hotspots of this gritty, trendy city, which exudes the energy of a capital reborn, but remembers being on the frontline of many pivotal and, at times, dark moments in the 20th century.

Berlin Facts and Figures

Population: **3.4 million (of which 86 percent ethnically German; 23.4 percent between ages of 18 and 35)**
Area: **891 sq km (344 sq miles)**
Buildings destroyed in World War II: **34 percent**
Visitors staying overnight per year: **14.6 million**
Hotels, hostels and pensions: **576**
Theatres: **52**
Museums: **125**
Cinemas: **288**
Number of *Bezirke* (boroughs): **12**
Largest lake: **Grosser Müggelsee**
Tallest building: **the Fernsehturm (368m/1,207ft)**

Division and Reunification

On 9 November 1989, with the eyes of the world watching, the Berlin Wall fell. The frontier at which East met West, the Wall had ripped through the centre of Berlin since 1961 and been the most visible and poignant emblem of the Cold War. After a century of profound tumult in Germany – wars, privation, dictatorships, division – at which Berlin had often found itself at the epicentre, the city was finally in a position to move forward.

And move forward it has. The history of Berlin since that night has been one of the most complete urban transformations in history. In the years since reunification, the redesigned Reichstag is once again the centre of government, Europe's biggest construction site has turned out a glittering new architectural playground, and many parts of central Berlin that had remained piles of rubble since the final days of World War II have finally been regenerated. Meanwhile, musicians, artists, students and entrepreneurs from around the world have flocked to Berlin to be a part of the city's re-emergence.

Berlin's Neighbourhoods

Visitors to Berlin who knew the city 20 years ago would no doubt be astounded by the shifts in the personalities of the various *Bezirke* (boroughs). Located in the eastern part of Germany, less than 100km (62 miles) from the Polish border, Berlin is buffered by the leafy Grunewald forest and the Havel river to the west. The Spree river crosses the centre of the city and is a main inland waterway; the city is criss-crossed with many canals. The centre of Berlin is Mitte, where the major cultural institutions are located. Tiergarten with its leafy park is to Mitte's west and leads to Charlottenburg, which is upscale, if less prominent since the fall of the Wall. South of the centre is Kreuzberg, home to many of the newer landmarks and a neighbourhood legendary for its alternative youth culture and large Turkish population. Schöneberg sits just west and is more gentrified, with a prominent gay scene. Meanwhile, northern district Prenzlauer Berg has transformed from a grey, poor district into a trendy hub of café culture and boutiques.

Below: in line with German tradition, when the sun comes out, locals head to a beer garden.

Berlin Today

Two decades since the fall of the Wall, the subway system is reconnected and the centre of Berlin is again a thriving hub of business and politics, not to mention riches of culture. This has come at a literal price: Berlin has considerable municipal debt due to redeveloping the city, while unemployment runs above the national average. Nevertheless, as Mayor Klaus Wowereit quipped, Berlin is 'poor but sexy'. He might be on to something. Compared to London and Paris, Berlin certainly appears less affluent and more gritty. Yet it maintains an avant-garde flair that has been largely priced out of these other capital cities; the cost of living in Berlin is still comparatively cheap. Meanwhile, though it is not the hotbed of Weimar-era decadence depicted in the film *Cabaret*, Berlin is still permissive. The city's nightlife scene is legendary, heavy drinking and smoking do not yet raise eyebrows, and Berliners generally take a liberal view of others' sexual proclivities.

Gradually, Berlin is becoming more established, with increasing tourism and fewer cranes, as the landscape of the city settles down. Nevertheless, there is still a good deal of edgy energy to keep Berlin distinct. With so much recent history that it can almost be touched, an exploding cultural scene and the sense of a city still building its identity, what better time to explore the old and the new in Berlin?

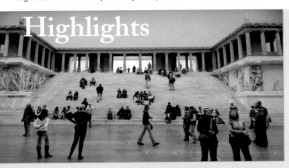

Highlights

▲ **Pergamonmuseum** An immense ancient collection: do not miss the Pergamon Altar.
▶ **Berlin Wall** Bernauer Strasse and the East Side Gallery are the best places to see the remains of this potent Cold War symbol.

▲ **Fernsehturm** An icon of communist East Berlin; ascend to the observation deck to take in the great panoramic city views.

▶ **Reichstag** From Sir Norman Foster's dazzling glass cupola, see the history-packed seat of the German parliament.

▲ **Schloss Charlottenburg** The palace reflects Berlin's Hohenzollern past, while the park is idyllic.
▶ **Jüdisches Museum** Striking architecture houses a broad and unflinching look at Jewish history.

Mitte

Mitte means 'middle', and this central Berlin district is truly both the geographical and historical centre of the city. It includes the two islands where Berlin began, the remnants of the old Hohenzollern Kaisers' residences and many of its contemporary cultural institutions, from the Museumsinsel to the Berliner Ensemble. Mitte is also the home of some of Berlin's most bombastic icons, such as the Brandenburger Tor, as well as some of its most sombre monuments. Sidelined during its days in East Germany, Mitte has sprung back into life since the Wall came down and regained its rightful place at the administrative and cultural heart of the city.

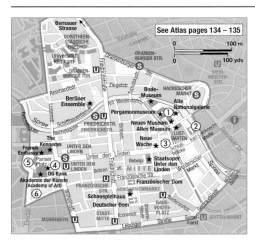

See Atlas pages 134 – 135

Berlin was actually founded on two islands, but they have been physically merged for years. Still, Fischerinsel, the island where the city's fishermen lived, is a nice break from the hustle of Mitte, with old boats in the historical harbour district, and shaded waterfront walks.

Museumsinsel

Running down the centre of Mitte is **Unter den Linden**, the city's grand promenade. At its start, it is bisected by the **Museumsinsel** ①, the island that is home to much of the city's immense collection of art treasures, divided up between the **Altes Museum**, the **Neues Museum**, **Alte National-algalerie**, **Pergamonmuseum** and the **Bode-Museum**. The Altes Museum not only contains masterpieces, it is itself a masterpiece of neoclassicism designed by Karl Friedrich Schinkel, the architect who did so much to shape Berlin's look

in the early 19th century. It is framed by the huge lawn, the **Lustgarten** (Pleasure Garden) of the Kaisers, as well as the imposing hulk of the **Berliner Dom** ②, the Protestant cathedral of the Evangelical Church in Germany, in whose basement much of the Hohen-zollern dynasty is buried.
SEE ALSO ARCHITECTURE, P.28; CHURCHES, SYNAGOGUES AND MOSQUES, P.44; MUSEUMS, P.86, 89

Unter den Linden

Across the **Schlossbrücke**, with its statues glorifying Prussian military virtues, the large pink building is the

former Prussian armoury, which today houses the **Deutsches Historisches Museum** ③ (German Histori-cal Museum), with its surpris-ing addition by I.M. Pei out of view in the rear. On the other side of the street stands the Kommandatur, the Prussian army headquarters.

Next to the Zeughaus is another Schinkel building, the **Neue Wache**, the guardhouse for the palace, which today is a memorial to the victims of German fascism and contains a statue by Käthe Kollwitz, *Mother with Her Dead Son*. Across the street is the **Staats-oper Unter den Linden**, still a major opera house.

Next door is **Bebelplatz**, where in 1933 the Nazis, including many students from the University, burned books by authors they deemed un-German; there is a sunken memorial to the book-burning in its centre. Most of the

Left: the Brandenburger Tor, Berlin's most iconic site.

the **Französischer Dom**, both Protestant churches. Today, the Französischer Dom is a museum dedicated to the Huguenots who settled in Berlin and played an instrumental part in starting the local Industrial Revolution.

Across the Spree is the **Berliner Ensemble**, the theatre built by the East Germans for returning playwright Berthold Brecht. Continuing up Friedrichstrasse, the **Dorotheenstädtische Friedhof** is Berlin's celebrity cemetery, with the graves of Bertolt Brecht, Heinrich Mann, G.W.F. Hegel, Karl Friedrich Schinkel and many others. Next door stands Brecht's house, which contains a **museum** and a fine **restaurant** in its basement.

Bernauer Strasse, the infamous **death strip** of the **Berlin Wall**, contains two of the remaining stretches of the Wall, as well as numerous historical markers provided by the Wall Documentation Centre at Bernauer Strasse and Ackerstrasse.

SEE ALSO ARCHITECTURE, P.30; LITERATURE, P.80; MONUMENTS AND MEMORIALS, P.82; MUSIC, P.96; RESTAURANTS, P.112; THEATRE AND DANCE, P.126

books were looted from the Staatsbibliothek, the national library next to the University. The huge building overlooking Bebelplatz is the law school of Humboldt, nicknamed the *Kommode* ('chest of drawers'). The **Reiterdenkmal Friedrichs des Grossen** (statue of Frederick the Great) in the centre of the street marks the end of the monuments of Imperial Berlin.
SEE ALSO MONUMENTS AND MEMORIALS, P.82–5; MUSEUMS, P.87–8; MUSIC, P.97

Brandenburger Tor

Continuing down the street, one of the few remaining relics of Russian post-war power stands, the Russian Embassy. Nearby, the **Hotel Adlon** ④ (a reproduction of the one which burned down in 1945) marks the beginning of Pariser Platz, which is dominated by the most recognisable symbol of Berlin, the **Brandenburger Tor** (Brandenburg Gate) ⑤.

The structures around the Brandenburger Tor are all recent, including the Akademie der Künste (Academy of Art), the French Embassy and the **DG Bank**, a Frank Gehry building. **The Kennedys**, a small museum, is in one of the buildings flanking the Gate, and beyond it is the recent **Denkmal für die ermordeten Juden Europas** (Memorial to the Murdered Jews of Europe) ⑥.
SEE ALSO HOTELS, P.71; MONUMENTS AND MEMORIALS, P.83; MUSEUMS, P.88

Elsewhere in Mitte

A couple of blocks south of Unter den Linden, near Friedrichstrasse, stands the group of buildings which are considered Schinkel's masterpiece, the impressive **Gendarmenmarkt** complex. Centred on the **Konzerthaus Berlin**, a theatre which is now used as a symphony hall, it is flanked by the **Deutscher Dom** and

Below: classical sculpture in the Pergamonmuseum.

Around Alexanderplatz

Alexanderplatz was once Berlin's commercial centre, a booming district of shops, trams and pedestrians. The German Democratic Republic (GDR) rebuilt much of this area after it was flattened in World War II, in a reconstruction which does little credit to East German architecture, being mostly the prefab buildings known as *Plattenbau*. Still, the iconic Fernsehturm is just one of the attractions here. With grandiose architecture, cutting-edge galleries and the historical districts of the Nikolaiviertel and Scheunenviertel, Alexanderplatz and the areas around it are distinctive parts of Mitte that are well worth visiting.

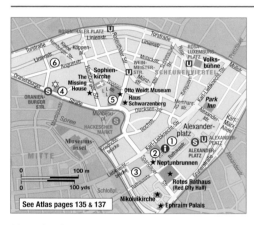

See Atlas pages 135 & 137

Death fresco and, if you're lucky, a recital on the 18th-century Walther organ.

SEE ALSO ARCHITECTURE, P.30; CHURCHES, SYNAGOGUES AND MOSQUES, P.44; HOTELS, P.73

The Nikolaiviertel

Just west of Alexanderplatz lies the **Marx-Engels-Forum** ③, a park dominated by the twin statues of the founders of communism and a collection of impressive stainless-steel stelae, in which are engraved photographs of the history of socialism and world revolution. Just beyond it, dominated by the twin steeples of the **Nikolaikirche**, is the Nikolaiviertel neighbourhood, which contains some of Berlin's oldest buildings, many of which were imported for the 750th anniversary of the city's founding in 1987. The church itself is now a museum of early Berlin history. Other historic buildings nearby include the **Ephraim Palais**, once the home of the court jeweller. On nice days, the restaurants and bars along the river here are a great place to relax.

SEE ALSO CHURCHES, SYNAGOGUES AND MOSQUES, P.44; PALACES AND HOUSES, P.105

Alexanderplatz

Alexanderplatz is dominated by two of Berlin's tallest buildings. The **Park Inn** hotel was previously one of three in which visitors from outside East Germany could spend the night instead of returning to the West at midnight. The other sky-scraping edifice is the **Fernsehturm** ① (Television Tower), built in the late 1960s to show East German superiority over the West, in particular the **Funkturm** (Radio Tower) in far West Berlin. From the observation deck there is an unparalleled view of the city.

Back on the ground, the **Rotes Rathaus** (Red City Hall), named for the bricks, not the politics practised therein, is a welcome early 20th-century relief from the Socialist architecture that dominates this area. During the city's division, East Berlin was administered from here, while West Berlin used Rathaus Schöneberg.

In the park in front of it, one of the last remnants of the Prussian castle, the **Neptunbrunnen**, spouts water from all manner of bronze sea creatures. At the northwestern corner of Alexanderplatz, the **Marienkirche** ②, one of Berlin's oldest churches, is worth a visit for its Plague-era *Dance of*

Left: the Fernsehturm (Television Tower).

The rest of the courtyard, known as **Haus Schwarzenberg,** is one of the prominent collections of artists' studios in the Mitte area. Apart from being a treasure chest of classical art, Mitte is known as a gallery hub and international art venue, due largely to the **Kunst-Werke Institute of Contemporary Art** ⑥ in Auguststrasse, which launched the Berlin Biennial for Contemporary Art in 1997. The art scene is part of what makes Scheunenviertel such a trendy area, packed with bars and restaurants.

SEE ALSO ARCHITECTURE, P.28; CHURCHES, SYNAGOGUES AND MOSQUES, P.44; GALLERIES, P.62; MONUMENTS AND MEMORIALS, P.83

Karl-Marx-Allee

East of Alexanderplatz is Karl-Marx-Allee, formerly Stalinallee, a massive architectural project undertaken by the GDR. The overall effect is a study in Russian bombast; the history is given on bilingual placards placed along both sides of the avenue. Starting at Strausberger Platz and extending to Frankfurter Tor, it makes an interesting walk on a day with good weather.

SEE ALSO ARCHITECTURE, P.30

Monbijou Park, on Oranienburger Strasse, is named for a minor palace which stood there until destroyed by bombing. It was built in 1703, and had numerous outbuildings in various fanciful styles. Today, its location on the banks of the Spree hosts the Strandbar, a fake beach which comes to life each summer and is hugely popular with locals and visitors.

The Scheunenviertel

North of Alexanderplatz, several bridges lead to the Scheunenviertel, a neighbourhood mostly built in the 19th century for Eastern European immigrants, many of whom were Jews. The Scheunenviertel has a rich Jewish history, and fittingly, its skyline is dominated by the **Neue Synagogue** ④, built in the 1860s as a sign of Jewish Berlin's prosperity. A park on Grosse Hamburger Strasse is the former site of the Alte Synagogue's **cemetery**; only the grave of Moses Mendelssohn remains.

Next to it, the **Grosse Hamburger Strasse Memorial** commemorates the Jews who were gathered in a former building there, before being deported to concentration camps. Similarly sombre is the **The Missing House** art installation by French artist Christian Boltanski, on the other side of the street. Here, the names and occupations of the former residents of a bombed-out house are affixed to the wall next to where their apartments once were.

The **Sophienkirche** is a masterpiece of Northern German Baroque architecture. Sophienstrasse, to the rear of the church, contains a number of restored 18th-century houses, as well as an entrance to the **Hackescher Höfe** ⑤, one of the most impressive collections of linked courtyards, now full of shops and bars.

Below: the Nikolaikirche, in one of Berlin's prettiest areas.

9

Tiergarten

The Tiergarten district is named after one of Berlin's most agreeable features, the huge 'central park' once used as a hunting preserve (its name means 'animal garden') by the Electors. It contains many monuments and sculptures, as well as the Zoo Berlin. The Tiergarten district is something of a showcase for post-reunification architecture, containing Potsdamer Platz, entirely rebuilt after the city's reunification in 1989. This is now the home of the annual Berlinale, Berlin's film festival, but the area around here yields many year-round cultural pleasures. For many, though, the highlight of this area will be a trip to the Reichstag.

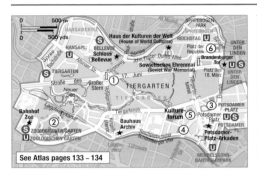

See Atlas pages 133 – 134

In 1955, an architectural competition was held to build new 'classic modern' residences in a bombed area just off the Tiergarten known as the Hansaviertel. Architects like Aalvar Aalto, Walter Gropius and Oscar Niemeyer were among the winners, and today, architecture students still walk its streets taking notes. A map on Bartningallee near the Hansaplatz S-Bahn station is the most convenient one for matching up architects with buildings.

The Tiergarten

Past the Brandenburger Tor (Brandenburg Gate), Unter den Linden becomes the Strasse des 17 Juni, its name commemorating a workers' uprising in East Berlin in 1953 that was put down by Soviet tanks. The broad boulevard stretches towards the **Siegessäule** ①, the victory column raised after the Franco-Prussian War. Just past the Brandenburger Tor is the **Sowjetisches Ehrenmal** (Soviet War Memorial), on the site of a mass grave of Russian soldiers killed in the battle for Berlin.

Venturing north into the park brings you to the **Haus der Kulturen der Welt** (House of World Cultures), known to the locals as the 'pregnant oyster', a gift to West Berlin from the United States. It serves as a venue for exhibitions and concerts.

At the end of John-Foster-Dulles-Allee is **Schloss Bellevue**, an 18th-century hunting lodge which is now the residence and office of Germany's President, a ceremonial figure whose presence is signalled by a flag atop the building.

South and west of the Siegessäule, trails lead past artificial lakes fed by the nearby Landwehrkanal along the periphery of the **Zoo Berlin** ②. The Zoo itself is immense, one of the largest collections of animals in the world, with one of its residents being an international star, the orphaned polar bear Knut. Across from the Zoo's main entrance is Bahnhof Zoo, once West Berlin's main train station, now replaced by the shiny new **Hauptbahnhof**.

SEE ALSO ARCHITECTURE, P.31; CHILDREN, P.41; MONUMENTS AND MEMORIALS, P.84–5; PARKS AND GARDENS, P.108

Potsdamer Platz

Next to Alexanderplatz, Potsdamer Platz was the most important square in pre-war Berlin and a centre of local culture. Bombed flat, it was caught in the no man's land between the Wall, languishing until unification made it the hottest piece of real estate in Europe. A campaign to bring corporate headquarters and commercial activity there resulted in a flurry of high-

Left: the roof of the Sony Center in Potsdamer Platz.

legislature. Its burning in 1933 was the catalyst for the Nazis seizing complete power, and the staged images of the victorious Russian army raising the hammer and sickle are part of Berlin's iconography. Standing on the western side of the Wall, with the border running just metres from its back door, the Reichstag lay empty for years after being reconstructed. With the country's reunification, it regained its former prominence as the home of the *Bundestag* (government). Sir Norman Foster designed a new dome and made it a focal point for the public, who can look down and watch the parliament at work. It is Berlin's top tourist attraction for Germans and always has long queues on the steps, although they move relatively quickly.

Past the Reichstag, lining the banks of the Spree, is the **Spreebogen** complex of government buildings, notable for their transparent architecture and occasional grandiosity. Some feature outdoor cafés and bars, which are extremely popular during the summertime.
SEE ALSO ARCHITECTURE, P.31

profile architectural projects. A huge cinema complex was built to house the **Berlinale**, and several grand hotels were built to house visitors. Despite all this, there's little to do in Potsdamer Platz itself once you've visited the excellent **Deutsche Kinemathek** and admired Helmut Jahn's **Sony Center** ③ and some of the other buildings; the Potsdamer Platz Arkaden is principally a shopping mall, and the majority of the restaurants are undistinguished.

It is, however, the jumping-off point to see two of Berlin's most important museums, the **Neue Nationalgalerie** ④ and the **Gemäldegalerie** at the **Kulturforum**, as well as being within walking distance of the **Philharmonie** ⑤, home of the renowned Berlin Philharmonic and the **Musikinstrumentenmuseum**.

Not far from them, across a narrow section of the park, is the **Bauhaus Archiv**,

which documents the important 1920s architectural and crafts movement with regular exhibitions.
SEE ALSO ARCHITECTURE, P.31; FESTIVALS AND EVENTS, P.54; FILM, P.57; MUSEUMS, P.90, 91; MUSIC, P.96

The Regierungsviertel

Few of Berlin's buildings are invested with as much history as the **Reichstag** ⑥, built in 1894 to house Germany's

Below: posing outside the Reichstag.

Charlottenburg

Before reunification, Charlottenburg *was* Berlin for Western visitors. Hotels and shops lined the Kurfürstendamm (or Ku'damm, as the locals call it), and a visit to the KaDeWe department store and its legendary food floor was mandatory. With a visit to Mitte or the palace of Sanssouci in Potsdam requiring going into GDR territory, the best glimpse of the Hohenzollern past was a tour of Schloss Charlottenburg. Today, the East is open and the choice of hotels is wider, but although less trendy, Charlottenburg retains its attractions and remains the best place to get a sense of the most established and sophisticated side of Berlin.

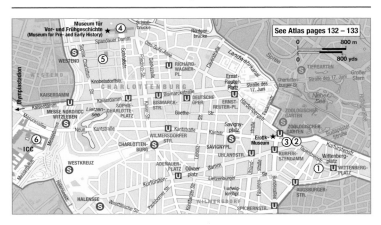

The Kurfürstendamm

For visitors, the Ku'damm starts in the section of Tauentzienstrasse by Wittenbergplatz U-Bahn station, a beautifully reconstructed Weimar-era facility with vintage advertisements on its walls. **Wittenbergplatz** is home to an understated memorial for victims of the concentration camps. At the end of Wittenbergplatz is the **KaDeWe** ①, Berlin's most famous and largest department store. The Kaufhof des Westens, as it is officially called, opened in 1907 and has served as a temple of luxury goods ever since. Its luxurious and decadent

food hall, on the sixth floor, is particularly worth a visit.

Other large department stores can be found nearby, and at the point where Tauentzienstrasse becomes the Ku'damm stands one of Berlin's rare skyscrapers, the **Europa-Center** ②, with its Mercedes star revolving on top. Next door, the **Kaiser-Wilhelm-Gedächtniskirche** (Kaiser Wilhelm Memorial Church) ③ was left in its partially bombed state by the Evangelical Church as a war memorial. Services are held in the tubular building adjacent. From here, the Ku'damm becomes the familiar tree-lined boulevard that evokes

pre-war Berlin, although increasing real-estate prices have seen a rise in chain stores and fast-food outlets and a decline in luxury retailers. A surprising discovery is the X-rated **Erotik-Museum** upstairs from the huge Beate Uhse store on Joachimsthaler Strasse near Zoo Station, home to a serious collection of historic erotica.

In the waning days of the Weimar Republic, Christopher Isherwood (or his alter ego in his *Berlin Stories*) would come over here for louche entertainment. At that time, numerous wealthy theatre people and other arty bohemians lived in huge apartments, whose

Left: shopping on the Kurfürstendamm.

with artefacts collected by Heinrich Schliemann and local Bronze Age discoveries. Across from the Schloss is the **Bröhan-Museum** ⑤, one of Europe's best collections of Art Nouveau, Art Deco, and Functionalism.

SEE ALSO MUSEUMS, P.91; PALACES AND HOUSES, P.104; PARKS AND GARDENS, P.108–9

Western Charlottenburg

South and to the west of the Schloss, Berlin's immense **Internationales Congress Centrum (ICC)** houses regular trade shows and conventions. Hard as it may be to believe now, its Eiffel Tower-like **Funkturm** ⑥ caused the envious East Germans to raise the Fernsehturm in Alexanderplatz *(see p.8)*.

A couple of U-Bahn stops away is the **Olympiastadion**, erected by Hitler for the 1936 Olympics and completely modernised for the 2006 World Cup. Some of the monumental Nazi sculpture is still plainly visible. Berlin's Hertha soccer team calls it home, and it also plays host to the likes of the Rolling Stones on tour.

SEE ALSO SPORTS, P.125

To immerse yourself fully in the feeling of a shopping stroll up the Ku'damm in the old days, stop for *Kaffee und Kuchen* (coffee and cake) at the Kranzler-Eck (Kurfürstendamm 21) or soup at Bovril (Kurfürstendamm 184).

---

buildings can still be seen, even if the apartments have long been subdivided.

Shoppers are advised to visit the Ku'damm side streets to the south, like elegant Fasanenstrasse, for interesting boutiques and galleries with a Berlin flair. This is where **Wilmersdorf** starts, with its upscale residential quarters and Wilhelminian buildings. For a taste of bourgeois lifestyle, try the smart street cafés and sophisticated shops around **Ludwigkirchplatz**.

SEE ALSO CHURCHES, SYNAGOGUES AND MOSQUES, P.45; FOOD AND DRINK, P.59; LITERATURE, P.80; MUSEUMS, P.91; SHOPPING, P.120

Schloss Charlottenburg

Best approached by walking up Schlossstrasse, **Charlottenburg palace** ④ was built by Frederick III as a summer residence for his wife, Sophie Charlotte, in 1699, back when this part of the city was deep in the countryside. New parts were added to the building over the years, and it was used as a secondary palace until the start of the 20th century. Today, it contains a museum with the largest collection of 18th-century French art outside of France and a large Baroque garden, which takes up the majority of the property and is a must-see in summer. Schloss Charlottenburg is one of Germany's most elegant houses, something of a rarity in austere Prussia.

In the palace grounds, there is another museum, the **Museum für Vor- und Frühgeschichte** (Museum for Pre- and Early History),

Below: at the gates of Schloss Charlottenburg.

Prenzlauer Berg

Prenzlauer Berg is the New Berlin writ large. Formerly a grey, working-class district, its large number of undamaged buildings attracted the first redevelopers after the fall of the Wall, and a new population demographic followed. Today, Prenzlauer Berg is one of the hippest and most revitalised parts of the city. More upscale than bohemian, its streets are filled with galleries, boutiques, restaurants and bars that serve an upwardly mobile, international populace. There are few traditional sights here, but the café culture and attractive streets make this an enjoyable place in which to wander.

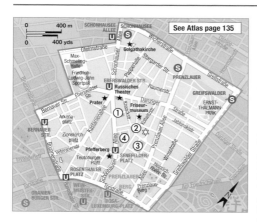

See Atlas page 135

Windmills and Breweries

Berlin is so flat that the gentle rise on which this neighbourhood sits earned it the half-ironic status of a 'mountain'. Until the last half of the 19th century, that rise was sufficient to catch the prevailing winds, and so Prenzlauer Berg was Berlin's milling centre, with dozens of windmills providing flour to the city's bakeries. Then came the breweries, with Joseph Pfeffer opening the first in 1841 at the site on Schönhauser Allee which is now the entertainment complex **Pfefferberg**. In 1853, Jost Schultheiss took over a brewery at Schönhauser Allee and built his

empire there. Today it is the **Kulturbrauerei** ①, a mixed-use complex of bars, restaurants, cinemas, offices and shopping. Others followed, such as the Bötzow on Prenzlauer Allee and Königstadt on Saarbrücker Strasse.
SEE ALSO NIGHTLIFE, P.103

Prenzlauer Berg in the 20th Century

The district's real expansion came towards the end of the century, when workers' housing, the so-called *mietskasernen* (rental-barracks) were thrown up in a

frenzy of construction to house the thousands of new Berliners attracted by the industry which had grown up in the city. With so little industry, and so much housing, the district was spared the bombing of World War II, and although the GDR did little to rebuild or renovate the *mietskasernen*, they survived. The spacious apartments attracted East German intellectuals and artists, particularly around **Kollwitzplatz** ②, the park across from where artist Käthe Kollwitz, memorialised by a statue in the park, once lived. The Café Westphal at Kollwitzstrasse was a meeting place for dissident intellectuals during the years before 1989 (it is now the **Istoria** restaurant). Another famed centre of dissent was the Golgotha Church on

Right: Prenzlauer Berg has a thriving café culture.

Left: stall selling GDR-era clothes in Kollwitzplatz.

prisoners during Nazi times, and the **Jüdischer Friedhof** (Jewish Cemetery) ④ on Schönhauser Allee, which dates from 1827 and has been rebuilt in recent years. It contains the remains of composer Giacomo Meyerbeer, painter Max Liebermann and publisher Leopold Ullstein.

Reflecting its popularity, Prenzlauer Berg is Berlin's first district with its own tourism bureau. Located in the Kulturbrauerei cultural centre, the Tourist Information Centre sells tickets and provides English-language cultural and architectural tours of Prenzlauer Berg (TIC Kulturbrauerei Maschinenhaus, Schönhauser Allee 36; tel: 4435 2170; www.tic-berlin.de; Sun–Wed noon–6pm, Thur–Sat noon–8pm; tram: M1, M10, U2: Eberswalder Strasse; map p.135 D4).

SEE ALSO MUSIC, P.99

StarStargarder Strasse, some of whose parishioners had been involved with sheltering Jews during the Nazi regime.

After the Wall came down, the cheap apartments drew a new group of bohemians from around the world, and the so-called LSD district (named for the boundary streets, Lychener Strasse, Stargarder Strasse and Danziger Strasse) became a hot centre of Berlin creativity, although the area south of Danziger Strasse between Schönhauser Allee

and Prenzlauer Allee was also notably chic. Today, Prenzlauer Berg attracts a young, multilingual going-out crowd from all over Berlin every night, filling up the countless bars, clubs and restaurants.

Kastanienallee

In a spherical building on Prenzlauer Allee there is a huge Zeiss planetarium, and many of Berlin's large-scale concerts take place in the nearby **Max-Schmeling-Halle**. The area makes for great walking, particularly on **Kastanienallee** (dubbed 'Casting Alley' by the locals), or in the streets around Kollwitzplatz, where there is great people-watching during the Saturday organic market.

Historical attractions in Prenzlauer Berg are few, but there are a couple of notable sights: the **Wasserturm** (Water Tower) ③ near Kollwitzplatz was a secret detention centre for political

Neighbouring sub-district Weissensee has Europe's largest Jewish cemetery, covering 42 hectares (105 acres) and containing over 110,000 graves, including those of hotelier Berthold Kempinski and department store magnate Hermann Tietz. The mausoleum of opera singer Joseph Schwartz has a secret passage leading to a small room, where Jews hid during World War II. Dedicated in 1880, the cemetery survived the Nazi era largely unscathed, but is now in a dilapidated state and largely overgrown by vegetation. With its simple tombstones and imposing marble mausoleums, it tells the stories of humble and famous Jewish Berliners (Jüdischer Friedhof Weissensee; Markus-Reich-Platz 1; tours by appointment; tel: 925 3330).

Schöneberg

Schöneberg is one of Berlin's most architecturally pleasant areas. It is not awash with historical sights, but has been the scene of many of Berlin's famed cultural moments: John F. Kennedy made his famous *'Ich bin ein Berliner'* speech outside Rathaus Schöneberg. Meanwhile, its established gay and party scene drew Christopher Isherwood and Marlene Dietrich in the 1920s, while David Bowie and Iggy Pop made Schöneberg their home in the 1970s. The media rediscover it as a *Szenekiez* (scene-neighbourhood) every few years, and there are numerous bars and restaurants that set the tone for the rest of Berlin culture.

See Atlas page 137

At Goebenstrasse and Potsdamer Strasse there is a housing project which is built across the street. What gives it its structural integrity is a huge Nazi air-raid bunker, which would have cost more to tear down than the property was worth, so the city simply used it as part of the building's foundation.

Around Rathaus Schöneberg

Each of Berlin's *Bezirke* (districts) has an administrative building, or *Rathaus* and it was in **Rathaus Schöneberg** ① that the West Berlin government was housed after the traditional Berlin city hall wound up in East Berlin. It was here, on 26 June 1963, that President John F. Kennedy gave his famed *'Ich bin ein Berliner'* speech, which solidified American support for West Berlin. A

model Liberty Bell within the building commemorates this.

Nearby is Bayerischer Platz, which displays another commemoration. This area was the site of a real-estate development of luxury apartments which were marketed to wealthy Jews by Jewish developers, people who were among the first victims of the Nazis' anti-Semitic laws. In 1993 two artists, Renata Stih and Frieder Schnock, erected signs with excerpts from the

laws ('Jews are allowed to buy foodstuffs only from 4.00 to 5.00 in the afternoon. 4 July 1940') around the Bayerisches Viertel neighbourhood. Maps of their location are in the park and elsewhere in the area. Keep walking north from Bayerischer Platz and you'll find **Viktoria-Luise-Platz** ②, one of Berlin's most charming pocket parks, surrounded by outdoor cafés which are great for lingering in on warm afternoons.

The Motzkiez

When the British writer Christopher Isherwood came to Berlin in the 1930s to write the stories which eventually became the play *I Am A Camera* and the musical *Cabaret*, it was largely because it was possible to live as an openly gay man. He is remembered with a plaque on his house at Nol-

Left: the weekend flea market by Rathaus Schöneberg.

quality you won't find any-where else in the city, but the customers are a perfect example of the neighbour-hood's bourgeois residents. Continuing out of the square, past the church, is the start of Goltzstrasse, the hot cen-tre of Schöneberg's 'scene', which continues as the street crosses Grunewaldstrasse and becomes Akazien-strasse. The bars, restau-rants, cafés and shops change with bewildering speed, but if you can find a local versed in this week's line-up of happening hang-outs, you'll be presented with glimpses of the lifestyles of the cool and the stylish.
SEE ALSO FOOD AND DRINK, P.59

Hauptstrasse

Hauptstrasse is, as its name makes clear, Schöneberg's 'main street' and has a couple of points of interest, starting at Kleistpark, where there is a building in which the Allied command was housed. **Neues Ufer**, an unprepos-sessing gay bar formerly known as Das Anderes Ufer, entered Berlin lore when David Bowie rented an apart-ment behind it at number 155 in the mid-1970s and used the bar as his main hangout.

Many of the houses on this part of Hauptstrasse were built by nouveau riche farmers who sold their property in the late 19th century to develop-ers desperate to throw up apartments; those which were spared bombing are still impressive. At the end of Hauptstrasse stands the **Alt-Schöneberg Dorfkirche**, an 18th-century reconstruc-tion of an older village church from when the *bezirk* was an independent town.

lendorfstrasse 17 (although whether it is on the right house remains a subject of debate), which is right in the Motzkiez, as the area around **Motzstrasse** has been dubbed. It has been a gay hub since the 1920s; a plaque commemorating the homosexuals killed by the Third Reich is affixed to Nol-lendorfplatz U-Bahn station. Motzstrasse is also the epi-centre of the annual **Christo-pher Street Day** and **Gay Pride Day** celebrations in the spring. Local bars, shops, small hotels and cinemas all cater to gay men (and women, to a lesser extent), as does the helpful drop-in centre **Mann-O-Meter**.

Not in the Motzkiez itself, but still in Schöneberg, is the renowned **Wintergarten Varieté** ③, where acrobats, magicians and other perform-ers provide entertainment with an edge in the decadent style of Weimar-era Berlin.

SEE ALSO CABARET, P.39; FESTIVALS AND EVENTS, P.55; GAY AND LES-BIAN, P.64–5; LITERATURE, P.80

The Szenekiez

The quintessential Schöneberg experience can be had on a Wednesday or Saturday in summertime by walking around the outdoor market in **Winterfeldplatz** ④. Not only are the goods on display, mainly food, of a

Below: the plaque at Nollendorfplatz U-Bahn.

17

Kreuzberg and Friedrichshain

W hen the Wall went up, Kreuzberg found itself isolated. Many buildings were abandoned, and the cheap rents attracted Turkish guestworkers, while the empty houses enticed squatters; before long, it was one of Berlin's most vibrant areas. Today, Kreuzberg is known for being a buzzing centre of art, culture and nightlife, not to mention the thriving Turkish-German culture. Neighbouring Friedrichshain retains its gritty charm and is home to the last big stretch of the Wall, now the East Side Gallery.

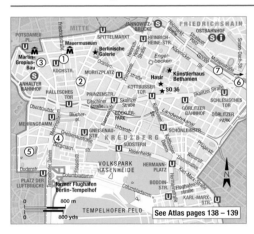

See Atlas pages 138 – 139

In years past, May Day was riot day in East Kreuzberg, with supermarkets ritually trashed and regular confrontations with the police. This has abated considerably in recent years, but the walls of Kreuzberg are still filled with graffiti and political posters year-round, and are a good barometer of the hot issues of the day.

Landwehrkanal, the twice-weekly **Turkischer Markt** (Tuesday and Friday) on Maybachufer sells fresh vegetables, as well as household goods and more kinds of olives than seem possible. The banks of the canal on the other side of Kottbusser Damm are a favourite place to lounge in the sun, and **Böcklerpark** and **Görlitzer Park** come alive at weekends, with locals grilling outdoors.

SEE ALSO FOOD AND DRINK, P.59; RESTAURANTS, P.119

East Kreuzberg

East Kreuzberg refers to the part that was closest to the Wall, with **Oranienstrasse** its main street. Also referred to by locals as 'Kreuzberg 36', in contrast to the slightly more bourgeois 'Kreuzberg 60' in the West, it is packed from one end to the other with Turkish shops, cafés and alternative bookshops, and remains a definitive slice of radical, edgy Berlin life.

The **SO 36** bar was an early hot centre of alternative art and had already made its mark when it became an important venue for Berlin punk rock. Just off Oranien-

strasse, on Adalbertstrasse, is **Hasir**, a Turkish restaurant where in 1971, the *döner kebap* was invented, as a variation on Turkish cuisine to suit German tastes. An old hospital on Mariannenplatz was a squat for artists in the 1970s and has become the **Künstlerhaus Bethanien**, where artists from around the world receive grants to work.

The former warehouses along the river on Köpenicker Strasse now play host to clubs and luxury condominiums, as well as providing space for Berlin's IT industry. Further south, down **Kottbusser Damm** where it intersects the

North Kreuzberg

At the border with Mitte are some of Berlin's most famous sights, such as **Checkpoint Charlie** ①, although the hut there is a reproduction and the 'soldier' is an actor. A **museum** across the street has a strident political agenda, but some fascinating

Left: the Turkischer Markt on Maybachufer.

SEE ALSO BARS AND CAFÉS, P.37; GAY AND LESBIAN, P.65; PARKS AND GARDENS, P.109

Friedrichshain

Connected by the neo-Gothic red-brick **Oberbaumbrücke** ⑥ bridge that spans the Spree river at Warschauer Strasse station, both Kreuzberg and Friedrichshain have come from largely run-down-edgy to trendy-edgy since the Wall came down, and both boast offbeat shopping and a lot of nightlife options.

In recent years, the latter has become a favourite with Berlin's younger crowd; some even consider it the most happening district. The streets around **Simon-Dach-Strasse** brim with bars and restaurants, most of them packed all night. Parts of Friedrichshain are still quite rough around the edges, rents are cheap and the punk spirit is alive.

However, developers have now arrived, and even parts of the **East Side Gallery** ⑦, the artist-painted longest stretch of Wall still intact, have had to make way for a new entertainment complex.

SEE ALSO GALLERIES, P.63

Below: the Oberbaumbrücke, Berlin's prettiest bridge.

exhibits on escape attempts. Turning east on Kochstrasse from Checkpoint Charlie will bring you to a small museum district containing the bold **Jüdisches Museum** ② and the **Berlinische Galerie**, while turning west takes you to the **Martin-Gropius-Bau**, which usually has a couple of fine exhibitions and the **Topography of Terror** ③, located in the excavated remains of the Gestapo headquarters.

SEE ALSO MONUMENTS AND MEMORIALS, P.82; MUSEUMS, P.93, 94

West Kreuzberg

Southern and Western Kreuzberg is more bourgeois than its neighbour, with houses in a better state of repair. **Bergmannstrasse** is also lined with alternative businesses and Turkish shops, from its market hall (one of the few remaining indoor markets from the 19th century) to Mehringdamm.

On Hasenheide's southern perimeter is **Flughafen Tempelhof**, the Nazi-built airport. Tempelhof had the world's eyes on it during the Berlin Airlift, when planes loaded with crucial supplies landed, unloaded and took off again in minutes, breaking the Russian blockade of Berlin. It has ceased to serve as a commercial airport and at the moment its future is uncertain.

On Mehringdamm, you'll find the **Schwules Museum** (Gay Museum) ④. Crossing Mehringdamm leads to **Viktoriapark** ⑤, which contains the 'cross hill' which gives the entire district its name. The monument with the cross marking the Napoleonic Wars on top of the hill is by Schinkel and dates from 1821. On summer nights, the nearby beer garden is packed. The hill, one of Berlin's few natural ones, is high enough to be a perfect place to orient yourself with the city.

Western Districts

Zehlendorf and Spandau form the western edge of Berlin. Rich in forests, lakes and waterways, as well as historical landmarks, they are always good for an outing. Spandau, on the western edge of Berlin, has large forests and more than 100km (62 miles) of shoreline, comprised by the Havel river and several lakes. While Spandau is traditionally also an industrial area, Zehlendorf has always been the residence of the rich and famous, with its villas set in leafy surrounds. Dahlem, meanwhile, is best-known for its collection of excellent museums, and those looking for a break from urbanity will find relief in Grosser Wannsee and beautiful Pfaueninsel (Peacock Island).

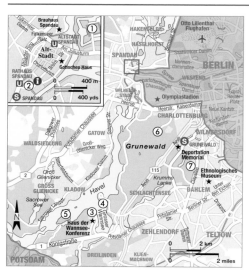

Outside Germany, Spandau was long associated with the **War Criminals Prison** south of the old town, where several prominent Nazis sentenced at the Nuremberg Trials were imprisoned after World War II. Inmates included Albert Speer and Rudolf Hess, Hitler's deputy, who, after the release of the others, was the only prisoner here for two decades until he committed suicide in 1987. The prison was torn down soon after his death.

Spandau

Founded as a Slavic settlement at the confluence of the Spree and Havel rivers, Spandau was a town in its own right until 1920 and is still distinctive from Berlin proper. The Spandauers are proud of this, as well as of their preserved buildings, which reflect 500 years of history. Spandau has a distinct medieval small-town atmosphere, which is best experienced at its Christmas Market, which stands out as one of Berlin's most picturesque.

The **Zitadelle Spandau** (Citadel) ① is one of the best-preserved Renaissance fortresses in Germany, with some parts dating back to the 12th century. The Zitadelle has a history museum, a great medieval-style restaurant, and provides a perfect backdrop for open-air concerts. Less known is that it also serves as winter quarters for 10,000 bats.

The **Gotisches Haus** (Gothic House) ② dates back to the 15th century and is the

oldest residence in all of Berlin. Today it houses the Spandau Information Office and is the starting point for town walks. Don't miss the crooked medieval half-timbered houses near Marien-kirche (St Mary's church) at the quiet north end of the old-town island. Pay a visit to the fortress-like **Brauhaus Spandau** brewery nearby and have a home brew in the charming beer garden.
SEE ALSO FESTIVALS AND EVENTS, P.55

Zehlendorf

Zehlendorf is the city's most genteel district, a leafy suburb in Berlin's southwest. This is where the well-to-do reside, while the less affluent flock to

The Grunewald

The Grunewald is an enormous forest stretching between the districts of Charlottenburg, Wilmersdorf, Zehlendorf and the Havel river, shared by city-worn humans, their dogs and several wild boar that habitually appear on nearby roads, raiding the rubbish bins for leftover lunches.

The Grunewald has a few sights. **Teufelsberg** ('Devil's Mountain') ⑥ was constructed from rubble after World War II. The abandoned US radar station at its summit (crowned by a white ball-shaped dome) was one of the premier listening posts of the Cold War. Other history is felt at the Grunewald S-Bahn station, where platform 17 is the **Deportation Memorial** to the 55,000 Berlin Jews sent from this station on trains bound for concentration camps.

Dahlem

Dahlem is a residential part of Zehlendorf, distinguished by its number of exquisite museums, such as the **Brücke Museum** ⑦, dedicated to the German Expressionist painters group of the same name whose works were defamed as 'degenerate art' by the Nazis, as well as the **Ethnologisches Museum** (Ethnological Museum), with 500,000 artefacts from all over the world, and the **Museum für Asiatische Kunst** (Museum of Asian Art).
SEE ALSO MUSEUMS, P.94

the district's woods and beaches at the weekend. The glamour of past times can be felt in the **Max-Liebermann-Villa** ③ (now a museum) at Grosser Wannsee, where the famous painter lived until his death in 1935. Just around the corner is the **Haus der Wannsee-Konferenz**, the notorious villa where the 'Final Solution' was devised by Nazi bureaucrats in January 1942. It houses a museum telling the story of how the hatred towards Jews was fuelled and how the terror that led to the Holocaust was organised.
SEE ALSO PARKS AND GARDENS, P.110

Around Wannsee

Europe's largest inland beach, **Strandbad Wannsee** ④, boasts almost a mile of sandy beaches and can be found on the shores of **Grosser Wannsee**. For the past century, Berliners have come here for a day out, a boat ride, a steamer cruise to Potsdam or coffee and cake at the café overlooking the lake.

Located south of Grosser Wannsee in the southern Havel river is **Pfaueninsel** ⑤, where 60 peacocks strut the grounds. Accessible only by ferry, it is listed as a Unesco World Heritage Site and is probably Berlin's most beautiful natural sanctuary.
SEE ALSO PARKS AND GARDENS, P.110; SPORTS, P.125

Below: Glienicker Brücke.

The inconspicuous **Glienicker Brücke** (*left*) spanning the Havel river connecting Berlin and Potsdam became known as the Cold War trading post for spies and other undesirables.

Treptow
and Köpenick

Treptow and Köpenick form a large district stretching from the city centre to the southeastern suburbs of Berlin. For visitors, Treptow's main point of interest is the large park named for the area, where the bombastic Soviet war memorial stands. Köpenick, meanwhile, gained fame through 'The Captain of Köpenick' and his antics. Today both districts, with their lakes, waterways and forests, offer plenty of recreational options, while Friedrichshagen is a picturesque place in which to spend time.

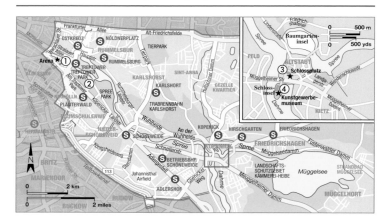

Treptow

Treptow is a mostly industrial district in the former East Berlin that is, however, rich in waterways and parks. The giant modern sculpture of the **'Molecule Man'** ① in the Spree river connects the glistening **'Treptowers'** skyscrapers of post-Wall Treptow with **Treptower Park**, a monument to its past. The **Sowjetisches Ehrenmal** (Soviet War Memorial) ② found here recalls World War II and the Stalinist period to follow. **Treptower Park** is also home to the 1896 Archenhold observatory, housing what was then the world's longest refractor telescope.

The area of Treptow was once best-known for the Johannisthal Airfield, Germany's first airport, where competing Fokkers and Junkers built in the local workshops were tested and the first commercial flights took off in the 1920s. Parts of the aviation laboratories, wind tunnels and hangars have been preserved and are historical landmarks today.

Some former industrial sites were reinvented as cultural venues or party locations, the largest of them being the **Arena** (a former bus depot) on the banks of the Spree that comes with a floating swimming pool in an old barge.

Treptow is a convenient starting point for boat tours of the southeast lakes of Berlin and to Köpenick and Grünau. SEE ALSO MONUMENTS AND MEMORIALS, P.85; MUSIC, P.98; PARKS AND GARDENS, P.110

Köpenick

For many people, Köpenick is associated with 'The Captain of Köpenick'. Founded as a Slavic settlement back in the 9th century, Köpenick is one of Berlin's oldest parts. The former fishermen's village raised on an island (**Schlossinsel**, the location of Schloss Köpenick) has preserved its small-town charm with narrow lanes,

Left: in Treptower Park, the Sowjetisches Ehrenmal.

Kunstgewerbemuseum (Museum of Decorative Arts). SEE ALSO PALACES AND HOUSES, P.104

Friedrichshagen

A very lovely part of Köpenick is the Friedrichshagen quarter. From the S-Bahn station of the same name, walk down picturesque 18th-century **Bölschestrasse** with its small ornate buildings, charming shops and good restaurants to **Müggelsee**, Berlin's largest lake. In one of the many beer gardens by the water, you can sit under old chestnut trees and enjoy the view of sailing boats passing by. Even more attractive is **Neu-Venedig** ('New Venice'), a lagoon neighbourhood where the Müggelspree river branches into numerous canals, lined by cottages and fish restaurants.

Overlooking the Grösser Müggelsee are the Müggel- berge hills, a large forested area popular with hikers and mountain bikers. The some- what derelict 1960s Müggel- turm tower offers scenic views. Swimmers flock to **Strandbad Müggelsee** beach, a lido similar to its counterpart on Grösser Wannsee in the West.

The story of *Der Hauptmann von Köpenick* (The Captain of Köpenick) is legendary. In 1906, ex-convict Wilhelm Voigt exposed the Prussian blind belief in military authority when he marched into the Köpenick town hall disguised as a captain and confiscated the town finances.

At the neo-Gothic town hall, **Rathaus Köpenick** ③, a bronze statue commemo- rates the Captain *(see box, left)*. Hearty German cuisine is served in the Ratskeller restaurant here, which is also a popular venue for jazz concerts.

Divided from the old town by wooden bridge and located right on the water is **Schloss Köpenick** ④, the restored palace, housing the

restored old buildings and the red-brick *Rathaus* (town hall). As three-quarters of Köpenick are covered by lakes and forests, this is a popular place to visit for fresh air and the outdoors.

The colourful history of Köpenick is reflected in the **Altstadt**, the car-free old town around Schlossplatz, uniquely located at the confluence of the Spree and Dahme rivers. Here, where little old ladies with hats idle away the day in the cafés near the old parish church, clocks seem to tick more slowly.

Below: Schloss Köpenick.

Potsdam

Potsdam is Berlin's neighbour, a small city with a historical importance that outweighs its size. Its main attraction is the Sanssouci Palace, built for Frederick the Great. The entire park is a Unesco World Heritage Site and contains numerous buildings, large and small, which can take an entire day to explore. Potsdam also has a charming city centre studded with 18th-century buildings, including entire neighbourhoods built to look Dutch and Russian. The nearby Babelsberg film studios provide the central impetus for the Filmmuseum Potsdam, housed in 17th-century military stables.

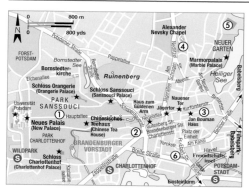

Sanssouci

Sanssouci ① was begun in 1747 on the orders of Frederick the Great, who found the royal residence in Berlin not to his liking. With construction continuing into the 19th century, this ensemble of palaces, gardens and pleasure spots is considered by many to be the equal of Versailles. The park itself can be enjoyed for free, although small vending machines by the entrances ask for a voluntary admission charge to help maintain the grounds. With the majority of attractions here being open only from May to October, most visitors get to see the gardens in their full formal splendour, with fountains splashing in the sunlight.

The **New Palace** is open year-round and is central to Frederick the Great's history, since it was his main residence. **Sanssouci Palace**, the older of Frederick's two palaces here, is adjoined by the **Picture Gallery**, stuffed with 18th-century art, and the **New Chambers** is a former orangery turned into a guest palace for noble visitors.

Elsewhere in the grounds, perhaps the most charming building is the **Chinese Tea House**, built 1754–7 from a sketch by Frederick and used for tea parties on fine porcelain which is displayed there today. Frederick is buried, along with his dogs, who also merit tombstones, next to Sanssouci Palace. Post-

Fredrician Sanssouci includes the **Charlottenhof Palace**, the **Orangery Palace** and the **Church of Peace**, all built in the early to mid-19th century by Friedrich Wilhelm IV.

Historic City Centre

Just outside Sanssouci, by the exits by the Picture Gallery or Church of Peace, one can see Potsdam's own **Brandenburger Tor** (Brandenburg Gate) ②, dating from 1770. This provides an entrance to the historic city centre, which continues down Brandenburger Strasse and its surrounding side streets, most of which are pedestrianised. At Hermann-Elfleim-Strasse 3 is the **Haus zum Güldenen Arm**, built and brilliantly decorated by the brewer and wood-sculptor August Melchior Erhart. Across

that the 1945 Potsdam Conference, which decided the fate of post-war Germany, was held. The round table where the Allies sat is still on view, and the surrounding grounds also contain the **Marble Palace**, created as a summer residence on the Heiliger See, and dating from 1791.

Outside of Potsdam proper, but easily reached by public transport, the suburb of Babelsberg has not only its own park with a palace designed by Schinkel, but also the **Filmpark Babelsberg**, on the site of the UFA Studios, where much classic German cinema was made. Today, it is an amusement park not unlike Universal Studios in California, with rides and stunt shows mostly geared towards the German television-viewing audience. People with a serious interest in what was accomplished in Babelsberg by directors such as Fritz Lang and G.W. Murnau would be better off in central Potsdam at the **Filmmuseum Potsdam** ⑥, which has well-curated exhibitions on German film history, as well as a cinema programme in the evenings.

Friedrich-Ebert-Strasse, the building materials abruptly change from plaster to brick. The **Holländisches Viertel** (Dutch quarter) ③ was erected in the 1730s to house Dutch builders who were invited by the Kaiser to build in Potsdam. The 134 houses have been reconstructed from the disrepair they had fallen into and now house galleries and restaurants as well as private residences and offices. The **Jan Bouman Haus** at Mittelstrasse 8 has reconstructed a typical residence of an 18th-century Dutch builder and provides a good history of the area in its museum.

Heading up Friedrich-Ebert-Strasse, one comes to **Alexandrowka** ④, a cluster of wooden Russian peasant houses built by Friedrich Wilhelm III in 1826 to house Russian musicians who had been taken by the Kaiser as spoils of war in the Napoleonic Wars. The Alexander

Nevsky Chapel above the settlement contains a number of important icons, and the area is another Unesco World Heritage Site.

Cecilienhof and Babelsberg

The last palace built by the Hohenzollerns, the **Cecilienhof** ⑤, was finished in 1917 and became a luxury hotel after World War I. It was here

Below: the distinctive shape of the Einsteinturm.

One of the most distinctive buildings in Potsdam is the Expressionist **Einsteinturm** (Einstein Tower), built in 1921 as an astrophysics observatory for the astronomer Erwin Finlay-Freundlich to conduct experiments in support of the Theory of Relativity. Albert Einstein's verdict on the avant-garde building? 'Organic.' Despite a large-scale conservation project in 1999, the tower is fragile, so take a guided tour while you can (tours run Oct–May).

A–Z

In the following section Berlin's attractions and services are organised by theme, under alphabetical headings. Items that link to another theme are cross-referenced. All sights that fall within the atlas section at the end of the book are given a page number and grid reference.

Architecture

Like no other European capital, Berlin's buildings bear witness to the chaotic history of the 20th century, from the beginning of urban planning for a working-class population, the creative, experimental years of the Bauhaus and the birth of modernism, the hubris and destruction during the Nazi period, the city divided in the Cold War to its rebirth as Germany's capital after the fall of the Berlin Wall. These listings demonstrate Berlin's tumultuous modern history through its architecture, as well as some key buildings from the Prussian era that have survived; for more of these, *see Palaces and Houses, p.104–5.*

The Prussian Legacy

St Hedwigs Cathedral (1773)
Bebelplatz; S1, S2, S25, S5, S7, S75, S9, U6: Friedrichstrasse, U2: Französische Strasse; map p.136 C1
Built by Johann Baumann, this Baroque Catholic cathedral was meant to demonstrate the predominately Protestant state's support for religious freedom.

Neue Schönhauser 8 (1785)
U8: Weinmeister Strasse; map p.135 C3
This apartment house is believed to have been built by Georg Christian Unger and is a typical Berlin residence from during the city's expansion in the late Baroque period. There are several houses on this street, such as numbers 12–14, with well-preserved facades and back courtyards that are exemplary of their time.

Neue Synagoge (1866)
Oranienburger Strasse 28–30; S1, S2, S25, S26: Oranienburger Strasse; map p.134 C3
Berlin's Jewish citizens erected what was once the city's largest synagogue with an oriental appearance, reflecting the tastes of the time. It was built by Eduard Knoblauch and Friedrich August Stüler. Ironically, it was largely undamaged during the Nazis' Kristallnacht pogrom but nearly destroyed by Allied bombing and later demolished under the GDR. It was restored after unification.
SEE ALSO CHURCHES, SYNAGOGUES AND MOSQUES, P.44

> Karl Friedrich Schinkel gave Mitte much of the appearance that we recognise today, being responsible for the **Altes Museum** *(see Museums, p.86)*, the first museum in Germany and only the third in Europe, after the Prado in Madrid and the British Museum in London. Other Schinkel masterpieces include the **Neue Wache** *(see Memorials and Monuments, p.85)*, the **Konzerthaus** *(see Music, p.96–7)* and the **Schinkel-Pavillion** in the grounds of Schloss Charlottenburg *(see Palaces and Houses, p.104)*.

City Life, Pre-World War I

Proskauer Strasse Apartments (1898)
Proskauer Strasse 14/15/17; U5: Frankfurter Tor
In the years before World War I, it was the German Miets-haus, a combination apartment building and rented space for shops, that shaped the face of the city. Proskauer Strasse, designed by Alfred Messel, was cutting-edge. It opened up the traditional inner courtyard to bring in light and create room for children. The building won a prize at the Paris World's Fair in 1900.

Hackescher Höfe (1907)
Rosenthalerstr 40–41; S3, S5, S7, S9: Hackescher Markt; map p.134 C3
Built by Kurt Berndt and August Endell, this was the largest combined residential and commercial complex in Europe. Its inner courtyards were a labyrinth of working class apartments, shops and small factories. The neighbouring station Hackescher Markt and the surrounding neighbourhood still give an impression of turn-of-the-century Berlin.

Left: GDR-era architecture on Karl-Marx-Allee.

sion. A GDR-era mural can be seen on the Leipzigerstrasse side of the building. In 2000, it became the finance ministry.

Olympiastadion (1936)
Olympischer Platz 3; U2, S75, S9: Olympiastadion
The stadium was designed by Werner March with some adjustments by Albert Speer. After the war, Germans feared that National Socialist architecture would breed fascism and so they destroyed many buildings such as Hitler's new chancellery. But if any building was meant to demonstrate Hitler's vision for Germany as an empire in the classic sense, it is the Olympiastadion, modelled on Rome's Colosseum. To get a true feel for this venue, try to get tickets to a Hertha BSC football match and absorb the atmosphere of where the 1936 Olympics were held. The tribune where Hitler and his cohorts watched Jesse Owens triumph over German athletes is still intact.
SEE ALSO SPORTS, P.125

Flughafen Tempelhof (1941)
Platz der Luftbrücke 1–6; U6: Platz der Luftbrücke; map p.138 B3
In its day, Tempelhof Airport was the largest building in the world. While the building was doubtless meant to

Modernism

Hufeisen-Siedlung (Horseshoe Housing Project) (1927)
Fritz-Reuter-Allee, Buschkrugallee, Parchimer Allee; U7: Parchimer Allee
This was a joint project of architects Bruno Taut and Martin Wagner and is a classic Bauhaus. It is one of the first big German housing estates, with more than 1,000 apartments. Simplification and mass production was meant to make the homes affordable for the working class. Nevertheless, workers still couldn't afford to live there. Clerks and civil servants moved in.

Berolina-Haus (1932)
Alexanderplatz 1; U2, U5, U8, S5, S75, S9: Alexanderplatz; map p.137 E2
The Berolina-Haus and the neighbouring Alexanderhaus are all that remain of the planned Weimar-era redesign of busy Alexanderplatz. Designed by Peter Behrens, the two buildings were meant to serve as gates to this central traffic hub and commercial district. On the top floor of Berolina-Haus was

the very hip Swing-era Café Braun, accessible via ultra-modern escalators and paternosters.

National Socialism

Bundesfinanzministerium (Ministry of Finance) (1936)
Wilhelmstrasse 97, Leipzigerstrasse 6–7; U2, S1, S2, S25: Potsdamer Platz; map p.134 B2
It was from here that Hermann Göring's *Reichsluftfahrtministerium* (aerospace ministry) directed the air war against Britain. It was designed by Hitler's architect Ernst Sagebiel, who also designed Flughafen Tempelhof. After the war, East Germany used it for its Central Planning Commis-

Below: the redeveloped Hackesche Höfe.

demonstrate Nazi power and Germany's technological prowess, Sagebiel's efficient design also became a model for airports around the world. Nazi symbols were removed from public after the war, but you can still see the German eagle adorning Tempelhof buildings.

Hochbunker (1943)
Albrechtstrasse 24–25; S3, S5, S7, S9, S75, U6, Tram M1 and 12: Friedrichstrasse; U6, Tram M1, M6 and M12: Oranienburger Tor, S1, S2: Oranienburger Strasse

Planning for war, Hitler built a massive civilian bomb-shelter system – enough to contain 7 percent of the population. To speed up the process after the war began, he built huge above-ground bunkers. This one was too costly to tear down and it served as a venue for an underground raver club after the Berlin Wall fell; today, it is sometimes used for art exhibits.

East Berlin

Karl-Marx-Allee (1951–4)
Block C: Karl-Marx-Allee 71–91B, Karl-Marx-Allee 72-90; U5: Strausberger Platz Station, Weberwiese; map p.135 E2

The Frankfurter Tor welcomed visitors from the East to central Berlin and was designed by Hermann Henselmann for Stalinallee, renamed Karl-Marx-Allee, which was intended to be Germany's first Socialist boulevard in the style of Moscow. For 260m the

> One of a series of three *Unités d'Habitation* that Le Corbusier designed as a solution to the housing shortages across Europe following World War II, the Corbusierhaus in Charlottenburg is possibly the ultimate example of Berlin's modern-architecture housing blocks. You can even choose to stay in one of the furnished flats available (www.domizil-berlin.com).

boulevard is flanked by what were luxurious housing blocks reserved for state functionaries in the days of East Berlin. Architect Richard Paulinck combined elements of classicism with Socialist aesthetics. This is where East German leaders held their annual military parades. Its value as architecture is disputed, but it is reminiscent of a Berlin that is rapidly disappearing. Take the subway to Frankfurter Tor, then walk back along Karl-Marx-Allee and visit old East Berlin landmarks like Café Moskau, a popular Soviet restaurant back in the day that now sports a dance club, or the egg-shaped Filmtheater Kosmos, East Germany's cinema for film premières.

Berlin Wall (1961)
Bernauer Strasse; www.die-berliner-mauer.de; U8: Bernauer Strasse, Schwarzkopfstrasse, U6: Schwarzkopfstrasse, Niederkirchnerstrasse, Kochstrasse, or U2, S1, S2, S25: Potsdamer Platz; map p.134 B4

The other major East Berlin

construction project, the Berlin Wall was erected in a single night and became the world's symbol of the Cold War. There are few stretches of the original Wall left standing; the best places to see it are here at the former 'Death Strip' on Bernauer Strasse or at the **East Side Gallery** across from the Ostbahnhof.
SEE ALSO GALLERIES, P.63

Fernsehturm (1969)
Alexanderplatz; U2, S5, S7, S75, S9: Alexanderplatz; map p.135 C3

When construction was completed, East German leaders praised the futuristic TV tower as the 'work of the working class'. However, locals say the arch-Socialist GDR head of state, Erich Honecker, hated the fact that the sun setting in the west reflected in a cross on the East's tower. Nevertheless, the Fernsehturm has become a Berlin icon, and the rotating restaurant on top with its stunning view of the city is a popular tourist stop.
SEE ALSO CHILDREN, P.43

Below: the Olympiastadion, modelled on the Colosseum in Rome.

Left: the Corbusierhaus.

The New Berlin

Jüdisches Museum (1998)
Lindenstrasse 9–14; tel: 2599 3300; www.juedisches-museum-berlin.de; U6, U1: Hallesches Tor; map p.134 C1

The mesmerising Jewish Museum building is based on the shape of an exploded Star of David. Its architect, Daniel Libeskind created empty spaces between the folds that can neither be entered nor crossed, as if to express the unspeakable, the annihilation of Jews under Hitler.
SEE ALSO MUSEUMS, P.93

Reichstag (1999)
Platz der Republik 1; S3, S5, S7, S9, S75: Hauptbahnhof; map p.134 A3

Sir Norman Foster placed special emphasis on transparency in redesigning the parliament's plenary hall in this building that was the parliament of Weimar's fragile democracy and later Hitler's stage. The glass cupola on the roof of the Reichstag allows citizens to observe their elected officials at work.

Potsdamer Platz 1 (2000)
S1, S2, S25, U2: Potsdamer Platz; map p.134 B2

The 20-storey flat iron-shaped red-brick office building recalls Potsdamer Platz's pre-war role as Europe's busiest intersection, architects Hans Kollhoff and Helga Timmermann creating a building that combines contemporary design with elements of a classic New York-style skyscraper.

Sony Center (2000)
Potsdamer Strasse 2; daily 24 hours; S1, S2, S25, U2: Potsdamer Platz; map p.134 A2

A massive tent-like roof seems to whirl above the main square of this entertainment and office complex designed by German-American architect Helmut Jahn. One of the most impressive new complexes in post-Wall Berlin, the Sony Center is a popular attraction with locals and tourists alike.

Bundeskanzleramt (2001)
Willy-Brandt-Strasse 1; S3, S5, S7, S9, S75: Hauptbahnhof; map p.134 A3

Berliners nickname everything, and have dubbed the new chancellery the 'washing machine' for its squat shape and glass front. Architects Axel Schultes and Charlotte Frank designed the building to symbolise the unification of Germany's two halves.

Neues Museum (2010)
Bodestrasse, Museumsinsel; tel: 2664 24242; www.neues-museum.de; daily 10am–6pm, Wed until 10pm; map p.137 D2

After seven decades of closure, the Neues Museum of ancient treasures re-opened in 2009. The bombed out ruin was painstakingly transformed by English architect, David Chipperfield, who incorporated as much of the original shell as he could, including fire-damaged columns and bullet-marked walls which contrast starkly with the modern white stairways. It is now one of the finest public buildings in the city (see p.89)

Below: the slick exterior of the Deutsche Bahn building.

West Berlin

Haus der Kulturen der Welt (1957)
John-Foster-Dulles-Allee 10; S3, S5, S7, S9, S75: Hauptbahnhof; map p.134 A3

Post-war building in West Berlin was largely functional and unsensational. That's why the former Kongress-halle stands out as a West Berlin icon and the optimism of the early 1960s. Built by Hugh Stubbins, it was a gift from the US.

Neue Nationalgalerie (1968)
Potsdamer Strasse 50; tel: 266 2951; www.smb.museum; U2, S1, S2, S25: Potsdamer Platz; map p.134 A1

The first building to open as part of West Berlin's new culture forum at Potsdamer Platz, the steel-and-glass construction is the only building that Mies van der Rohe would build in post-war Germany. The former head of the Bauhaus in Dessau, van der Rohe had fled from the Nazis in 1938.

Bars and Cafés

A lot of time is spent in bars and cafés in Berlin. In fact, the distinction between the two can be hard to make, as the same place will often host people enjoying the ritual *Kaffee und Kuchen* (coffee and cake) in the middle of the afternoon and then another crowd sipping beer, wine and cocktails at night. Of course, there are also *Konditorei*, which are bakeries with dining facilities, not mention bars that are just bars. Of the thousands in the city, those listed below provide a taster of Berlin drinking and café culture. *Prost! See also Gay and Lesbian, p.65–7; Nightlife, p.102–3; and Restaurants, p.112–19.*

Mitte

Opernpalais

Unter den Linden 7; tel: 202 683; www.opernpalais.de; daily 9am–midnight; U2, S5, S7, S9: Hackescher Markt; map p.137 C1

In a 1733 building which was once the residence of the Hohenzollern princesses, a well-dressed clientele sips coffee and tea and enjoy a bewildering selection of pastries; there are over 40 types of cake alone on offer each day. In winter, it serves as a great break from one of Berlin's best Christmas markets, held right outside.

Strandbar

Monbijoupark; www.altes europa.com; daily 10am–late; S3, S5, S7, S9: Hackescher Markt; map p.137 C2

It's a simple enough concept: dump a bunch of sand on the shore of the Spree river opposite the Bode-Museum, set up a couple of shacks with beer taps and refrigerators, and people will come. In fact, so many of them come that this popular evening spot is often full. The nearby Hexenkessel Hoftheater

> Berlin is not as noted for its *Kaffee und Kuchen* (coffee and cake) culture as some other German cities, but that doesn't prevent the locals from stopping each afternoon around 3pm for refreshment. You can often get breakfast until late in the afternoon, particularly in establishments favoured by Berlin's huge student population, and a bite to eat late at night is also easy come by at these places.

(either on its fixed stage or on the ship Marie in the river, depending on production) draws crowds to its performances of Shakespeare in German. The enticing sight of people stretched out in the sun makes you want to join the fun.

Weinbar Rutz

Chausseestrasse 8; tel: 2462 8760; www.rutz-weinbar.de; Tue–Sat 4–11pm; U6: Zinnowitzer Strasse; map p.134 B4

Top-drawer wines from around the world are on offer at this upscale bar. It is pricey, but one of the best places to taste excellent vin-

tages in Berlin. Light snacks are also available, and there is a restaurant upstairs.

Around Alexanderplatz

Altes Europa

Gipsstrasse 11; tel: 2809 3840; www.alteseuropa.com; daily noon–late; U8: Weinmeisterstrasse; map p.134 C3

Idiosyncratic bar on the site of the Gipsdiele, a notorious dive of the inter-war years made famous by Joseph Roth, decorated with kitschy oil paintings and the odd obscene fresco. The food is all but inedible, but there's excellent beer and, surprisingly for a Berlin bar, the featured wine is usually both superb and a bargain.

Gorki Park

Weinbergsweg 25; tel: 448 7286; www.gorki-park.de; daily 10am–8pm; U8: Rosenthaler Platz; map p.135 C4

This offshoot of Prenzlauer Berg's Pasternak Restaurant is a popular meeting place for locals, as well as a fine place to have an authentic Russian lunch. Free wi-fi, good cof-

Right: Weinbar Rutz.

Left: lunchtime at Café Einstein.

ers. The apple cake sets a high standard, though, and the brew is good enough to have given birth to a city-wide franchise of coffee houses.

Caffè e Gelato
Alte Potsdamer Strasse 7, Potsdamer Platz Arkaden (top floor); tel: 2529 7832; www.gelato-berlin.de; Mon–Sat 10am–10pm; S1, S2, U2: Potsdamer Platz; map p.134 A1
This ice-cream parlour is a hit among locals and visitors alike. Always packed and with long queues for takeaway cones but worth the short wait. As close as you can get to real Italian ice-cream in Berlin and with so many flavours to chose from, you are bound to make a return trip.

Schleusenkrug
Müller-Breslau Strasse; tel: 313 9909; www.schleusenkrug.de; daily 10am–late; S3, S5, S7, S9, U7, U2: Tiergarten or Zoologicher Garten; map p.133 D2
Located by a lock in the Landwehrkanal and within earshot of the Zoo, this pop-

fee, Russian beer and vodka, and a popular Sunday brunch from 10am onwards.

Hackbarth's
Auguststrasse 69a; tel: 282 7704; daily 9am–3am; U8: Weinmeisterstrasse; map p.134 C3
Hackbarth's was a bakery once upon a time, and it still opens to serve breakfast. A crucial part of the early post-Wall scene in the Mitte area, it is still the favourite watering-hole of local artists and

curators. Light meals are also available.

Tiergarten
Café Einstein
Kurfürstenstrasse 58; tel: 261 5096; www.cafeeinstein.com; daily 8am–1am; U1, U15: Kurfürstenstrasse; map p.133 E1
A Berlin institution in the mansion of a once-famous silent-screen actress. A Viennese coffee house with style, and staffed by haughty wait-

Above: when in Germany... do as the Germans do.

ular spot in the Tiergarten has been a favourite since it opened in 1954, although since 1996, new management has made it as noted for its organic sausages as its central location and pleasant grounds. A perfect retreat after a visit to the Zoo.

Charlottenburg

Café Hardenberg
Hardenbergstrasse 10; tel: 312 2644; www.cafe-hardenberg.de; daily 9am–1am; U2: Ernst-Reuter-Platz; map p.133 C2
The Café Hardenberg pretty much defines the West Berlin student café: located near both the Technical University and the Art College, it hums day and night with students and others out and about in the neighbourhood enjoying a light meal, breakfast, or one of those huge cups of *Milchkaffee*.

Want a beer? Be prepared to wait: German tradition says seven minutes is what it takes to draw a decent beer, waiting for the head to subside and then shooting a bit more in. Does it make a difference? Probably not, but tradition is tradition.

Café im Literaturhaus
Fasanenstrasse 23; tel: 882 5414; www.literaturhaus-berlin.de; daily 9.30am–1am; U15: Uhlandstrasse; map p.137 D4
Housed in a beautiful 1889 Belle Époque villa off the Ku'damm and frequented by accomplished and aspiring writers, this small café-cum-restaurant in the building's winter garden makes for a great break from city-trotting, even if it is just for a cup of coffee. The Mediterranean-inspired food does not quite come up to the setting.

Café Kranzler
Kurfürstendamm 18; tel: 887 183 925; www.cafekranzler.de; daily 8.30am–8pm; S5, S7, S9: Zoologischer Garten, U2: Kurfürstendamm; map p.133 D1
The refined ladies who gathered for *Kaffee und Kuchen* here in days gone by would hardly recognise the Kranzler today. Not that there aren't still refined ladies and *Kaffee und Kuchen* here, but this Ku'damm landmark, a survivor of an institution which opened on Unter den Linden in 1835, moved to the Ku'damm a century later and was destroyed in World War II, to be rebuilt after the conflict. It has now been integrated into a huge office and shopping complex, its vintage architecture intact. A defining old-school Berlin place every bit as much as the KaDeWe and the Ku'damm itself.

Schwarzes Café
Kantstrasse 148; tel: 313 8038; www.schwarzescafe-berlin.de; daily 24 hours; U2, S5, S7, S9: Savignyplatz; map p.133 C1
If ever there were a typical Berlin café, this raucous institution would be it. Rough around the edges and full of attitude, it has always been there, is always open and everyone else goes there, which gives it a certain distinct charm.

Universum
Kurfürstendamm 153; tel: 8906 4995; www.universum lounge.com; daily 6pm–3am; U7: Adenauerplatz; map.136 B4
With a space-age theme, this is one of Berlin's most distinctive concept bars. Situated in the same building as the Schaubühne theatre, Universum has a clock set to Houston time and a fun ambience thanks to all the moon mission emphemera.

Vienna Bar
Kantstrasse 152; tel: 3101 5090; www.vienna-bar.de; Mon–Sat 5pm–1am; U2, S5, S7, S9: Zoologischer Garten; map p.133 D1
A bit friendlier than next-door neighbour Paris Bar, although owned by the same folks, the Vienna Bar's high-end inter-

national clientele is a cross section of the movers and shakers around Berlin's media and business worlds. It has yet to develop a distinctive style, but it is in the right location, so expect it to find a niche.

Zwiebelfisch
Savignyplatz 7; tel: 312 7363; www.zwiebelfisch-berlin.de; daily noon–4am; S5, S7, S9: Savignyplatz; map p.133 C1

An older, well-educated crowd gathers here to peruse the many magazines and newspapers on offer and discuss the news and views contained therein.

If your German and your knowledge of current events are up to it, you can join in. If you're lucky enough to be able to go with a regular, you'll be royally entertained.

Prenzlauer Berg

Café Schwarz Sauer
Kastanienallee 13; tel: 448 5633; www.schwarzsauer.com; daily 9am–late; U2: Eberswalder Strasse

The central location on 'Casting Allee', so called because of the beautiful people posing at the kerbside tables during the summer. Schwarz

Above: perfectly in-season fruit pastries.

Sauer is probably the best-known, best-loved bar on the street and is a favourite meeting place for young and budget-conscious residents of the neighbourhood, many of whom are British and American expats.

Prater-Garten
Kastanienallee 7–9; tel: 448 5688; www.pratergarten.de; Mon–Sat 6pm–late, Sun noon–late, garden open Apr–Sept; U2: Eberswalder Strasse

Claiming to be Berlin's oldest beer garden, the Prater has been around since 1837, when someone named Porath opened a beer bar on the site. In 1852, the Kalbo family took it over and soon established a small theatre to entertain the drinkers with songs and revues. In 1946, the property was taken over by the Volksbühne theatre, which became the focus of activity on the property, but in 1996, a major remodelling of the property put the beer garden back in business, where it remains an extremely popular gathering place today. Enjoy a Prater Pilsner, a charcoal-grilled Wurst, and an ambience that looks not too unlike the photo on the

Left: drinking at a bar in Hackescher Höfe.

A good café will never offer fruit pastries out of season. This means berries in the spring, peaches and plums later in the year, and apples, pears and dried fruit in the autumn.

1912 postcard pictured on the Prater's website.

Weinstein
Lychener Strasse 33; tel: 442 1842; www.weinstein.eu; Mon–Sat 5pm–2am, Sun 6pm–2am; U2: Eberswalder Strasse

Somewhere between a restaurant, a café and a wine bar, Weinstein has grown out of a wine wholesale business into one of the neighbourhood's top tips. The food is good, and the selection of wines from obscure corners of Europe, particularly Eastern Europe, is incredible.

Wohnzimmer
Lette Strasse 6; tel: 445 5458; www.wohnzimmer-bar.de; daily 9am–late; U2: Schönhauser Allee

In this bohemian-chic dive bar, the residents of Prenzlauer Berg come and hang out on vintage furniture. *Wohnzimmer* translates as 'living room', and with breakfast, cakes and drinks available, this laid-back pub is ideal for relaxing in like it was your own trendy lounge.

Yes
Knaackstrasse 14; www.yes berlin.de; Tue–Sat 8pm–late; U2: Senefelderplatz; map p.135 D4

Very eccentric bar owned and presided over by a very eccentric Spaniard with excellent taste in background music, beer and spirits. Yes also sits right by the Wasserturm, making it a good stop during an evening out in Prenzlauer Berg. If the owner offers you some of his whisky, though, just say no.

the tiny front garden during the day. English is spoken at the bar, although note that one of the owners is named Chaos for a reason.

Kreuzberg and Friedrichshain

Barcomi's
Bergmannstrasse 21; tel: 694 81 38; www.barcomis.de; Mon–Fri 9am–midnight, Sat 8am–midnight, Sun 10am–midnight; U7: Gneisenaustrasse; map p.138 B3

Cynthia Barcomi, an American, got tired of Berlin's bad coffee and became the first person in town to introduce home-roasted beans in her house blend. There are also cookies and brownies; unsurprisingly, this is the American cake-lover's home from home.

Café Milagro
Bergmannstrasse 12; tel: 692 2303; www.milagro.de; daily 9am–1am; U7: Gneisenaustrasse; map p.138 B3

A fixture of the Bergmannstrasse scene since 1990, the Milagro is open round the clock, and offers food until midnight. Its two floors are often packed with locals of every description, eating, drinking and trying to read in the dim light on a winter's afternoon.

CSA
Karl-Marx-Allee 96; tel: 2904 4741; www.csa-bar.de; daily May–Oct: 8pm–late, Nov–Apr: 7pm–late; U5: Weberwiese; map p.135 E2

This upmarket drinking den is somewhat different from most of the drinking options in scruffy, anarchic Friedrichshain. CSA has been sleekly designed from the former offices of the Czech Republic's airline of the same

---

As of January 2008, smoking has been theoretically prohibited in Berlin's bars and restaurants, although a separate smoking area is legal. Many bars have resisted this, but the chances are you'll be able to drink in a smoke-free environment.

Schöneberg

Bar am Lützowplatz
Lützowplatz 7; tel 262 6807; www.baramluetzowplatz.de; Sun–Wed 6pm–2am, Thur–Sat 6pm–4am; U3, U7: Nollendorfplatz; map p.133 E1

Berlin's longest cocktail bar, stretching throughout the length of the block, is a favourite of visitors. Seeing Mao Zedong's visage at the head of it may set off some cognitive dissonance though, even without the help of one of their superb selection of single malts, champagnes (one of the largest collections in the world) or distinctive cocktails.

Café Berio
Maassenstrasse 7; tel: 216

1945; Sun–Thur 8am–midnight, Fri–Sat 8am–1am; U2, U3, U4: Nollendorfplatz; map p.137 E4

A mainstay of Berlin's gay and lesbian community for over 50 years, the Berio is also a favourite place to stop after shopping at the Winterfeldtplatz market for its excellent coffee and pastries. Friendly service, and lovely tables outside during summer months.

Pinguin-Club
Wartburgstrasse 54; tel: 781 3005; www.pinguin-club.de; daily 6pm–4am; U7: Eisenacher Strasse; map p.137 E3

Since 1986, this merry pub has been serving a mix of Germans and expats, most of whom have remained regulars as they've aged. Elvis, Billy Wilder and Horst Buchholz on the set of *One, Two, Three*, as well as various forgotten German pop stars stare down from the walls, there's a kiddy-car made into a table and a disco ball on the ceiling. In recent years, they've started serving icecream in the summertime in

One daunting fact about Berlin is that its bars can, legally, be open round the clock. This, however, doesn't mean 24 hours: an hour a day has to be set aside for cleaning, although customers can remain in the house while service is suspended. Bars tend just to close when they close, usually late at night after the customers stop coming.

Above: enjoying a sunny day at an outdoor table.

name, and has put an elegant spin on the Soviet-era architecture, to make this bar something quite special.

Floating Lounge
Mühlenstrasse 73–7; tel: 6676 3806; www.floatinglounge-berlin.com; Mon–Sat 3 or 4pm–late, Sun 9am–late; S3, S5, S7, S9: Warschauer Strasse; map p.135 E1

Part of the Eastern Comfort Hostel Boat, this chilled out lounge is ideal for having a drink in while watching the sun set over the Oberbaum-brücke.

Golgatha Tanzbar und Biergarten
Dudenstrasse 40 (in Viktoria-park); tel: 785 2453; www.golgatha-berlin.de; Apr–Sept daily 10am–6am; U7: Yorck-strasse, U6: Platz der Luft-brücke, S1, S2: Yorckstrasse; map p.138 B3

Leave it to irreverent Berliners to name a beer garden on a hill with a cross on top of it after the garden where Jesus spent his last night, even if they do (intentionally) mis-

spell it. Live bands, occasional firework displays and lots of beer make this a lively and occasionally rowdy place in the summertime. Best to go with a local if you don't speak *Berlinisch*, but it's a genuine slice of Berlin life. Enter on Katzbachstrasse where Monumentenstrasse ends, then take the first right inside the park. You should hear it before you see it.

Solar
Stresemannstrasse 76; tel: 163 765 2700; www.solar berlin.com; Sun–Thur 6pm–2am, Fri–Sat 6pm–4am; S1, S25: Anhalter Bahnhof; map p.134 B1

Step into the glass lift on the side of a nondescript high-rise building near the Anhalter Bahnhof and

whoosh up to a glamorous cocktail lounge with killer views out over the city.

Western Districts

Loretta am Wannsee
Neue Kreisstrasse 50, Wannsee; tel: 803 5156; www.loretta.de; daily 11am–11pm; S1, S7: Wannsee

Berlin's Wannsee is a large lake with the biggest inland beach in Europe, so it's not surprising that there is a tree-shaded, 1,000-seat beer garden serving a variety of food and Berlin, Bavarian and Czech beers on draught just 150m (164yds) from the S-Bahn station. A perfect way to finish a day's boating, a visit to the Pfaueninsel, or any of the other activities in the region.

Below: the view of the Oberbaumbrücke from Floating Lounge.

Overseas visitors who've never experienced Continental ice-cream concoctions can be in for a shock: piles of ice-cream and fruit are often doused with liquor and then topped with whipped-cream, with a few cookies stuck in for good measure. A quality *Eiscafe* will have an illustrated menu.

Cabaret

Since the days of Christopher Isherwood's experiences in Berlin's sexual underground during the Weimar Republic years, the city has been widely considered to be a capital of cabaret shows, an impression compounded by the famous musical and film *Cabaret*, inspired by Isherwood's stories. Today, there remain a few venues in Berlin to experience top-class performances, including on some of the legendary old stages, such as the Wintergarten Varieté, while general theatres often provide a platform for well-known *travestie* artists. For further listings of theatres, see *Theatre and Dance, p.126–7.*

Entertainment Forms

Be aware of the distinctions between cabaret, *travestie* and *varieté*, or you could be in for something of a surprise. *Travestie* is effectively revue in drag, while *varieté* is more of a mixed, circus-like show with a sprinkling of all different types of entertainment.

A little history

Berlin's cabaret *(Kabarett)* scene has its roots in the pre-World War I era when variety shows hinted at political satire and criticism. However, it was not until the post-war fall of the Empire, and the subsequent lifting of censorship, that it really began to come into its own. Although owing something to the cabarets of Paris, with song and dance acts introduced by a compère, the German – and particularly Berlin – version was to become one of the most subversive and sharp theatrical movements in the world. Its heyday was during the Weimar Republic (1919–33) when stars such as Werner Finck, Paul Graetz

and Anita Berber pushed the boundaries of political satire and sexual liberation. The cabaret scene also attracted some of the best and brightest of Germany's literary talents, including Bertolt Brecht and Klaus Mann, and was also given considerable impetus by the work of the great theatre director Max Reinhardt.

With the rise of National Socialism cabaret's days were numbered and during the 1930s many of its stars fled abroad. There was a brief renaissance of the genre after World War II when the divided country began to deal with the issues of its Nazi past but by the 1960s it had lost its cutting edge and had been absorbed into mainstream entertainment on the television.

During the 1990s, however, a new cabaret scene began to form, especially in the east, and with the fall of the wall Berlin again became, briefly, the centre of a vibrant, satirical theatre. In recent years, though, as the city has settled into its new role as a

gentrifying capital city, audiences have have once again begun to ebb away.

Cabaret

Bar Jeder Vernuft
Schaperstrasse 24, Wilmersdorf; tel: 883 1582; www.bar-jeder-vernunft.de; daily, Mon–Sat 8pm, Sun 7pm, other shows vary; admission charge; U3, U9: Spichernstrasse; map p.137 D4
In a multi-mirrored circus-style tent, see popular performers in slick, entertaining shows, some in English. This is a fun place to indulge in classic Berlin entertainment.

Kleine Nachtrevue
Kurfürstenstrasse 116, Schöneberg; tel: 218 8950; www.kleine-nachtrevue.de; show Wed–Sat 11.15pm; admission charge; U1, U2, U3: Wittenbergplatz; map p.133 E1
Burlesque, nude ballets and torch songs by a male Marlene Dietrich impersonator make up the late-night programme at this playful cabaret, ideal for experiencing the decadent fantasy.

Scheinbar Varieté
Monumentenstrasse 9; tel: 784 5539; www.scheinbar.de; show

A major attraction at Hackescher Höfe, Chamäleon's influence on the development of German *varieté* extends well beyond Berlin. A beautiful theatre in one of the city's original theatre venues.

Friedrichstadtpalast
Friedrichstrasse 107; tel: 2326 2326; www.friedrichstadt palast.de admission charge; S3, S5, S7, S9, S75, U6, Tram M1, 12: Friedrichstrasse; map p.134 B3
One of the biggest attractions in Berlin for more than a century, Friedrichstadtpalast has survived two world wars, two dictatorships, and continues to draw crowds from all over to its musical and dance shows.

Wintergarten Varieté
Potsdamer Strasse 96; tel: 588 433; www.wintergarten-berlin.de; admission charge; U1: Kurfürstenstrasse, or S1, S2: Potsdamer Platz; map p.134 A1
Wintergarten has been described as Europe's most beautiful *varieté* theatre, and its extravagant shows are reminiscent of 1920s Berlin.

8.30pm, check programme for performance dates; admission charge; S2, S25, U7: Yorckstrasse; map p.138 A3
This theatre is about as big as your living room, seating up to 60 guests for its popular 'open stage' evenings when anyone can perform and the stage hosts professional and amateur clowns, jugglers or pantomime artists. Make reservations, by phone only.

Travestie

Ikenna Cabaret Berlin
Marlene-Dietrich-Platz 1; tel: 176 646 32 362; www.ikenna. de; check website for performance dates; admission charge; U2, S1, S2: Potsdamer Platz; map p.134 A1
The *travestie* artist Ikenna performs regularly in New York, Los Angeles, Paris, Cannes and Salzburg, and is known for her soulful singing. In Berlin, Ikenna hosts a number of visiting *travestie* artists. There are two shows each night.

Theater im Keller
Weserstrasse 211; tel: 623 1452; www.theater-im-keller.de;

admission charge; U7, U8: Herrmannplatz; map p.139 D3
This is a cosy basement theatre with just 43 seats and a changing programme. Check local listings for current events.

Varieté

Chamäleon Theater
Rosenthaler Strasse 40–41; tel: 400 0590; www.chamaeleon berlin.com; admission charge; S3, S5, S7, S9, S75, U8: Hackescher Markt; map p.135 C3

Below: a glamorous cabaret performer.

Children

Berlin's prime attractions might not seem immediately suitable for travelling with children, but the city is surprisingly child-friendly. Walking the wide streets of Berlin can be a tiring experience for little feet, but there are exciting alternatives: a front-seat ride past all the sights on a city double-decker bus, a visit to the world's largest dinosaur skeleton, petting a koi in the Zoo Aquarium, licking ice-cream 200m (656ft) above the city on the TV tower or exploring Berlin in miniature at the city's Legoland. Meanwhile, playgrounds and parks can be found in virtually every neighbourhood.

Activities

Domäne Dahlem (Dahlem Domain)

Königin-Luise-Strasse 49, Zehlendorf; tel: 666 3000; www.domaene-dahlem.de; farm grounds daily 24 hours, museum Wed–Mon daily 10am–6pm; farm grounds: free, museum: admission charge; U3: Dahlem-Dorf

Germany's only working farm with underground access. In the 15-hectare (37-acre) open-air museum of farming, kids can tour the fields on a tractor, pet the hogs, learn old crafts and learn about nutrition and organic farming in the old manor. A shop sells organically grown products, and for the parents there is an on-site beer garden (May–Oct 11am–8pm).

Jacks Kids World

Miraustrasse 38, Reinickendorf; tel: 8862 4464; www.jacks-kids-world.de; Tue–Fri 2–7.30pm, Sat–Sun 10am–7pm; admission charge; map p.133 D1

Mini-Go Karts, trampolines, jungle gyms, climbing maze, tunnel slides, cinema show-ing Disney cartoons and a nap room for infants and toddler area. Kids over 4 can be dropped off while parents go shopping and sightseeing.

Kinderbad Monbijou

Oranienburger Strasse 78, Mitte; tel: 282 86 52; www.berliner baederbetriebe.de (German only); daily 10am–7pm; admission charge; S1, S2, S25, S26: Oranienburger Strasse; map p.134 C3

On a hot summer day, there is hardly a better alternative than cooling off in centrally located Monbijou children's pool. Officially, only children are allowed to bathe here, but you can accompany your toddler in the shallow pool. Camp out on the lawn under old trees. Good to combine with a visit to Hackesche Höfe.

Legoland Discovery Centre

Potsdamer Strasse 4, Tiergarten; tel: 301 0400; www.legolanddiscoverycentre.com; daily 10am–7pm, last admission 5pm; admission charge; S1, S2, S25, U2: Potsdamer Platz; map p.134 A2

A good deal for very active families is the 'Welcome Card Berlin and Potsdam' (sold in tourist offices), which is a two- or three-day public transport and discount pass valid for one adult and up to three children.

A small indoor amusement park in the Sony Center on Potsdamer Platz, complete with rides, 4D cinema, a build-and-test area for creative lovers of the little bricks, a miniature Berlin, a cafeteria and a gift shop. Best for kids aged 3–7, but beware, no child discounts mean it is expensive.

Loxx MiniaturWeltenBerlin

Grunerstrasse 20, Mitte; tel: 4472 3022; www.loxx-berlin.com; daily 10am–8pm; admission charge; U2, U5, U8, S5, S7, S75, S9: Alexanderplatz; map p.135 D3

One of Berlin's newest attractions. A huge computer-controlled model railway world on 2,500 air-conditioned sq m (3,000 sq yds). Trains and highlights of Berlin are presented on a 1:87 scale, including an

Left: considering a splash in the Lustgarten.

Zoo Berlin
Hardenbergplatz 8, Tiergarten; tel: 25 40 10; www.zoo-berlin.de; daily 9am–7pm; admission charge; combined tickets for Zoo and Aquarium; U2, U9, S5, S7, S75, S9: Zoologischer Garten; map p.133 D1

The Zoo Berlin, home to Knut, the famous polar bear born in captivity in 2006, is a centrally located classic with a compact yet pleasant display of the largest variety of animals shown anywhere in the world including panda bears, gorillas and black rhino. There are public feedings, a petting zoo and huge playgrounds. Parents will also be interested to note the Zoo's blend of historic architecture, like the Elephant Gate, as well as the modern animal houses like the fascinating, glass-domed Hippopotamus House.

General Information

ACCOMMODATION
Some hotels have family rooms sleeping up to four; one extra bed or cot in a double is usually not a problem. Renting an apartment with a full kitchen is often good value.
SEE ALSO HOTELS, P.70–77

airport serviced by model planes: big fun for kids and dads.

Sea Life Berlin
Spandauer Strasse 3, Mitte; tel: 992 800; daily 10am–7pm; admission charge; S5, S7, S75, S9: Hackescher Markt; U2, U5, U8: Alexanderplatz; map p.135 C3

Displays of local and European water life. The attached Aquadom is really something: a slow elevator ride through a huge round fish tank full or coral fish. Overall though, the cost means the Aquarium is better value for families.

Zoo-Aquarium
Budapester Strasse 32, Tiergarten; tel: 254 010; www.aquarium-berlin.de; daily 9am–6pm; admission charge; combined tickets for Aquarium and Zoo; U2, U9, S, S5, S7, S75, S9: Zoologischer Garten; map p.133 D1

A hands-on experience of biodiversity, this aquarium, the largest in Europe, has a record number of species in fish tanks and terrarium, including breathtaking displays of sharks, stingrays, piranhas and coral reef fish, as well as the opportunity to pet the kois.

Below: the Elephant Gate at Zoo Berlin leads to many creatures, from flamingos to a curious giraffe.

Above: playgrounds can be found in many Berlin parks.

BABYSITTING
Although you can almost certainly arrange a babysitter for a few hours through your hotel, this is an alternative:

Kinderinsel (Children's Island)
Eichendorffstrasse 17, Mitte; tel: 4171 6928; www.kinderinsel.de; S2: Nordbahnhof; U6: Zinnowitzer Strasse; map p.134 B4
Kinderinsel is a day care centre-cum-hotel. The multilingual professional staff look after children aged 0–14 around the clock, entertain them with ghost parties or take them out on city adventure tours. In emergencies (sick children or parents), they pay house visits.

DISCOUNTS
Almost everywhere, there are discounts for children under 14. Toddlers are mostly admitted for free. Most Berlin museums are free for kids under 16.

EATING OUT
Children are welcome but expected not to disturb other guests in restaurants. Most places have children's menus or serve an extra plate if you want to split a meal. Most restaurants will also have high chairs for young guests.

HOSPITALS
DRK Krankenhaus Westend
Spandauer Damm 130; tel: 30350; S41, S42, S46: Westend and 5 minutes' walk
A hospital with 24-hour children's emergency service and English-speaking staff.
SEE ALSO ESSENTIALS, P.48–9

SUPPLIES
Baby food and supplies such as nappies are sold at every larger supermarket and at pharmacies.

Museums
Deutsches Technikmuseum
Trebbiner Strasse 9, Kreuzberg; tel: 902 540; www.dtmb.de; Tue–Fri 9am–5.30pm, Sat–Sun 10am–6pm; admission charge; U1, U7: Möckernbrücke; U1, U2: Gleisdreieck; S1, S2, S25: Anhalter Bahnhof; map p.138 B4
The Mecca for young railway, car and engineering aficionados. A few steps from the main building is the SPECTRUM Science Centre (entrance Möckernstrasse 26), offering several floors of playful physics experiments suited to kids aged from 4 upwards.

Museum für Kommunikation
Leipziger Strasse 16, Mitte; tel: 202 940; www.mfk-berlin.de (German only); Tue 9am–8pm, Wed–Fri 9am–5pm, Sat–Sun 10am–6pm; entrance charge; U2: Mohrenstrasse; U2, U6: Stadtmitte, S1, S2, S25: Potsdamer Platz; map p.134 B2
Kids can play football with cute-looking robots in the museum's foyer, while parents may marvel at the architecture of this beautifully renovated 19th-century building, the world's oldest

In winter, ice rinks are set up on Alexanderplatz and Potsdamer Platz where the winter playground (Winterwelt) is completed by a huge tobogganning hill *(see p.55).*

Make the trip up to one of Berlin's best viewpoints as a treat for both parents and little ones. The **Fernsehturm** (Television Tower) has good views of the city from the observation deck or the Telecafé restaurant with its rotating floor, over a meal or an ice-cream sundae *(see also p.30–1)*. Alternatively, you can avoid the queues at the **Reichstagskuppel** (dome of the **Reichstag** building) by entering the building on its right side entrance, which is reserved for families with young children *(see also p.31)*.

postal museum. In the basement, you can admire the Blue Mauritius and Bell's first telephone.

Museum für Naturkunde (Museum of Natural History)
Invalidenstrasse 43, Mitte; tel: 2093 8591; www.naturkunde museum-berlin.de; Tue–Fri 9.30am–6pm, Sat–Sun, holidays 10am–6pm; admission charge; U6: Zinnowitzer Strasse; S3, S5, S7, S9: Hauptbahnhof; S1, S2: Nordbahnhof; map p.134 B4
The star of Berlin's Natural History Museum's newly arranged dinosaur exhibition is the world's largest Brachiosaurus skeleton, measuring 12m high by 22m long (40ft by 70ft).
SEE ALSO MUSEUMS, P.88

Sightseeing

BY BOAT
Give those little feet a rest on one of the many sightseeing boats cruising on the Spree river and canals. Several companies operate on similar routes.
SEE ALSO TRANSPORT, P.129

Reederei Riedel
Landing Märkisches Ufer, Mitte;

tel: 6165 7930; www.reederei-riedel.de (German only); U2: Märkisches Museum; S3, S5, S7, S75, S9, U8: Jannow-itzbrücke; map p.135 D2
Go on a three-hour 'Brückenfahrt' (tour of bridges) along the Spree and the Landwehrkanal and discover that Berlin actually has more bridges than Venice.

Reederei Winkler
Landing Bahnhof Friedrich-strasse (outside the railway station), Mitte; tel: 349 9595; www.reedereiwinkler.de/en; Apr–Oct; S5, S7, S75, S9: Friedrichstrasse; map p.136 B2
Easy-to-find landing, one-hour city tours. Longer ones depart from Schloss Charlottenburg landing.

BY BUS
Kids will love seeing the city from the top deck of bus No. 100 or 200, or any official hop-on hop-off bus tour.

BY CYCLE-RICKSHAW
Call or simply hail a cycle-rickshaw at Brandenburg Gate, Potsdamer Platz, Kurfürstendamm or Hauptbahn-

hof for individual guided tours of the city.
Berlin Rikscha Tours
Tel: 0163 307 7297; www.berlin-rikscha-tours.de; spring–autumn: daily 24 hours
Velotaxi
Tel: 400 5620; www.velotaxi.de; spring–autumn: daily 24 hours

Toy Shops

Ratzekatz
Raumerstrasse 7, Prenzlauer Berg; tel: 681 9564; www.ratzekatz.de; Tue–Sat 9am–7pm; U2: Eberswalder Strasse
Angelina Jolie bought dinosaurs here for her son; the crammed shop stores everything from baby toys to model trains.
T.O.T.S.
The Original Toy Store
Unter den Linden 69, Mitte; tel: 2267 9081; www.tots.de; map p.136 A1
Quality toy paradise just a block away from Brandenburg Gate. Traditional Anker stone building sets and puzzles. Wooden toys. English-language children's books.

Right: a tour boat sets sail on the Spree.

Churches, Synagogues and Mosques

There's no Notre-Dame or Hagia Sophia here: for a European capital city, Berlin is a comparatively secular city, especially compared to many others in Germany, which are deeply imbued with Catholic or Protestant significance. Instead, the important churches and synagogues tie in to the larger historical picture; indeed, some of the most notable are more iconic as monuments than as houses of worship.

Mitte

Berliner Dom (Berlin Cathedral)

Lustgarten; tel: 2026 9110; www.berliner-dom.de; Mon–Sat 9am–8pm, Sun noon–8pm; admission charge; S3, S5, S7, S9, S75: Hackescher Markt; map p.137 D1

The central administrative building of the Evangelical Church was built in 1905 to replace a classic Schinkel structure. It's typical Wilhelmine bombast and the sanctuary's acoustics are not ideal for the many concerts held there, but the sheer detail of its interior is impressive. Admission also includes access to the dome, which has a fine view of Mitte, and the crypt, which contains 90 sarcophagi of various Hohenzollerns.

Around Alexanderplatz

Marienkirche

Karl-Liebknecht-Strasse 8; tel: 242 4467; www.marienkirche-berlin.de; daily 10am–6pm; free; S3, S5, S7, S9, S75, U2, U5, U8: Alexanderplatz; map p.137 E2

Begun around 1270 and gradually added to and rebuilt until Carl Gotthard Langhans, the architect of the Brandenburg Gate, finished it in 1790, this is one of Berlin's oldest structures. The *Dance of Death* fresco in the entrance hall is from 1485, during the time of the Plague. The Walther organ is one of Germany's finest. The church gained further prominence in 1989 as a centre for anti-government dissidence in East Germany, one of the few in Berlin.

Neue Synagogue

Oranienburger Strasse 28–30; tel: 8802 8316; www.cjudaicum.de; Sun–Mon 10am–8pm, Nov–Feb until 6pm, Tue–Thur 10am–6pm, Fri 10am–2pm, Apr–Sept until 5pm; admission charge; guided tour in English Thur 4pm; S1, S2, S25, S26: Oranienburger Strasse; map p.134 C3

Built in 1866 as a symbol of pride in Berlin's Jewish community, the New Synagogue, its Moorish dome filigreed with gold, towers over the Scheunenviertel. Although attacked on Kristallnacht in 1939, the thugs were turned away by a brave policeman, Wilhelm Krützfeld, who is honoured with a plaque on the synagogue front. The real damage came from an Allied bombing raid in 1945, which destroyed the sanctuary. Today, the structure is a museum for the Centrum Judaicum, a foundation which maintains a permanent collection celebrating the building's history and various temporary exhibitions dealing with various aspects of Berlin's Jewish history.

At the end of the 19th century, the Kaiser's wife, the Kaiserin, decreed that each of the city's *Bezirke* (districts) should have its own Evangelical church, which resulted in the skyline being dotted with steeples. None are particularly architecturally distinguished. Another decree was that non-Evangelical churches were permitted, but not allowed to have their front doors on the street, so neighbourhood Catholic and other Protestant churches are often hidden from view.

Left: the Neue Synagogue.

Kaiser Wilhelm I, and bombed in 1943, this church has become famous for its ruin. Instead of rebuilding it, the Evangelical Church shored up the remains and left it as a stark reminder of war amidst its gleaming modern surroundings. Services take place in the glass-encased tower next door.

Kreuzberg and Friedrichshain

Mosques

Although Berlin's mostly Turkish Muslim community has over 200,000 members, mosques tend to be hidden from view, with worship being conducted in converted factory buildings and unlabelled storefronts. As recently as April 2007, the laying of a cornerstone for a mosque in Kreuzberg attracted angry demonstrators. One of the few visible mosques is the **Ahmadiyya Mosque** in Wilmersdorf (Brienner Strasse 7–8; tel: 873 5703); a very impressive one is the **Sehitlik Mosque** in Neukölln (Columbiadamm 128; tel: 692 1118, tours on request), its minarets towering over the Hasenheide park. None of Berlin's mosques are open for inspection by the general public without prior notice.

Note that there is an armed police presence in front of all synagogues and other Jewish buildings in Berlin. This is a normal security procedure and not a cause for alarm.

Nikolaikirche

Nikolaikirchplatz; tel: 2400 2162; www.stadtmuseum.de; daily 10am–6pm; free, donations welcome; S3, S5, S7, S9, S75, U2, U5, U8: Alexanderplatz; map p.137 E1

Originally constructed in 1220 and added to through the 19th century, the Nikolaikirche forms the centre of the Nikolaiviertel historical district. The church was bombed heavily during World War II, but was faithfully reconstructed in 1987. Today it houses a history museum, focussing on Berlin's development as a city until the mid-17th century, and is occasionally used as a concert venue.

Charlottenburg

Kaiser-Wilhelm-Gedächtniskirche

Breitscheidplatz; tel: 218 5023; www.gedaechtniskirche-berlin.de; daily 9am–7pm; free; S3, S5, S7, S9, U1, U2, U9: Zoologischer Garten; map p.133 D1

Built in 1891–5 to honour

Below: the impressively detailed altar and ceiling of the Berliner Dom.

Environment

Berlin is a surprisingly 'green' city; surprising because of the scale of development the city is always undergoing and the cash-flow problems that the local government is suffering. However, there are measures in place to reduce once chronic problems of air pollution, while recycling is an inbuilt feature of the German lifestyle. Visitors will notice the provision made for recycling as well as the changes wrought by the recent smoking ban. Meanwhile, with 18 percent of the Greater Berlin area covered by greenery, many local species are thriving, and the urban population is never too far from a park, forest or even a beach.

Construction

Berlin is constantly renewing itself. Hard as it may be to believe, there is still damage from bombing raids during World War II, and unexploded bombs even turn up from time to time. In addition, much of the renovation done by the East German government was rather lacking, whether covering up a beautiful old facade with concrete or working with low-quality materials, and this, too, is having to be repaired. The days when the sky over Potsdamer Platz looked like a crane convention may be gone, but the building of new buildings continues at a lesser pace, especially in the East, where bombed buildings tended to be torn down and the lot left vacant.

Air Quality

A piece of good news for those who never felt at home in Berlin's smoke-infested bars and cafés: smoking is now banned in indoor public areas, apart from specially identified rooms. However, many Berliners still smoke, so some bars have avoided

Due to high-tech water purification and less industry in Berlin, the water quality of the Spree river has improved considerably over the past 20 years, but swimming is still neither allowed nor advisable here. However, 17 species of fish have recently been counted in the Spree, and the quality of the Berlin tap water is excellent.

the ban by re-inventing themselves as 'smoking clubs'.

With the replacement of coal stoves in old apartment buildings by more modern heating systems, the Berlin air *(Berliner Luft)* has lost the pungent smell that used to be so characteristic of winter in the city. Another measure aimed at improving the proverbial *Berliner Luft* has been the recent introduction of *Umweltplaketten*, green, yellow or red tags for cars, depending on their contribution to pollution. Without such a sticker, cars are not allowed into the Green Zone or *Umweltzone*, the inner-city area within the S-Bahn ring. If

you are planning to drive to Berlin, you can have a badge mailed to your house in advance by online registration at www.umweltplakette.de.

Flora and Fauna

Berlin is committed to protecting and preserving its 2,500 public parks, green spaces and old trees in the city, realising how much they contribute to Berliners' quality of life. The efforts pay: Berlin is considered a very habitable place by two- and four-legged creatures: Mandarin ducks, herons, wild boar and foxes can all be spotted in city parks, with a bit of luck. Recent surveys have shown that the number of species found per hectare of urban land in Berlin is actually higher than in rural areas of Germany. This is partly due to the slightly higher average temperatures in the city, providing comfortable conditions for some Mediterranean species.

Among animals feeling particularly at home in Berlin are bats: 10,000 of them spend the winters in the Spandau Citadel, making it

Left: cranes are an everyday presence in Berlin.

the Wall. The city pumped €4.5 million into laying it out. SEE ALSO PARKS AND GARDENS, P.108–11; SPORTS, P.124; TRANSPORT, P.129

Eco-initiatives

Berliners, like all good Germans, are renowned for separating their rubbish neatly into colour-coded bins or containers (plastic goes in yellow, paper in blue). What they are less conscientious about is cleaning up after their dogs, assuming that they are not paying their dog tax for nothing, so keep an eye on where you step.

Although the sky over Berlin is not often a sunny one, solar power is hot here. SolarEnergy, one of the world's most important renewable energy trade shows, is held under the Funkturm tower every two years, partly to meet the rising demand for the latest heating technologies. You can even charter a solar-powered boat for a tour on the Berlin canals (www.solarpolis.de). However, so far solar power only accounts for 1 percent of the city's energy consumption, but with the increasing popularity of this energy form in sunnier southern Germany, this may increase in the future.

one of Europe's most important hibernation areas for the winged mammals. Surviving old bunkers and abandoned buildings in the city are just as popular with them. The more natural setting of the Berlin forests includes a number of nature sanctuaries that are refuges for protected species.

An area well-suited to study how quickly nature reclaims abandoned developed sites is the Schöneberger Südgelände, barely 20 minutes away from Potsdamer Platz by S-Bahn. A unique landscape emerged here on 18 hectares (45 acres) of a former marshalling yard. Trees have grown between railway tracks ever since the yard was given up after the building of the Wall, resulting in a 'primary forest'. Public protests prevented a development of the area in the 1970s, so it was left untouched for decades. Numerous species of birds, butterflies, grasshoppers and wild flowers are flourishing

here now on dry meadows and in robinia forests.

Berlin also has 17,000 hectares (42,500 acres) of forest, several dozen lakes with beaches and 180km (112 miles) of navigable waterways, resulting in plenty of recreational options. A great way of exploring the city and its surroundings is by bicycle – Berlin has 620km (385 miles) of bike paths, and rental bikes are available from many places. For a bit of history with your nature, try the Berliner Mauer-Radweg path, a 160km (100-mile) bicycle trail along the former death strip, passing by the few surviving relicts of

Right: a recycling bin at an S-Bahn station.

Essentials

Berlin is an easy city to get around, and there is certainly no lack of things to do. Locals tend to be reserved but polite with strangers, and younger Berliners in particular may be happy to practise their English on you. The police in Berlin are generally friendly and helpful to tourists, but note that their command of English may be limited. Still, don't hesitate to approach them if you feel lost. The following listings detail practical information to help you get to grips with, among other things, locating an address, getting out cash and finding information on what events are happening during your stay.

Addresses

House numbers in Berlin do not necessarily progress in one direction. The name of the street and the numbers on that block are marked on street signs at most corners.

Climate

Summers are fairly warm in Berlin, with highs around 25°C (77°F) from June to August, but rainy days are not uncommon. Spring and autumn are pleasant seasons to visit, with moderate temperatures. Winters tend to be wet and cold, with few sunny days.
www.berlin-life.com/weather.php

Electricity

You will need an adaptor or transformer for most British and US plugs. German sockets have two round holes and supplies are 220 volts.

Embassies and Consulates

Australia
Wallstrasse 76–79, Mitte; tel: 880 0880
Canada
Leipziger Platz 17, Mitte; tel: 203 120

Republic of Ireland
Friedrichstrasse 200, Mitte; tel: 220 720
UK
Wilhelmstrasse 70, Mitte; tel: 2045 7579
US
Consulate: Clayallee 170, Zehlendorf; tel: 832 92
Embassy: Neustädtische Kirchstrasse 4–5, Mitte; tel: 238 6290

Emergencies

Polizei (Police): 110
Feuerwehr/Rettungsstelle (Fire Department/ Ambulance): 112
These numbers can be called toll-free from public phone boxes and mobile phones.

Health

DOCTORS AND HOSPITALS
Call a doc
Tel: 01804-22 55 23 62
Arranges appointments with English-speaking doctors.
Charité
Schumann Strasse 20–21; tel: 420 50; U6, S1 S2, S7, S9, S75: Friedrichstrasse; map p.134 B3
St Hedwig Krankenhaus
Grosse Hamburger Strasse 5; tel: 231 10; S5, S7, S9, S75: Hackescher Markt; map p.134 C3

MEDICAL TREATMENT
EU Nationals
Visitors from EU member states are entitled to reduced-cost (usually 70 percent) emergency treatment from doctors and dentists with a European Health Insurance card (EHIC). UK citizens can obtain it from post offices or online at www.dh.gov.uk.
North Americans
International Association for Medical Assistance to Travellers (IAMAT); 40 Regal Road, Guelph, Ontario N1K 1B5, Canada; tel: 519 836 0102
This is a non-profit group that offers members fixed rates for medical treatment. Members

Below: if in need of a pharmacy, look out for one of these.

Left: a good map is always useful for navigating city streets.

(phone cards) are sold at T-Punkt telecom shops.

Tourist Information

EX-BERLINER
The monthly *Ex-Berliner* English-language city maga-zine is good for listings of all kinds of events. Available from all better news-stands and tourist offices (limited contents on www.exberliner.de).

TOURIST OFFICES
The city tourist offices are called 'Berlin Infostore', and branches can be found at: **Hauptbahnhof; ground floor; daily 8am–10pm.** **Brandenburg Gate, Pariser Platz; daily 10am–6pm** **Berlin Pavilion at the Reichstag, Scheidemannstrasse; daily 10am–6pm** **Neues Kranzler Eck mall, Kurfürs-tendamm 21; daily 10am–6pm** Apart from making reserva-tions, providing maps and information, these places sell the **Berlin WelcomeCard** (travelcard and 50 percent dis-count on admission charges) and the new **WelcomeCard Culture** that includes free entry into 70 museums.

Visas
Visitors from the EU, the US, Canada and Australia don't need a visa for visiting Ger-many, just a valid national identity card (EU citizens) or a passport. Visitors from other countries need a valid passport and should check regulations with their local German Consulate.

receive a medical record com-pleted by their doctor and a directory of English-speaking IAMAT doctors in Germany, who are on call 24 hours a day. Membership is free.

PHARMACIES
Over-the-counter drugs are sold at *Apotheke* (pharmacies) which can be found every-where, marked by a red 'A'.

Internet
Many hotels, hostels and cafés, especially in the tourist areas, provide wireless inter-net, and there are numerous internet cafés all over town: **easyEverything** Kurfürstendamm 224; daily 6.30am–2am; U1, U15: Kurfürstendamm; map p.133 D1 The biggest internet café is very centrally located. Other branches, with shorter open-ing hours, at the **Sony Center** and **Friedrichstrasse** station.

Money
Germany's currency is the euro. For up-to-date exchange rates, consult: www.xe.com.
 Credit cards are not as universally accepted here as elsewhere in the world. Always carry some cash; small items are never paid for by card. ATMs are located all over the city but not as frequently as you might want. Many are sit-uated in banks; after hours, open the doors with your card. Most have an English menu but require numeric PINs.
 Wechselstuben (Bureaux de Change) offer slightly better exchange rates than banks. You find them at railway stations and airports.

Post
Post offices are rare these days, but they are about the only places selling stamps. **Postamt Friedrichstrasse** Georgenstrasse 12, Mitte; daily 8am–10pm; S1, S7, S9, S75, U6: Friedrichstrasse; map p.136 B2 The longest-opening branch.

Telephones
Berlin has many telephone shops where you can make long-distance calls at low fares. Compare prices, though, since most have a focus region in the world.
 Most phone boxes are card-operated. *Telefonkarte*

Useful Websites
www.berlin.de
www.visitberlin.de
www.berlin-info.de
www.berlin-life.com

Fashion

Berlin fashion has always been edgy. From the erotic masculinity of Marlene Dietrich to today's street-savvy style, it has long been known for its elegant toughness. In Marlene's day, Berlin was a fashion centre, a role it lost after World War II and did not recover until after the Berlin Wall fell and designers rediscovered the German capital. While those looking for the big international names will find them, Berlin's speciality is innovative, individual designers housed in quirky boutiques, as well as cutting-edge streetwear. For department stores that stock clothing, *see Shopping, p.120.*

The Berlin Fashion Map

International brands can be found in posh boutiques on **Kurfürstendamm** or **Friedrichstrasse**, while Berlin's new, young fashion is mainly situated in the Eastern part of the city, in small shops on **Kastanienallee** in Prenzlauer Berg, or in the winding side streets around **Hackescher Markt** in Mitte.

Berlin Designers and Boutiques

Adddress

Weinmeisterstrasse 12–14; tel: 2887 3434; www.adddress.de; Mon–Sat noon–7pm; U2: Rosa-Luxemburg-Platz; map p.135 C3

Andrea Vrajitoru launched her shop in 2003, determined to add a touch of elegance to

---

West Berlin's famous Kurfürstendamm is still a major fashion venue, where many high-street and international brands are found. Explore the side streets that lead off Ku'damm to find smaller boutiques with local designers.

---

daily life. Her womenswear mixes high-quality design with utilitarian sophistication, resulting in a raft of trendy designs fit for any occasion.

Anuschka Hoevener

Kastanienallee 47, Prenzlauer Berg; tel: 4431 9299; www.anuschkahoevener.de; Tue–Fri 2–6pm, Sat noon–6pm; U8: Rosenthaler Platz; map p.135 C4

One of Berlin's avante-garde designers, Hoevener celebrates natural materials like silk and wool, incorporating sculptural forms into her minimalist designs for women. She is also gaining a devoted following in the US and Japan.

Butterflysoulfire

Mulackstrasse 11; tel: 9488 9181; www.butterflysoulfire.com; Mon–Fri 10am–6pm; Sat by appointment; S8, S41, S42: Greifswalder Strasse

As its name suggests, this young label for men and women seeks a metamorphosis of styles that combine street cool with evening elegance. Proud of its Berlin roots, it calls its label A1, 'a tribute to the hood'.

Above: the hallmark knitwear at Claudia Skoda Level.

C'est tout Berlin

Mulackstrasse 26, Mitte; tel: 2759 5530; www.cesttout.de; Mon–Sat noon–7pm; U8: Rosenthaler Platz; map p.135 C3

As its designer, Katja Fuhrmann defined MTV Germany's look. Now she's turned to the appearance of women everywhere with urban, elegant and feminine designs.

Claudia Skoda Level

Alte Schönhauser Strasse 35, Mitte; tel: 280 7211; www.claudiaskoda.com;

Left: shopping at the clubwear and streetwear shop, Planet.

map p.135 C3

One of the most internationally celebrated of the new designers, the men's fashion by design duo Carl Tellessen and Daniela Biesenbach captures the spirit of change in the new Berlin.

Heimspiel
Niederbarnimstrasse 18, Friedrichshain; tel: 2068 7870; www.heimspiel-berlin.de; Mon–Fri 1–8pm; U5: Samariterstrasse

At this multi-label store, small is beautiful. It is a retail outlet for no less than 30 young Berlin designers, offering everything from clothes and accessories to art and crafts.

Molotow
Gneisenaustrasse 112, Kreuzberg; tel: 693 0818; www.molotowberlin.de; Mon–Fri 2–8pm, Sat noon–4pm; U7: Mehringdamm; map p.138 B4

This boutique is a showcase for both established and emerging local designers and sells fresh, elegant items that are both innovative and wearable.

Mon–Fri noon–8pm, Sat 11am–7pm; U8: Weinmeisterstrasse; map p.135 C3

An icon of the Berlin avant-garde and the city's most established local designer, Claudia Skoda transformed knitwear into a modern design statement and became known internationally. She hung out with Bowie and Iggy Pop in West Berlin and spent the '80s in New York before returning home to take part in the revival of Berlin. Men's and women's lines available.

Creation Pia Fisher
Eisenacher Strasse 69, Schöneberg; tel: 7895 0915; www.creationpiafischer.de; Mon–Fri noon–6pm, Sat 10am–2pm; U7: Eisenacher Strasse; map p.137 E3

Pia Fischer is definitely not a disciple of the No Logo school; her unique creations are akin to an extravagant patchwork of 'utensils of haute couture': labels, buttons, zippers and ribbons.

Ebner Hosen Berlin
Schlesische Strasse 36, Prenzlauer Berg; tel: 5369 6486; www.florindaschnitzel.de;

Tue–Sat noon–8.30pm; U1: Schlesisches Tor; map p.135 E1

In addition to its collections of hip trousers, shirts, capes and skirts, Ebner offers a 'racing and tuning' service to breathe new life into your favourite old clothes.

Firma
Mulackstrasse 1 tel: 4005 4047; www.firma.net; Mon–Fri noon–8pm, Sat noon–6pm; U8: Weinmeisterstrasse; S3, S5, S7, S9: Hackescher Markt;

Below: women's and men's fashions at Molotow.

Above: popular street fashion at IrieDaily.

Stoffrausch

Gabelsbergerstrasse 8, Friedrichshain; tel: 2966 5151; www.stoffrausch.com; Mon–Fri noon–8pm, Sat noon–4pm; U5: Samariterstrasse

Designers Steffi di Freddi and Dominik Muun say their clothes are for 'crazy city-dwellers and other lunatics', and indeed, their street hip jackets, trousers and sweat-shirts are ideal for the urban individualist.

Thatcher's Shop

Kastanienallee 21; tel: 2462 7751; Mon–Fri 11am–7pm, Sat noon–6pm; U2: Eberswalder Strasse

Inspired by photography, music, architecture and digit-al arts, Ralf Hensellek and Thomas Mrozek have been among the most popular Berlin designers since they first opened Thatcher's in 1995.

Other Designer Boutiques and Department Stores

Peek & Cloppenburg

Tauentzienstrasse 19, Charlottenburg; tel: 212 900; www.peek-cloppenburg.de; Mon–Sat 10am–8pm; U2: Wittenbergplatz; map p.133 D1

This is the flagship store of the upmarket fashion chain. It offers a wide variety of brands, from quality casual wear and basics to business attire, young fashion and designer brands, often at a discount.

Quartier 206

Friedrichstrasse 71, Mitte; tel: 2094 6800; www.department-store-quartier206.com; Mon–Fri 11am–8pm, Sat 10am–6pm; U2: Stadtmitte, Französische Strasse; map p.134 B2

This is where the stars shop when they come to Berlin. A sophisticated temple to shopping, Quartier 206 restores Friedrichstrasse's cosmopolitan flair. The heart of the Quartier is Anne Maria Jagdfeld's, with her stunning collection of top designers, beauty products and gor-geous flowers.

Size Conversions
Women: 36 (UK 8, US 6); 38 (UK 10, US 8); 40 (UK 12, US 10); 42 (UK 14, US 12); 44 (UK 16, US 14); 46 (UK 18, US 16).
Men: 87 (UK/US 34); 91 (UK/US 36); 97 (UK/US 38); 102 (UK/US 40); 107 (UK/US 42); 112 (UK/US 44)

Specialist Clothing

Devils Child

Kreuzbergstrasse 31, Kreuzberg; tel: 7889 5002; www.devils-child.com; Mon–Fri noon–6pm, Sat noon–2pm; S2, S25, U7: Yor-ckstrasse; map p.138 B3

This local t-shirt maker has a wide variety of Berlin prints, but customers can also choose their own designs.

Rocking Chair

Gabriel-Max-Strasse 13, Friedrichshain; tel: 2936 4291; www.rockingchair-berlin.de; Mon–Fri noon–7pm, Sat 10am–4pm; U5: Samariter-strasse

Look closely and you might spot Elvis at this fashion shop that features '50s clothes, rockabilly attire, punk outfits and a large selection of retro-style bowl-ing jerseys and Hawaiian shirts.

Sexy Mama

Lychener Strasse 52, Prenzlauer Berg; tel: 5471 4338; www.sexy-mama.de; Mon, Thur–Fri noon–7pm, Tue–Wed 10am–7pm, Sat 11am–5pm; U2: Schönhauser Allee or Eber-swalder Strasse

Catering to an influx of young families in Berlin's hippest neighbourhood, this boutique offers locally designed clothing for fashion-conscious mothers-to-be.

Trüffelschwein
Rosa-Luxemburg-Strasse 22, Mitte; tel: 7022 1225; www.trueffelschwein berlin.com; Mon–Sat noon–8pm; U2: Rosa-Luxemburg-Platz; map p.135 C3
Named for the pig used to sniff out delicious truffles in the woods, this men's fashion store is arranged like an attic to go rummaging in for timeless clothing that defies any passing trend. No suits or tuxedos here, but everything else a man might need.

Streetwear

East Berlin
Alte Schönhauser Strasse 33–4; tel: 4404 6090; www.east berlin.net; Mon–Sat 11am–8pm, Sat 11am–7pm; U2: Eberswalder Strasse
Trendy young fashion that screams out its love of Berlin on t-shirts and sweatshirts bearing local icons such as the TV Tower on Alexanderplatz or the Bundesadler, the eagle that is Germany's national symbol.

IrieDaily
Depot 2, Oranienstrasse 9, Kreuzberg; tel: 611 4655; www.iriedaily.com; Mon–Sat 11am–8pm; U1: Görlitzer Bahnhof; map p.135 D1
Beloved, iconic Kreuzberg brand selling skater-influenced urbanwear. Very Berlin and increasingly successful, but still true to its edgy, street-style roots. Pick up a classic hoodie.

Planet
Schlüterstrasse 35, Charlottenburg; tel: 885 2717; www.planetwear.de; Mon–Fri 11.30am–7.30pm, Sat 11.30am–6pm; U1: Uhlandstrasse; map p.132 C1
Looking for some proper rave kit to hit Berlin's legendary club scene in? Planet is brimming with dancefloor-ready clothes and shoes, in addition to more standard streetwear styles. Pumping music helps get clients in the mood.

Footwear

Budapester Schuhe
Kurfürstendamm 43, Charlottenburg; tel: 8862 4206; www.budapester.eu; Mon–Fri 10am–7pm, Sat 10am–6pm; U1: Uhlandstrasse; map p.133 C1
For the latest in designer shoes, this is a one-stop shop, packed with designs from the most coveted brands, as well as some spe-

Above: Berlin is a great place for finding funky shoes.

cialists in handmade footwear.

Riccardo Cartillone
Savignyplatz 5, Charlottenburg; tel: 312 9701; www.riccardo cartillone.com; Mon–Sat 10am–8pm; S5, S7, S9, S75: Savignyplatz; map p.133 C1
Cartillone emigrated to Germany and discovered a demand for well-designed hand-made Italian shoes and boots. In his Berlin stores he sells top brands as well as his own creations for men and women, often marked down (many other branches in the city, see website for details).

Below: utter elegance at Riccardo Cartillone.

Festivals and Events

The city of Berlin is chronically broke, but certainly not in spirit. It seems that there is always something to celebrate here, with many events culminating in ceremonial fireworks. The biggest one of these, on New Year's Eve at the Brandenburger Tor (Brandenburg Gate), attracts a million visitors every year. In the months preceding this big party, Berlin plays host to a number of special events and large-scale festivals. Of these, the most famed is the prestigious Berlinale International Film Festival.

January

Grüne Woche (Green Week)

Late January; exhibition ground Messe Berlin, Wilmersdorf; tel: 3069 6969; www.gruene woche.de; admission charge; S41, S42, S46: Messe Nord, ICC; map p.132 A1

The annual Green Week farming and food fair is a spectacular gourmet extravaganza. Visitors come to sample exotic goods, while proud farmers present their organic produce.

Lange Nacht der Museen

Late January; museums throughout the city; www.lange-

Below: crowds gather outside a cinema during the Berlinale.

nacht-der-museen.de; admission charge

A hundred museums keep their doors open until 2am, presenting not just their collections but an ambitious programme of video installations, concerts, shows and recitals. All venues are connected by free shuttle busses leaving in front of the Berliner Rathaus near Alexanderplatz.

February

Berlinale International Film Festival

Early/mid-February; cinemas around Potsdamer Platz; www.berlinale.de; admission charge; map p.134 B2

Playing in the same league as Venice and Cannes, the Berlinale is one of Europe's most important film festivals and the largest cultural event of the year. All of Berlin seems to go film-mad for two weeks. With 200,000 tickets sold, the Berlinale is the place where film professionals and the audience meet; dedicated cineastes take two weeks off so they can watch five films a day.

SEE ALSO FILM, P.57

March

Spandauer Frühlingsfest (Spandau Spring Festival)

Early/mid-March; Festplatz am Brauhaus, Oranienburger Tor; www.spandauer-fruehlings fest.de; free; daily 2–10pm; U7: Altstadt Spandau

Admission is free to this fun-fair in idyllic Spandau. Enjoy the rides and the hearty German food and beer.

May

Karneval der Kulturen

Blücherplatz; www.karneval-berlin.de; Whitsun weekend; free; map p.138 B4

The Carnival of Cultures is an immensely popular four-day street festival that reflects Berlin's diversity. All around Kreuzberg, dancers and musicians take to the streets in Mardi Gras style and draw huge crowds of onlookers. Bands, acrobats, wizards, percussionists perform on every corner around Blücherplatz.

June

ISTAF Golden League Athletics

Olympiastadion, Olympischer Platz 3; tel: 3068 8100;

Left: the famous Christmas market at Gendarmenmarkt is a winter treat not to be missed.

For two weeks in October, dozens of public and private buildings, major landmarks on Unter den Linden and around the Ku'damm are illuminated. 'Lightseeing' tours are provided by various operators.

November/December

Christmas markets

Berlin hosts more than 50 Christmas markets in all parts of the city, each with distinct atmospheres. Most open in late November and close at Christmas or in early January. The most notable ones are:

Gendarmenmarkt The square of the same name provides a beautiful setting for one of the most exquisite Christmas markets in Germany.

Nostalgischer Weihnachtsmarkt on Unter den Linden offers a wealth of traditional German crafts and seasonal food and drink.

Spandauer Weihnachtsmarkt in the pedestrian old town of Spandau has a small-town feel.

Winterwelten on Potsdamer Platz. Apart from hosting an Alpine-style Christmas market, the area is transformed into a giant winter playground complete with an ice rink and sledging hill.

New Year's Eve Party at the Brandenburg Gate

31 Dec, from 6pm around Brandenburg Gate and on Strasse des 17. Juni, up to Siegessäule, Tiergarten

Every year, a million Berliners and visitors see in the New Year in a festive mood, watching the spectacular midnight fireworks and listening to live music at the Brandenburger Tor, once marking the separation of East and West.

Public Holidays

1 Jan: Neujahr (New Year); Karfreitag (Good Friday); Ostermontag (Easter Monday); 1 May: Tag der Arbeit (Labour Day); Himmelfahrt (Ascension Day); Pfingsten (Whit Monday); 3 Oct: Tag der Deutschen Einheit (Day of German Unity); 25–6 Dec: Weihnachten (Christmas)

---

www.olympiastadion-berlin.de; admission charge; U2, S75, S9: Olympiastadion

A day of highly competitive athletics action hosted at the Olympiastadion. The ISTAF meeting, part of the Golden League series, attracts the top athletes in the world.

Christopher Street Day (CSD)

Late June; city centre; www.csd-berlin.de; free

Christopher Street Day sees thousands of scantily clad gay and lesbian folk proudly take to the streets on decorated floats, demonstrating for equal rights and having fun, cheered by the onlookers, many of them in town for a 'Pride Week' of events preceding the CSD.

August

Berliner Gauklerfest

Two weeks in August; around the Opernpalais restaurant, Unter den Linden 5; tel: 206 2673; www.gauklerfest.de; admission charge; bus: 100, 200: Staatsoper, U2: Hausvogteiplatz; map p.137 C1

In one of Berlin's most charming annual street festivals, the city's best restaurants and bars run a gourmet trail, while visitors can shop for crafts and antiques in an intimate market atmosphere, entertained by jugglers, tightrope walkers and puppeteers.

September

Berlin Marathon

Start at Brandenburg Gate; tel: 3012 8810; www.real-berlin-marathon.com; registration fee for participants

Watch and cheer 40,000 runners, skaters and wheelchair athletes attracted to this fast course past all the major Berlin sights.

October

Festival of Lights

Mid-October; tel: 3267 9887; www.city-stiftung-berlin.eu

Film

Berlin has been Germany's cinema central since the medium began. The UFA Studios in nearby Babelsberg produced some of the most famous and, during the Nazi era, notorious films Germany has made, including Fritz Lang's *Metropolis* and Josef von Sternberg's *The Blue Angel*. The Berlinale, Berlin's international film festival, is one of the top cinematic showcases, and films like *Goodbye, Lenin!*, *Downfall* and the Oscar-winning *The Lives of Others* are bringing Berlin cinema to a new audience. However, for many, the myth of Berlin is embodied cinematically in the 1972 film of *Cabaret*.

The Beginnings of Berlin Cinema

Berlin is the birthplace of cinema. In 1895, a film was projected onto a screen in the Wintergarten, a month before the Lumière brothers showed their first film in Paris. With the rise of film occuring during the artistic years of the Weimar Republic, it's not a coincidence that Berlin was the setting of much early German cinema. One of the first abstract documentaries was Walter Ruttmann's *Berlin: Symphony of a Great City* (1927), which 'orchestrated' images of Berlin in motion.

A young Billy Wilder began his film career here with *People on Sunday* (1929). At Babelsberg Studios near Potsdam, Fritz Lang's seminal classics *Metropolis* (1927) and *M* (1931) were filmed, as was the film that made Marlene Dietrich famous, *The Blue Angel* (1930).

Post-War Cinema

The coming of the Nazis saw the near-wholesale defection of German film's talent, most of whom were Jewish or anti-Nazi. The most notorious film of this period is Leni Riefenstahl's *Olympia* (1938), a still controversial piece of Nazi propaganda.

After the war, Berlin slowly re-emerged as a film setting, in Roberto Rossellini's *Germany Year Zero* (1948), a story of post-war corruption, and in Billy Wilder's lighter tale, *A Foreign Affair* (1948). George Seaton's *The Big Lift* (1950) is a comedy about the Berlin Airlift and was filmed in and around the actual scene of events, Flughafen Tempelhof.

> Filmed on location in West Berlin and in other parts of Germany, Bob Fosse's 1972 adaptation of the musical *Cabaret*, itself adapted from Christopher Isherwood's *Berlin Stories* (see also Literature, p.80) and subsequent play, *I am a Camera*, is enduringly popular and critically acclaimed. The on-screen portrayal of Weimar Republic-era Berlin is key to how many visitors imagine the city. For a taste of the nightlife portrayed so evocatively here, *see Cabaret, p.38–9.*

Berliners' favourite film about their city is probably Billy Wilder's comedy *One, Two, Three* (1961). In a development Wilder couldn't have anticipated, the Wall went up during shooting and was deftly incorporated into the film.

The city has served as a backdrop for numerous Cold War spy thrillers, most notably Martin Ritt's *The Spy Who Came in from the Cold* (1965), as well as in lighter films such as the Bond caper *Octopussy* (1983). Wim Wenders's cult clasic, *Wings of Desire* (1987), uses the divided city as a character equal to the human actors and is an invaluable look at Berlin in the last years of the Wall.

Contemporary Film

Post-Wall, Berlin has turned into a choice location, and it is common to come upon a film crew set up on a backstreet somewhere, filming in an apartment or restaurant. Berlin as a location was used to great effect in Tom Tykwer's *Run, Lola, Run!* (1998). The traumas of 20th-century history have been revisited

Left: Liza Minelli evokes Weimar-era Berlin in *Cabaret*.

new, historic and documentary fare in its original language. Once there at the Filmhaus, you may want to check out the exhibits of the Deutsche Kinemathek and the fabulous museum shop.
SEE ALSO MUSEUMS, P.90

Cinemaxx Potsdamer Platz
Potsdamer Strasse 5; tel: 01805 2463 6299; www.cinemaxx.de; U2, S2, S25: Potsdamer Platz; map p.134 B2
The biggest multiplex in town, showing English-language films on at least two of its 19 screens.

CineStar Berlin
Sony Center, Potsdamer Strasse 4; tel: 2606 6400; www.cine star.de; U2, S2, S25: Potsdamer Platz; map p.134 B2
Comfortable multiplex screening all the US blockbusters and a few art-house films in their original format.

Hackesche Höfe Filmtheater
Rosenthaler Strasse 40–41; tel: 283 46 03; www.hoefekino.de; S5, S7, S75, S9: Hackescher Markt; map p.135 C3
Once you've mastered five flights of stairs, you can sit back and watch original-language movies.

Below: still from Fritz Lang's *Metropolis*, at the Deutsche Kinemathek *(see p.90)*.

recently, in Oliver Hirschbiegel's *Downfall* (2004), while the East Germans' story has joined the narrative and made a great impact, with the comedy *Goodbye Lenin!* (2003) and the Oscarwinning tragedy, *The Lives of Others* (2006).

Festivals

The **Berlinale** is a prestigious international film festival held each year, with major films from around the world vying for the high prize of the Golden Bear. There are so many screenings that it is often possible for the general public to see a film. If you are hoping to attend any part of the Berlinale, it is wise to make all your plans at least six months in advance. The event runs a very comprehensive website with all the information you'll need about what's playing and where to get tickets at: www.berlinale.de.
SEE ALSO FESTIVALS AND EVENTS, P.54

The Berlinale is far from the only show in town, however. There's a **Fantasy Film Festival** in July and August, a

Human Rights Film Festival in the autumn, **Verzaubert**, a gay film festival, in April and plenty of smaller festivals at independent cinema houses throughout the year.

Cinemas

The majority of Berlin's big cinemas play dubbed versions of Hollywood films, although the Potsdamer Platz houses frequently show them in the original version with subtitles. The best way to find out what's on is to pick up a listings magazine like **tip** or **Zitty** and look for films labelled *OF* (*Originalfassung*, original version), *OmU* (*Original mit Untertiteln*, original with subtitles) or, for non-German or English-language films, *O m engl U*, indicating English subtitles. Note that cinemas tend to use the German titles for films, even when they are going to be screening in English.

Arsenal
Potsdamer Strasse 2; tel: 2695 5100; www.arsenal-berlin.de; U2, S2, S25: Potsdamer Platz; map p.134 A1
The Arsenal is devoted to art-house cinema, screening

Food and Drink

Even within Germany, Berlin has never really been considered a food destination; even famous German specialities like bread and beer are not considered particularly special. However, quality is on the up generally, with increasingly good Italian, Japanese and German regional cuisines on offer; meanwhile, there is a certain rough charm to traditional Berlinese food, although it is becoming harder to hunt it down. Nevertheless, you can indulge in Berliners' favourite street foods, such as *Currywurst* and *Döner Kebap*, all over the city. For food and drink vocabulary, *see Language, p.79,* and *Restaurants, p.119.*

Local Dishes

Berlin's signature dish is considered to be *Eisbein*, a pig's trotter. Served with boiled potatoes and mashed peas or sauerkraut, it's hardly exalted fare and today only turns up on the most traditional menus.

Another famous concoction is *Königsberger Klopse*, pork meatballs served with a white, caper-studded gravy. There are also various roast pork dishes, like *Schweine-haxe* (*Eisbein*, but roasted) and *Krustenbraten* (roast pork with a crunchy crust).

Beef is hardly eaten, although *Tafelspitz*, sliced

roast beef pounded very thin and sautéed with an egg-wash crust, is an Austrian dish common in restaurants. Chicken and saltwater fish outside of various preparations of herring and smoked salmon is not common, but a few freshwater fish like *Zander* (pike-perch) and *Viktoria-barsch* (a type of perch) can be found on some menus.

Street Food

Street food is more likely to provide a satisfactory taste of Berlin cuisine. A *Thüringer Bratwurst*, a pale sausage seasoned with powdered caraway, is a recommended lunch, as is *Currywurst*, which sounds much worse than it

tastes: a sausage, cut into coins, has mild curry powder and paprika sprinkled heavily over it and is then doused in warm curry ketchup. Served with *Pommes* (french fries) and ketchup or mayonnaise, it is not healthy food by any means, but at **Bier's** outside Friedrichstrasse Station or **Konnopke's** in Prenzlauer Berg, it can be seen how this is often considered the definitive Berlin cuisine.

Oddly enough, this status is also conferred on the *Döner Kebap*, which has become a ubiquitous European snack. The sandwich-style version was invented in Berlin in 1971, consisting of meat shaved off a column, packed into a toasted quarter of Turkish *peda* bread, dressed with tomato, cabbage, onion and cucumber and topped off with one of several sauces.

Beer

Local beer took a huge leap in quality when the Wall opened up, as East Berlin beer was still made like it always had been, unlike the factory-processed Western variations.

Frühstück (breakfast) is a big deal in Berlin, with weekend brunches being particularly popular. Almost all cafés that open in the morning will serve some sort of *Frühstück*, and it will often be served most of the day to accommodate party animals sleeping off the previous night's excesses. A typical *Frühstück* will involve a variation on scrambled eggs, bread, cheeses and cold cuts, served with juice and coffee.

Below: *Frühstück.*

Left: eating local favourite, *Wurst und Brot.*

the likes of Paul Bocuse.

Kollwitzplatz Market
Kollwitzplatz, Prenzlauer Berg; Thur noon–7pm, Sat 9am–4pm; U2: Senefelder Platz; map p.135 D4

Saturday at Kollwitzplatz is packed with local families, but you will find some of Berlin's finest produce, pasta and bread for sale if you can make your way to the stands. Thursday is calmer and smaller.

Rogacki
Wilmersdorfer Strasse 145–146, Charlottenburg; tel: 343 8250; www.rogacki.de; Mon–Wed 9am–6pm, Thur 9am–7pm, Fri 8am–7pm, Sat 8am–4pm; U2: Bismarckstrasse; map p.132 B2

Since 1928, the Rogacki family has been selling fish and meat to a select clientele. There is also some cheese and other deli items, but the emphasis is on fish you cannot get anywhere else, every kind of sausage imaginable, and game in season. A major draw is the dining area, where many locals come for lunch.

Turkischer Markt
Maybachufer, Kreuzberg; Tue, Fri noon–6.30pm; U1, U8: Kottbusser Tor; map p.139 D4

Shop for fruit and vegetables of widely varying quality, nuts and sweetmeats, oils and seasonings and Turkish breads in the company of local Turkish housewives.

Wochenmarkt Winterfeldplatz
Winterfeldplatz, Schöneberg; Wed 8am–2pm, Sat 8am–4pm; U1, U2, U4: Nollendorfplatz; map p.137 E4

Well-dressed locals come out for high-quality organic vegetables and baked goods, olives, Spreewald pickles and potted herbs. It is all fun to look at, but prioritise the food, some of the best in town.

Although the Eastern firms have long since been gobbled up by the Western ones, the quality remains the same, thanks to a large consumer base. Try *Berliner Pilsner* or *Berliner Bürgerbräu. Berliner Weisse* is a sour, lactic beer that is never drunk straight, but mixed with raspberry or woodruff syrup and drunk with a straw in the summer.

Buying Food
Some of the best food on offer can be found on the lower levels of department stores like **Kaufhof**, **Hertie** and **Karstadt**, instead of Berlin's supermarkets, which generally lag behind. Individual fruit and vegetable shops will also generally have higher-quality produce. 'Bio' stores such as **Demeter**, **LPG** and **eo** can also be a good choice.

Galeries Lafayette
Friedrichstrasse 76–78, Mitte; tel: 209 480; www.galeries-lafayette.de; Mon–Sat 10am–8pm; U6: Französische Strasse; map p.134 B2

The basement food department is a bit of France in the middle of Berlin. Here, you can

Above: fresh chillies on display at the Turkischer Markt.

get genuine Poilâne bread, registered chickens from Bresse, a serious selection of cheese, and an unparalleled French wine selection.

KaDeWe
Tauentzienstrasse 21–24, Charlottenburg; tel: 21 210; www.kadewe-berlin.de; Mon–Thur 10am–8pm, Fri 10am–9pm, Sat 9.30am–8pm; U1, U2: Wittenbergplatz; map p.133 D1

Ordering for much of the legendary department store's food halls has been taken over by a supermarket chain, and it shows. However, many independent boutiques remain, as do mini-restaurants run by

Galleries

Besides all the treasures of the past in Berlin's museums, the city is fairly bursting with commercial galleries showing off the works of some of today's finest talents. Many artists have been drawn to live here because of the low rents for studio space and the creative energy of the city, as well as the buzzing scene this has created. For an idea of what is on display during your visit, free programme folders are available in most reputable galleries and list the current shows, as well as provide a map showing the locations of all the galleries listed. For art museums, see *Museums, p.86–95*.

Art Galleries

MITTE

Arndt

Potsdamer Strasse 96; tel: 2061 3870; www.arndt-partner.com; Tue–Sat 11am–6pm; U2: Stadtmitte; map p.134 B1

Long-established gallery representing a wide range of emerging talents and the occasional underground star (Joe Coleman), Arndt has positioned itself as a champion of the international avant-garde.

Contemporary Fine Arts

Am Kupfergraben 1; tel: 288 7870; www.cfa-berlin.com; Tue–Fri 11am–6pm, Sat 11am–4pm; S3, S5, S7, S9: Friedrichstrasse; map p.136 C2

Contemporary Fine Arts lives up to its name, with a roster that pretty much defines Germany's favourite contemporary artists, among them Georg Baselitz, Peter Doig, Jörg Immendorf,

A good resource for information on the current exhibitions showing around town is: www.indexberlin.de.

Above: at Galerie Eigen + Art.

Raymond Pettibon, Jonathan Meese, Chris Ofili and Daniel Richter. Its glittering new headquarters opposite Museuminsel just confirms its position as one of Berlin's most important galleries.

Klosterfelde

Potsdamer Strasse 93; tel: 283 5305; www.klosterfelde.de; Tue–Sat 11am–6pm; U2: Stadtmitte; map p.134 B1

Another pioneer in Mitte's gallery boom, Klosterfelde long outgrew its tiny backyard space and moved into more spacious digs. Working with a number of conceptual artists and others far outside

the mainstream, it has helped build the reputations of the likes of Matt Mullican, Dan Peterman, Rivane Neuenschwander and Kirsten Pieroth.

Mehdi Chouakri

Edisonhöfe, Invalidenstrasse 117; www.mehdi-chouakri.de; tel: 2839 1153; Tue–Sat 11am–6pm; S1, S2, S25: Nordbahnhof; U6: Zinnowitzer Strasse; map p.134 B4

Iranian-born Chouakri cruises the outer limits of the avantgarde to present some of the most challenging art on the scene, often with a wry sense of humour. Shows here can be quite outrageous.

Left: a photography exhibit at Kicken Berlin.

'New British Artists', introducing several of them to Berlin before they became famous back home. She continues to seek out fresh young talent while holding on to many of her old clients, including Julian Opie and Fiona Banner.

Galerie Berinson
Lindenstrasse 34; tel: 2838 7990; www.berinson.de; Tue–Sat 11am–6pm; S1, S2, S25: Oranienburger Strasse; map p.134 C3

Hendrik Berinson is one of the best-known dealers of historical photography, including many important German photographers of the 1920s and 1930s. Among the artists he shows are Georg Grosz, Stanley Kubrick, Friederich Seidenstücker, Lee Miller and Marianne Brandt.

Galerie Eigen + Art
Auguststrasse 26; tel: 280 6605; www.eigen-art.com; Tue–Sat 11am–6pm; S1, S2, S25: Oranienburger Strasse; map p.134 C3

Eigen + Art made its splash by arriving early on Auguststrasse and aggressively promoting artists from the former East Germany, includ-

AROUND ALEXANDERPLATZ

Alexander Ochs Galleries
Sophienstrasse 21; tel: 2839 1387; www.alexanderochs-galleries.com; Tue–Fri 10am–6pm, Sat 11am–6pm; U8: Weinmeisterstrasse; map p.134 C3

Nobody has been more instrumental in promoting the art of the new Chinese avant-garde in Berlin and building bridges to allow artists from the Far East to come and work in Berlin than Alexander Ochs. As a result, he's had his pick of the finest young talent China has to offer, whose work is often shown first in the West – or in the world – at this gallery in an impressive red-brick courtyard.

DNA
Auguststrasse 20; tel: 2859 9652; www.dna-galerie.de; Tue–Sat 11am–6pm; S1, S2, S25: Oranienburger Strasse; map p.134 C3

Die Neue Actionsgalerie came about after Johann Nowak was turfed out of his popular bar-cum-gallery at Hackescher Markt and found that the international, Berlin-based artists he had been showing in its basement were beginning to attract attention. This cavernous, two-level space has some of the most audacious, hair-raising artists on the scene, which makes it a must on the Augustrasse gallery-crawl.

Galerie Barbara Thumm
Markgrafenstrasse 68; tel: 2839 0347; www.bthumm.de; Tue–Sat 11am–6pm; S3, S5, S7, S9: Alexanderplatz; map p.137 E2

Thumm rode the wave of the

Below: Adam Szymczyk and Elena Filipovic, curators of the 5th Berlin Biennial for Contemporary Art.

ing Neo Rauch, who went on to become its first big star. A small but very select roster now includes Carsten Nicolai, Matthias Weischer and Christine Hill. The gallery wisely maintains a presence in Leipzig, where many new stars are rising.

Kicken Berlin

Linienstrasse 155; tel: 2887 7882; www.kicken-gallery.com; Tue–Sat 2–6pm; S1, S2, S25: Oranienburger Strasse; map p.134 C4

Kicken represents a virtual who's who of photography, from pioneers like Eugène Atget, through Arnold Newman and contemporaries like Robert Mapplethorpe. They've almost always got a fantastic show up, and serious collectors can make an appointment to view prints in their private gallery down the street.

Kuckei + Kuckei

Linienstrasse 158; tel: 883 4354; www.kuckei-kuckei.de; Tue–Fri 11am–6pm, Sat 11am–5pm; S1, S2, S25: Oranienburger Strasse; map p.134 C4

You'll either respond immediately to the Kuckei + Kuckei aesthetic or you won't; some find the works of the artists it represents cold and flat, while others find them filled with ideas. They prefer artists with a conceptual element to their work and have launched important careers.

Kunsthaus Tacheles

Oranienburger Strasse 54–56; tel: 2826 185; www.tacheles.de; U6: Orainenburger Tor; map p.134 B3

After the Wall came down, the bombed-out former department store on Oranienburger Strasse attracted young artists looking for studios. With minimum investment, the squatters from all over the world turned the ruin into a centre of creativity. While a few studios are still there and the courtyard is a playground for scrap-metal art, the building is now covered with random graffiti and beleaguered by tourists attracted by its morbid charm. There is a pleasant bar and a comfy cinema on the top floor but not for long – eviction orders have been issued by the owner.

Kunst-Werke (KW Institute for Contemporary Art)

Auguststrasse 69; tel: 243 4590; www.kw-berlin.de; Tue–Sun noon–7pm, Thur until 9pm; admission charge; S5, S7, S9: Hackescher Markt; S1: Oranienburger Strasse; map p.134 C3

Kunst-Werke is located in a

former margarine factory in the Scheunenviertel area in Mitte. In 1997 Kunst-Werke initiated the Berlin Biennale for Contemporary Art and partnered with New York's art-space P.S.1, with which it remains identified.

Wohnmaschine

Invalidenstrasse 50–1; tel: 3087 2015; www.wohnmaschine.de; Tue–Sat 11am–6pm; S1, S2, S25: Oranienburger Strasse; map p.134 C3

The only major gallery in Mitte before the Wall opened, Wohnmaschine moved out of its rickety quarters in 1998 and into this medium-sized space, where sometimes the art is so playful you'll see little kids pulling their parents over to look. Few of the artists who show here are household names yet, but

Left: innovative displays at the Kunst-Werke Institute for Contemporary Art.

Left: inside the Kunsthaus Tacheles.

the **Haus des Lehrers** (House of Teachers) on the east side of Alexanderplatz remains as a good example. One thing that Berlin excels at is street art, often extremely ephemeral. Well-known guerrilla artists like Banksy and Swoon have cut swathes through the city, primarily in Mitte, Prenzlauer Berg and Kreuzberg, but lots of locals get into the action and a close look at walls will turn up some very clever pieces.

East Side Gallery
Mühlenstrasse; www.eastside gallery.com; daily 24 hours; S3, S5, S9, S75: Ostbahnhof; map p.135 E1
Probably Berlin's best-known murals are the ones painted on the 1.3km (0.8-mile) remaining stretch of the Berlin Wall on Mühlenstrasse, known as the East Side Gallery. The largest open-air gallery in the world, its 106 wall sections were painted by groups of artists

Thanks to a subsidy to bring culture to the Eastern half of the city, a major gallery mile has sprung up on Auguststrasse and the surrounding streets, and Mitte remains the hot centre of Berlin's art market. Note that the location and existence of galleries is as volatile as the art market itself, with galleries opening and closing all the time.

from all over the world after reunification as a memorial to freedom of expression. There are also some newer murals representing contemporary graffiti artists. Unfortunately, the heavy automotive traffic on Mühlenstrasse and the degradations of vandals have conspired to destroy large parts of the gallery, including the famous image of Honecker and Brezhnev locked in a passionate kiss. Nevertheless, a non-profit organisation has been working on restoring the original images bit by bit, to preserve these unique images.

this is one gallery that's always worth a visit.

KREUZBERG AND FRIEDRICHSHAIN
Galerie Volker Diehl
Lindenstrasse 35; tel: 2248 7922; www.dv-art.com; Tue–Sat 11am–6pm; U6: Kochstrasse; map p.134 C1
Diehl often shows representational work by his roster of international artists, but none of it could be accused of being merely decorative. There's often an edge, psychological or physical, to the paintings, prints and occasional photographs on display here.

Street Art and Murals
It was a policy of the East Berlin government to paint murals 'beautifying' the blank sides of buildings, preferably with murals glorifying socialist virtues. Since 1989, most of these have vanished, although the mosaic one on

Below: a new mural at the East Side Gallery in progress.

Gay and Lesbian

Berlin has almost always been one of Europe's most gay and lesbian-friendly cities, and it is particularly so today. Pretty much anything goes here, so whichever side of the scene you are looking for, there is something happening to suit it. In Berlin, information is plentiful and easy to come by, the bars and clubs are inclusive and the scene goes on 24 hours a day. Meanwhile, the locals are welcoming and tolerant; indeed, in 2002, the city elected Klaus Wowereit as its first openly gay mayor and did not blink an eye when he declared, 'I'm gay and that's OK.'

History

In 1897, Dr Magnus Hirschfeld formed a committee in Berlin to look into the question of whether homosexuality was a disease or a naturally occurring condition. He lobbied tirelessly for the decriminalisation of homosexuality. His Institute for Sexual Research, founded in 1919, offered a huge library and doctors for medical consultations, but the Nazis burned the library and its papers in 1933. Hirschfeld went into exile in Nice, where he died in 1935. A monument to him now stands behind the Haus der Kulturen der Welt in the Tiergarten, near where the Institute was located.

By the 1920s, the area around Motzstrasse was already a center of gay activity, thanks in part to the Eldorado club, where Christopher Isherwood was a regular *(see Literature, p.80)*. When the Nazis came to power, homosexuals were forced to wear a pink triangle on their clothing and many were sent to concentration camps; the number

estimated to have perished at the hands of the Nazis ranges from 5,000 to 15,000. A monument to them is affixed to the Nollendorfplatz U-Bahn station near Motzstrasse today.

After the war, the West Germans held homosexuality in legal limbo, but the East Germans decriminalised it in the early 1950s, which meant that when the Wall opened, there was a ready-made scene for all to explore in East Berlin. Today, the gay scene is still very much where it used to be: in the **Motzkiez** in the West and in

Prenzlauer Berg in the East. One distinction between the East and West Berlin scenes is that the tradition in the East was for there to be mixed venues for gays and lesbians, while the two scenes were separate in the West. This has relaxed on both sides of town since the Wall opened up, but if you would rather not mix, choose your venue accordingly.

Resources
SCHÖNEBERG
Mann-O-Meter
Bülowstrasse 106; tel: 216 8008; www.mann-o-meter.de;

Below: exhibits at the Schwules Museum.

Left: out and proud at the Christopher Street Day parade.

array of gay listings and information is just a click away.

Shops

Bruno's

Büowstrasse 106; tel: 6150 0385; www.brunos.de; Mon–Sat 10am–10pm, Sun 1–9pm; U1, 2, 3, 4: Nollendorfplatz; map p.133 E1

An enormous men's emporium of DVDs, clothing, toys, condoms and much more (also at Schönhauser Allee 131).

La Luna

Dunckerstrasse 90; tel: 4432 8488; www.laluna-toys.de; Mon–Fri noon–8pm, Sat noon–6pm; U2: Eberswalder Strasse

A friendly lesbian shop with a good selection of books, sex toys and underwear.

RoB

Fuggerstrasse 19; tel: 2196 7400; www.rob-berlin.de; Mon–Sat noon–8pm; U1, 2, 3, 4: Nollendorfplatz; map p.133 E1

A rubber and leather specialist, RoB has some of the best-quality fetish gear to be found in Berlin, as well as an impressive selection of other toys for boys.

Sexclusivitäten

Fürbringerstrasse; tel: 693 6666; www.sexclusivitaeten. de; Fri noon–8pm, other times by appointment; U6, 7: Mehringdamm; map p.138 B4

The grande dame of Berlin's lesbian shops, founded by Laura Méritt to provide a relaxed and fun environment

---

Each of the more central city districts has its own gay neighbourhood or street. In Schöneberg, it is the **Motzstrasse** quarter, in Kreuzberg, it is **Oranienstrasse** and **Mehringdamm** and in Prenzlauer Berg, it is **Gleimstrasse** and **Greifenhagener Strasse**.

Tue–Fri 5–10pm, Sat–Sun 4–10pm; U1, U2, U4, U12, U15: Nollendorfplatz; map p.137 E4

Berlin's central gay resource centre has multilingual staff in touch with every facet of gay life in the city. Its website has a downloadable gay guide to the city, as well as a searchable database of bars, clubs, medical resources and anti-violence programmes. Men only.

KREUZBERG AND FRIEDRICHSHAIN

Schwules Museum (Gay Museum)

Mehringdamm 61; tel: 6959 9050; www.schwules museum.de; Wed–Mon 2–6pm, Sat until 7pm; admission charge; U6, U7: Mehringdamm; map p.138 B4

For years, this was the world's only museum devoted to gay life and culture, and its research division contributed greatly to the understanding of homosexuality. The library is probably the most thorough in Europe, containing archives of noted sexologists and thousands of books and periodicals. All information is available in English.

Publications and Websites

Siegessäule

Berlin's most established magazine for gay men, available free everywhere in the city gay men might conceivably go. Great listings and a website at www.siegessaeule.de. German only.

L-Mag

Bimonthly free magazine for lesbians, Siegessäule's sister publication is the best print resource around. Website at www.l-mag.de has podcasts, listings and more. German only.

Out in Berlin

This bilingual website, www.out-in-berlin.com, has a full

Gay pride annual mega-events include the **Christopher Street Day parade** (late June) and the **Schwul-Lesbisches Stadtfest** (street fair) around Nollendorfplatz in Schöneberg (mid-June). *(See Festivals and Events, p.55.)*

seminars, art events and cabaret, plus there's a coffee bar and Kneipe, which is a relaxed place to meet up and have a chat. There are regular 'Kneipenabend' where you can make new friends, as well as attend lectures and readings.

Hafen
Motzstrasse 16; tel: 211 4118; www.hafen-berlin.de; daily 8pm–late; U2, U3: Nollendorf-platz; map p.137 E4

A bar that advertises itself as being for 'Sally Bowles and her friends' is certainly trading on neighbourhood tradition, and the crowd here celebrates everything from Playboy bunnies to the Queen of Holland's birthday: any excuse for a party.

Nah-Bar
Kalckreuthstrasse 16, ecke Fuggerstrasse; tel: 3150 3062; www.neuebar.de; daily (Fri–Mon only during winter); U1, 2, 3, 4: Nollendorfplatz; map p.137 E4

A fun bar to hang out in, with regular events including the popular Dance Party, details pf which can be found on the website. This is a lesbian bar but it is pretty friendly and male friends are also welcome.

in which women can explore their sexuality. Salons with readings, workshops and other events are held on Fridays noon–8pm, while appointments can be made easily to visit at other times. Her on-line store has an amazing range of books and items.

Mixed Bars and Clubs

MITTE
Sharon Stonewall
Kleinen Präsidenterstrasse 3; tel: 2408 5502; www.sharon stonewall.com; U6: Oranienburger Tor; map p.134 B3

Stylish mixed bar with affordable and well-mixed cocktails.

PRENZLAUER BERG
Schall und Rauch
Gleimstrasse 23; tel: 448 0770; www.schall-und-rauch.de; daily 8am–3am; U2, S45, S46: Schönhauser Allee

The name may mean 'shallow

words' in German, but there's no mistaking the friendly atmosphere here. The food's good, the company's good, and a small guesthouse on the premises is well furnished.

Sonntagsclub
Greifenhagener Strasse 28; tel: 449 7590; www.sonntags-club.de; Mon–Thur 5pm–1am, Fri–Sun 6pm–2am; U2, S45, S46: Schönhauser Allee

Traditional pre-1989 East Berlin gay and lesbian hangout that is still a meeting place of choice for politically minded queers due to its mix of club nights, discussion events and film screenings.

SCHÖNEBERG
Begine
Potsdamer Strasse 139; tel: 215 1414; www.begine.de; Mon–Fri from 5pm, Sat from 7pm; U2: Bülowstrasse; map p.137 E4

This women-only space is used to hold workshops and

The opportunities for indulging in the sex scene are plentiful in Berlin generally, but most of the options are men-only. Listings of the latest happenings can be found in the main gay publications and websites *(see p.65)*. Saunas are also popular cruising grounds, as are the local parks. Anti-gay violence is less common than in other European cities, but does occasionally happen, so do keep alert and, of course, protected.

KREUZBERG AND FRIEDRICHSHAIN
Barbie Deinhoff's
Schlesische Strasse 16; www.barbiedeinhoff.de; Mon–Fri 6pm–late, Sat–Sun from 4pm; U1: Schlesisches Tor; map p.139 E4

Trashy, slightly naughty bar catering to a youngish crowd of playful, sex-positive gay and lesbian folk.

SchwuZ
Mehringdamm 61; tel: 629 0880; www.schwuz.de; usually 11pm–late, see website for details; U6, U7: Mehringdamm; map p.138 B4

Gay and lesbian culture centre in the same complex as the Schwules Museum (see p.65) hosts a variety of weekend events, including an all-lesbian event on the fourth Friday of the month and the Safer-Sex-Party at Christmas and New Year.

SO 36
Oranienstrasse 190; tel: 6140 1306; www.so36.de; 11am–late; U2, U8: Kottbusser Tor; map p.135 D1

Long-time venue for alternative lifestyles of all sorts. Current events include Gayhane on the fourth Saturday of the month, featuring Turkish and oriental dance music, and MfS, an all-female hip-hop party on the first Friday of the month.

Gay Bars and Clubs
PRENZLAUER BERG
Zum Schmutzigen Hobby
Rykestrasse 45; www.ninaqueer.com; daily 6pm–late; U2, S45, S46: Schönhauser Allee; map p.135 D4

Zum Schmutzigen Hobby is the hobby of celebrity drag queen Nina Queer, who presides every Wednesday over the Glamourquizz at 9pm. Fun, if a bit touristy, but then, some of the tourists are celebrities.

SCHÖNEBERG
Apollo Splash Club
Kurfürstenstrasse 101; tel: 213 2424; www.apollo-splash-club.com; Mon–Thur 1pm–7am; Fri 1pm–Mon 7am; map p.133 D1

Tropical theme in the bar; always crowded. Admission includes robe, towels, slippers. Foam parties; private rooms for rent.

Böse Buben
Sachsendamm 76–7; no phone; www.boese-buben-berlin.de; usually Wed, Fri–Sun from 9pm; S1: Schöneberg

'Bad Boys' is a fairly hardcore leather and fetish club for men only.

Prinzknecht
Fuggerstrasse 33; tel: 2362 7444; www.prinzknecht.de; Sun–Thur 3pm–2am, Fri–Sat 3pm–3am; U4: Viktoria-Luise-Platz; map p.137 E4

Refreshing to find a bar in this part of town which isn't fixated on the cult of youth. Large beer garden and rooms catering to all tastes.

Tom's Bar
Motzstrasse 19; tel: 213 4570; www.tomsbar.de; daily 10pm–6am; U1, U2, U3, U4: Nollendorfplatz; map p.137 E4

This Motzstrasse institution is not for the timid, although the front bar is friendly.

KREUZBERG AND FRIEDRICHSHAIN
Barbie Bar
Mehringdamm 77; tel: 6956 8610; www.barbiebar.de; daily 2pm–late; U7: Mehringdamm; map p.138 B3

Camp but relaxed and welcoming bar decorated with Barbie dolls. Special events held regularly; check the website for details.

Berghain
Am Wriezener Bahnhof; www.berghain.de; Fri–Sat midnight–late; S5, S7, S9: Ostbahnhof; map p.135 E2

Stylish, post-industrial nightclub in a former power station, attracting buff young men with its top-shelf dance music and sound system. A super-trendy hotspot for after-hours clubbing.

Below: drag queens at Sage Club (see Nightlife, p.102).

History

1244
Berlin, situated on the Spree on an adjacent island to the town of Cölln, is mentioned in contemporary records for the first time.

1307
Berlin and Cölln become a joint city under the Ascanian dynasty.

1319
The death of the last Ascanian precipitates the collapse of law and order in the province.

1411
Burgrave Frederick of Nuremberg, a member of the Hohenzollern family, brings peace by becoming governor and subsequently Elector of the Marches.

1448
A citizens' rebellion is crushed by Frederick II.

1535
The first Protestant elector, Joachim I Nestor, accedes to the throne, heralding the arrival of the Reformation in Berlin.

1618–48
Berlin is severely affected by the Thirty Years' War, losing half its population of 12,000. In 1640, Friedrich Wilhelm, the Great Elector, accedes to the throne.

1672
Jews and French Huguenot refugees are welcomed to Berlin. The city benefits from their industry and culture. A mass influx of persecuted European Protestants is sparked.

1701
After the Hollenzollern's acquisition of Polish land up to the Russian frontier, the Great Elector's successor, Elector Friedrich II, declares himself King of Prussia.

1740

The ascension to the throne of Friedrich II (Friedrich the Great) is the start of military expansion and administrative reform.

1791
The Brandenburger Tor, a monument to Prussian glory, is completed.

1806
During the Napoleonic Wars, Napoleon marches through the Brandenburger Tor, marking the start of two years of French occupation.

1813
Russia, Austria and Prussia defeat Napoleon at the Battle of Leipzig.

1840
Friedrich Wilhelm IV takes the throne and brings cultural greats to Berlin, but the poverty of the lower classes continues.

1848
Following revolutions in Paris and Vienna, Berliners take to the streets in the 'March Revolution', which results in the loss of 200 lives.

1862
Otto von Bismarck becomes Minister-President of Prussia and, later, the North-German Alliance.

1871
The German states' victory in the Franco-Prussian War is marked by the proclamation of the Second German Empire, with Berlin as its imperial capital.

1914–18

World War I, expected to be a six-month fight with a victorious outcome, results in rationing and famine in Berlin, as Germany is blockaded.

1918
Kaiser Wilhelm abdicates in November after the navy mutinies. Philip Scheidemann declares Germany a republic and Karl Liebknecht declares it socialist.

1919
The socialist Spartacus uprising is stopped and the Weimar Republic government formed, but has to agree to demanding peace terms at the Treaty of Versailles.

1920
The Kapp Putsch sees 6,000 soldiers occupy the government district. Only a general strike by workers forces the coup to end after four days. Greater Berlin takes today's geographical form after territorial reform unites the city with several surrounding towns.

1923

Hyperinflation hits its peak, with a US dollar buying 4.2 billion Reichsmarks. Mass poverty prevails and it is only when the Rentenmark is introduced that the economy becomes more stable. In November, Adolf Hitler's attempted putsch collapses in Munich, before his plan to march on Berlin is realised.

1923–9

Berlin becomes the focal point for the European arts and bohemian scene.

1929

The Wall Street Crash precipitates the worldwide Depression. By the end of the year, 2.9 million Germans are unemployed.

1933

Poverty and desperation leads to a surge in support for both the Communist Party and the Nazis. Hitler becomes Chancellor. Shortly after, the Reichstag is burnt down. A left-wing anarchist is blamed and Hitler tightens his grip over the country.

1936

Nazi tyranny is suspended for two weeks as Berlin hosts the 11th Olympic Games.

1938

During Kristallnacht (9 November) the SA target Jewish shops, homes and businesses.

1939

Outbreak of World War II.

1945

The Battle of Berlin. Hitler takes his own life in his bunker as Soviet troops close in. Germany surrenders. The de-Nazification of Berlin begins as the city is divided into four sectors.

1948–49

Conflicts between the occupying Allied forces result in the Soviets cutting off all transport into West Berlin for nearly a year. France, Britain and the US airlift supplies into the stranded city during the Berlin Blockade.

1949

The Federal Republic of Germany, with Bonn as its capital, and the German Democratic Republic (GDR) are formed.

1953

On 17 June, Soviet tanks hit the streets to crush the Workers' Uprising.

1961

With one in every nine GDR citizens having fled to West Germany and tension between Russia and the US at a high, transport links between the East and West are cut and the Berlin Wall is erected overnight.

1963

US President John F. Kennedy gives his 'Berliner' speech at Rathaus Schöneberg. Berlin is at the epicentre of the Cold War throughout the 1960s.

1972

The Berlin Agreement allows travel between West Berlin and the GDR.

1989

Hungary opens its border with Austria, leading to a mass exodus of East Germans to the West and bringing the local economy to the point of collapse. On 9 November, the Wall is declared open.

1990

On 3 October, Germany is officially reunified.

1999

The capital of Germany is moved to Berlin.

2001

Klaus Wowereit is elected mayor. A programme of cuts is announced in the face of Berlin's huge debts.

2006

Berlin hosts the FIFA World Cup final.

2010

Celebrations for the twentieth anniversary of German Reunification.

2011

Mayoral elections are held.

2012

Berlin's new international airport is scheduled to open.

Hotels

Berlin hotels are quite reasonably priced compared with other capitals in Europe, and if you avoid landing during peak periods, such as the Berlinale, some real bargains can be found. Hotels include the high-end and opulent, as well as the arty and boutique, but some of Berlin's guesthouses and hostels are a worthwhile alternative. For families or long-term stays in Berlin, a catered apartment, available in almost every district, may be the best option. Whether you have come to surround yourself with art and culture, to party all night or for a romantic weekend, there's a hotel in Berlin to suit your needs.

Mitte

Apartments am Brandenburger Tor
Behrenstrasse 1b; tel: 200 7570; www.apartments-mitte.de; €€€€; S1, S2, S25, bus TXL, bus 100: Unter den Linden; bus 200: Behrenstrasse; map p.134 B2
Self-catered modern apartments of different sizes in an unbeatable location just a stone's throw away from Unter den Linden and Brandenburger Tor, adjacent to the Holocaust Memorial. There are many restaurants and a supermarket within walking distance. Furniture is a little basic but comfortable. Best for families and groups: there is a washing machine and separate bedrooms. Great value for money.

> Hotel price ranges including tax, given as a guide only, for a standard double room in peak season, with bathroom but without breakfast unless otherwise stated:
>
> | | |
> |---|---|
> | € | under €70 |
> | €€ | €70–€100 |
> | €€€ | €100–€170 |
> | €€€€ | over €170 |

Arte Luise Kunsthotel
Luisenstrasse 19; tel: 284 480; www.luise-berlin.com; €€–€€€; S3, S5, S7, S9: Friedrichstrasse; map p.136 A2
Every room in this hotel has been created by a noted artist, including some big names, but this can mean the decor is not necessarily for the timid. Fortunately, you can look through the selection available in the hotel's 50 rooms on the website before you book, choosing from themes that range from the whimsical to the downright bizarre. Close to the main train station, it is in an ideal location and is a one-of-a-kind experience.

Artotel Berlin-Mitte (Ermelerhaus)
Wallstrasse 70–73; tel: 240 620; www.artotel.de; €€€–€€€€; U2: Märkisches Museum; map p.135 D2
An 16th-century Rococo mansion on the banks of the Spree has been converted into a luxurious contemporary hotel with a fine collection of Georg Baselitz paintings. Located on Fischerinsel, a charming, quiet village-like area that is nonetheless quite accessible by public transport from the rest of the city, it offers a number of rooms with wheelchair access. A favourite of art-loving visitors and those in search of something a bit different.

Hilton Berlin
Mohrenstrasse 30; tel: 302 0230; www.hilton.com; €€€€; U2, U6: Stadtmitte; map p.134 B2
Superb location on Gendarmenmarkt square (grand neoclassical architecture and one of Berlin's best Christmas markets), with a metro station right outside the hotel. Numerous sights and museums and Friedrichstrasse high-end shopping within walking distance. Excellent restaurants, but not much nightlife in the area. Friendly service, high-speed internet, spa, pool, 24-hour gym and an in-house Trader Vic's. Reserve a room overlooking the Gendarmenmarkt.

Honigmond and Honigmond Garden Hotel
Tieckstrasse 12 and Invalidenstrasse 122; tel: 284 4550; www.honigmond.de; €€–€€€; U6: Zinnowitzer Strasse, S1, S2: Nordbahnhof; map p.134 B4

Left: the grand lobby of the Hotel Adlon.

of it remained, it was finally demolished in 1984. After reunification, the building was rebuilt from original plans, and the new Kempinski Adlon opened its doors in 1997. Its many rooms and suites are some of the most luxurious in Berlin and have prices to match, but no other Berlin hotel offers a view of the iconic Brandenburger Tor and such quick access to Berlin's cultural centres.

Hotel de Rome
Behrenstrasse 37; tel: 460 6090; www.hotelderome.com; €€€€; U2: Hausvogteiplatz; bus TXL, bus 100, 200: Staatsoper; map p.134 C2
A Sir Rocco Forte hotel with a very central and yet quiet location just off Unter den Linden, mere steps away from the opera and Museuminsel. One of the few luxury hotels in Berlin housed in a historical building (it was once the head office of Dresdner Bank), it was recently converted into an elegant 5-star designer hotel, where most rooms are large with high ceilings and dramatic modern decor. The former bank vault was converted into a 20m (66ft) swimming pool.

It is not essential to book your room with breakfast. If you get a good rate, go for it. Otherwise, there are plenty of affordable alternatives in neighbourhood bakeries and coffee houses. Curiously, lower-priced hotels tend to include breakfast in the price of the room. Expect to spend anywhere from 5 to 20 euros for breakfast if it's not included.

Small, lovingly renovated romantic hotels (the name translates as 'honeymoon') in a central yet somewhat hidden old neighbourhood. Elegant rooms with stucco, parquet floors and colonial-style furniture. A good choice for summer, when breakfast is served in the lush back garden with a pond, fountains and pet rabbits. If you prefer croaking frogs over street noise, ask for a garden room. Within walking distance of happening Scheunenviertel with its boutiques and nightlife and the Dorotheenstädtischer Friedhof cemetery.

Hotel Adlon
Unter den Linden 77; tel: 22 610; www.kempinski.com; €€€€; U1, U2, U25: Unter den Linden; map p.136 A1
Probably Berlin's most famous address since it went up in 1907, the Adlon has paid host to scores of luminaries, from the crowned heads of Europe to Thomas Edison, Albert Einstein and Charlie Chaplin. Readers of Isherwood's *Berlin Stories* will recognise the name, and it was here that Marlene Dietrich was discovered. In 1945, having survived the war, it was destroyed by an accidental fire, and although bits

Below: a luxurious marble bathroom and a 'lady's bedroom' at the opulent Hotel Adlon.

Expect air conditioning only in hotels from 4 stars upwards. If these are out of your reach and you are planning to travel in the summer, opt for accommodation in an old (pre-war) building rather than a new one, as they tend to be cooler. However, do note that these may not have a lift.

Maritim Pro Arte

Friedrichstrasse 151; tel: 20 335; www.maritim.de; €€€; S3, S5, S7, S9, U6: Friedrichstrasse; map p.136 B1

The Maritim hotel chain seems just a little bit old-fashioned, but that's not necessarily a bad thing, as this fine hotel right by Friedrichstrasse station attests. A changing collection of first-rate contemporary German art is on display in the lobby and some of the rooms, which are comfortable without being overdone. A short walk to the Brandenburger Tor, Unter den Linden and shopping on Friedrichstrasse, it's an affordable place in the thick of things.

Meliá

Friedrichstrasse 103; tel: 2060 7900; www.meliaberlin.com; €€€; S3, S5, S7, S9, U6: Friedrichstrasse; map p.134 B3

This luxurious but affordable hotel on the banks of the Spree is a new arrival and being part of a Spanish hotel group, is something of a favourite with Spanish travellers. Bright, comfortable rooms (though not the rather aloof staff) offer a nice relief on one of Berlin's gloomy days and there is a good and authentic tapas bar.

mitArt Hotel + Café

Linienstrasse 139–40; tel: 2839 0430; www.mitart.de; €€; U3: Oranienburger Tor; map p.134 B3

This small hotel with very stark and simple rooms (no TV or phone) might not be to every-

one's taste, however, it does offer a good organic breakfast and is in a decent location for the price.

Park Plaza Wallstreet

Wallstrasse 23–4; tel: 847 1170; www.parkplaza.com; €€€; U2: Märkische Markt; map p.135 C2

This comfortable design hotel has hit on Wall Street-themed interiors as a unifying motif. As well as neat, striking rooms it also boasts its own cinema showing everything from classic films to the latest releases. A generous buffet breakfast is included in the price and the staff are very friendly and helpful.

The Regent

Charlottenstrasse 49; tel: 20 338; www.theregentberlin.com; €€€€; U2: Hausvogteiplatz; S5, S7, S75, S9: Friedrichstrasse; map p.134 B2

One of the world's best places to stay according to Condé Nast, The Regent Berlin is popular with visiting American celebrities like Brad Pitt and Tom Cruise. If you are into old-world elegance and opulent decor, this is the place for you. The deluxe rooms and suites overlook Gendarmenmarkt, and Fischers Fritz is the in-house gourmet restaurant, boasting two Michelin stars for its renowned fish and seafood dishes.

The Westin Grand

Friedrichstrasse 158–64; tel: 20 270; www.starwoodhotels.com/westin; €€€€; S5, S7, S75, S9: Friedrichstrasse; TXL bus, bus 100, bus 200: Unter den Linden; map p.136 B1

In a choice location on the corner of Friedrichstrasse and Unter den Linden, this 5-star non-smoking hotel boasts a grand sweeping lobby and old-world charm despite being newly renovated. The beautiful suites come with free butler service. Marble pool area, gym, spa

and a beauty salon make it an ideal setting for weddings or honeymoon trips. Ask for the quiet rooms overlooking the courtyard garden.

Around Alexanderplatz

Alexander Plaza

Rosenstrasse 1; tel: 240 010; www.alexander-plaza.com; €€–€€€; S3, S5, S7, S9: Hackescher Markt; map p.137 D2

An excellent choice for the Mitte area, this quiet hotel is within walking distance of the Scheunenviertel and Alexanderplatz and right by the S-Bahn and a major tram depot. The Thursday and Saturday markets at Hackescher Markt are minutes away, as are numerous dining possibilities.

The Circus

Weinbergsweg 1a; tel: 2839 1433; www.circus-berlin.de; €; U8: Rosenthaler Platz; map p.135 C4

One of Berlin's best-loved hostels, located within minutes of Kastanienallee in Pren-

Left: distinctive decor at the Arte Luise Kunsthotel.

this new hostel recommends itself for its superb yet quiet location, design and service. It has all the mod cons you can ask for, but they come in a charming historical package. The hostel has shared but lockable facilities and is sparklingly clean and secure. Alexanderplatz, Unter den Linden, Scheunenviertel and Museuminsel are all on your doorstep. It is also very easy to reach by direct TXL bus from Tegel airport.

easyHotel Berlin
Rosenthaler Strasse 69; www.easyhotel.com; €; U8: Rosenthaler Platz
This brand-new (December 2010), modern hotel offers designer style at a knock-down price. The rooms are simple but comfortable and attractive. The location is convenient for sightseeing with good transport links.

Hotel Hackescher Markt
Grosse Präsidentenstrasse 8; tel: 280 030; www.hotel-hackescher-markt.com; €€–€€€; S5, S7, S9: Hackescher Markt, S1, S2: Oranienburger Strasse, map p.134 C3
A hotel in the middle of trendy Scheunenviertel with its galleries, up-and-coming designer stores, bars and

restaurants, where you can sleep peacefully in a feel-good room overlooking an ivy-overgrown courtyard and have breakfast in the sun. This small and charming boutique hotel has it all; just remember to ask for a garden room. If you want to arrive in style, the hotel provides limousine pick-up at very little extra cost compared to an ordinary taxi.

Park Inn
Alexanderplatz 7; tel: 23 890; www.parkinn-berlin.com; €€–€€€; S3, S5, S7, S9, U2, U5: Alexanderplatz; map p.137 E2
Formerly the Stadt Berlin, one of only a couple of hard-currency hotels in East Berlin where Westerners were permitted to stay, the Park Inn is a favourite with discount-travel sites because, with 1,012 rooms and suites, there is almost always a vacancy. Rooms can be tiny, although with 39 floors, the views can be breathtaking. The 'classic' rooms on the top 10 floors tend to be bigger and more expensive, but there is no denying the central location here is a plus. Book a room on the Fernsehturm side.

Radisson Blu Hotel
Karl-Liebknecht-Strasse 3; tel: 238 280; www.radissonblu.com; €€€€; S5, S7, S75, S9: Hackescher Markt; map p.137 D1
A 25m- (82ft-) high cylindrical

zlauer Berg or the historical Scheunenviertel. It can get loud and raucous, but the staff are friendly and full of tips for the youthful clientele. There is bicycle rental available, a travel service, wi-fi and tickets for various events around town.

Citystay Hostel Berlin Mitte
Rosenstrasse 16; tel: 2362 4031; www.citystay.de; €; TXL bus, bus 100, bus 200: Spandauer Strasse, Marienkirche; S5, S7, S9: Hackescher Markt; map p.137 D2
Housed in a converted 19th-century department store,

> Hotel price ranges including tax, given as a guide only, for a standard double room in peak season, with bathroom but without breakfast unless otherwise stated:
>
> | | |
> |---|---|
> | € | under €70 |
> | €€ | €70–€100 |
> | €€€ | €100–€170 |
> | €€€€ | over €170 |

Below: a friendly welcome at the Hotel Brandenburger Hof.

Huge, modern 4-star hotel with a clear commitment to design in a convenient location near the Zoo, the Tiergarten and the Ku'damm. It is worth asking for a quiet room and a rate with breakfast included. In the hotel's 'Le Spa' pampering zone, you will find a gym, three saunas and Berlin's largest indoor pool, complete with cocktails served on a sun terrace.

Ritz-Carlton
Potsdamer Platz 3; tel: 337 777; www.ritzcarlton.com; €€€€; S1, S2, S25, U2, bus 200: Potsdamer Platz; map p.134 B2

Nice high-rise tucked away from the honky-tonkier bits of Potsdamer Platz, although with easy access to all the Berlinale's cinemas. Famous for its luxurious feather beds, it also features heated floors in its marble bathrooms. Ask for a room overlooking the Tiergarten or Potsdamer Platz's collection of modern architecture. An added plus is a very authentic French brasserie, Desbrosses & Desbrosses.

aquarium stocked with 2,500 tropical fish is the astonishing sight which greets you in the lobby of this luxury hotel across the Spree river from the Berliner Dom. Depending on your room, you'll have either the cathedral or the fish as a view. Rooms are not big, but they are comfortable and the location is excellent.

Tiergarten
Grand Hyatt
Marlene-Dietrich-Platz 2 (Potsdamer Platz); tel: 2553 1234; www.berlin.grand.hyatt.com; €€€€; S1, S2, S25, U2: Potsdamer Platz; map p.134 B2

The hub of the annual Berlinale film festival, the Grand Hyatt seems a bit austere at first glance, but the lobby furnishings of black marble and polished wood are echoed in the room decor, which is minimal but warm with smart touches, like Bang & Olufsen flat-screen televisions, Aveda

cosmetics in the luxurious bathrooms and fresh flowers to greet you each day. Top-rate, centrally located hotel.

Intercontinental Hotel Berlin
Budapester Strasse 2; tel: 26 020; www.berlin.intercontinental.com; €€€€; S3, S5, S7, S9, U2: Zoologischer Garten; bus 200 to Budapester Strasse; map p.133 E1

The Interconti, as abbreviation-prone Berliners call it, has been a landmark on West Berlin's skyline for 50 years. Its rooms are both up to date yet redolent of the era in which it was built. It may not be as close to the action as it once was, but is still nice to return to in the evening.

Pullman
Budapester Strasse 25; tel: 26 960; www.pullmanhotels.com; €€€; U2, S5, S7, S9, bus X9: Zoologischer Garten; bus 200: Budapester Strasse; map p.133 E1

Charlottenburg

Hecker's Hotel
Grolmanstrasse 35; tel: 88 900; www.heckers-hotel.com; €€–€€€; S1, S2, S25: Savignyplatz; map p.133 C1
Stylish 4-star boutique hotel in a quiet street off the Kurfürstendamm, a perfect shopping location. Savignyplatz with its bars and restaurants is a block away. Spacious rooms with king-sized beds and theme suites in colonial, Tuscan or Bauhaus style. Roof terrace, lavish buffet breakfast and lunch. The air of privacy and luxury makes it a preferred haunt for many a publicity shy showbiz star.

Hotel Art Nouveau
Leibnitzstrasse 59; tel: 327 7440; www.hotelartnouveau.de; €€€;

U7: Adenauerplatz; S5, S7, S9, S75: Savignyplatz; map p.132 C1
Charming boutique-style pension, decorated with a mix of discreet modernity and well-chosen antiques. Not only is breakfast included, but there is an 'honour' refrigerator packed with goodies for those midnight cravings.

Hotel Bleibtreu
Bleibtreustrasse 31; tel: 884 740; www.bleibtreu.com; €€€; U1: Uhlandstrasse; S5, S7, S9, S75: Savignyplatz; map p.133 C1
A good choice for the eco-conscious traveller, as a recent renovation of this hotel made extensive use of environmentally friendly materials. In keeping with the theme, options such as reflexology sit alongside traditional pampering services. Rooms are snug in size but smart, with an aesthetic somewhere between the earthy and the urban.

Hotel Brandenburger Hof
Eislebener Strasse 14; tel: 214 050; www.brandenburger-hof.com; €€€€; U3: Augsburger Strasse; map p.133 D1
Discreet, warm elegance at a grand, but not at all stuffy

hotel. The rooms' decor is in the Bauhaus style, and the winter garden is a lovely place to while away some time. Breakfast is included, and the Michelin-starred restaurant **Die Quadriga** is excellent.
SEE ALSO RESTAURANTS, P.116

Hotel Pension Dittberner
Wielandstrasse 26; tel: 881 6485; www.hotel-dittberner.de; €€€; U7: Adenauerplatz; S5, S7, S9, S75: Savignyplatz; map p.133 C1
If you are looking to live out a fantasy of Alte Berlin life, this traditional pension is an ideal place in which to do it. Well-chosen paintings and prints adorn the walls, and the decor is luxurious, with tactile fabrics and elegant furnishings. The charming proprietor makes guests feel at home. Free wifi and DSL.

Propeller Island City Lodge
Albrecht-Achilles-Strasse 58; tel: 891 9016; www.propeller-island.com; €€–€€€; U7: Adenauerplatz; bus 109, X10, M19, M29: Adenauerplatz; map p.136 B4
Eccentric 'habitable work of art in the heart of Berlin'. Every piece of furnishing is an artist-created, one-of-a-kind object; no two rooms resemble each other. Get inspired amid surreal colours, slanted floors, 'sound sculptures' and suspended beds. Alternatively, you can sleep in a coffin, a cage or a prison cell. Not all rooms have full bathrooms. There are no reception services or restaurant – not a problem since the lodge is just a block from the Ku'damm.

Q! Hotel
Knesebeckstrasse 67; tel: 810 0660; www.loock-hotels.com; €€€; U1: Uhlandstrasse; S5, S7, S9, S75: Savignyplatz; map p.133 C1

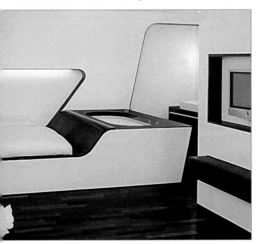

Left: note the bathtub by the bed at the futuristic Q! Hotel.

Left: elegant style at the Hotel-Pension Dittberner (*see p.75*).

lively Kollwitzplatz square with its organic farmers' market on Saturdays.

City Guesthouse Pension Berlin
Gleimstrasse 24; tel: 448 0792; www.pension-guesthouse-berlin.de; €–€€; U2: Schönhauser Allee

Friendly, B&B-style boarding house in a renovated 19th-century building. The pleasant, comfortable and well-equipped guest rooms and apartments with hardwood floors are very affordable, and the accommodating staff go out of their way to make your stay a memorable one. Only 10 minutes from Alexanderplatz by underground, and surrounded by bars, restaurants and shops.

Hotel Pension Kastanienhof
Kastanienallee 65; tel: 443 050; www.kastanienhof.biz; €€; U8: Rosenthaler Platz, then Tram 1: Schwedter Strasse; map p.135 C4

The 150-year-old Kastanienhof is a find: in a quiet location between Mitte and Prenzlauer Berg, it offers simply furnished rooms with incredibly helpful service. It has a rustic charm which the large number of repeat guests find restful. The huge, free breakfast buffet is another plus, and the short walk to the sights and sounds of the neighbourhood makes it a great place for travellers on a budget.

Park Plaza Prenzlauer Berg
Storkower Strasse 162; tel: 421 810; www.parkplaza.com; €€–€€€; S8: Storkower Strasse

Near trendy Prenzlauer Berg, this is a modern hotel with clean lines and free WiFi. The

A sexy hotel, decked out in futuristic style and popular with design-conscious magazines and their trendy readers. Despite its hipness, it is surprisingly comfortable, with a playfulness that belies its aesthetics, such as the bath that can be rolled into from the bed. There is also a fantastic spa on-site and a super-chic bar and restaurant.

Swissotel Berlin
Augsburger Strasse 44; tel: 220 100; www.swissotel.com; €€€–€€€€; S3, S5, S7, S9, U2: Zoologischer Garten; map p.133 D1

With its soaring atrium lobby and ultra-modern decoration, the Swissotel is located on

the corner of the Ku'damm. Rooms are comfortable, and the ones which don't look out onto the atrium have splendid views across the rooftops of Berlin. Each room is fitted with a Lavazza espresso machine.

Prenzlauer Berg

Ackselhaus/Bluehome
Belforter Strasse 21; tel: 4433 7633; www.ackselhaus.de; €€€; U2: Senefelder Platz; map p.135 D4

The Ackselhaus boarding house is a unique retreat in young and trendy Prenzlauer Berg. The terracotta-coloured 19th-century converted residential building offers a Mediterranean ambience, complete with a charming courtyard garden. It is easy to feel at home in tastefully decorated rooms with a personal touch. The Bluehome twin building next door focuses on a water theme, and the Balinese-style studios are a dream. It's located in a tree-lined street three blocks away from a metro station and

Hotel price ranges including tax, given as a guide only, for a standard double room in peak season, with bathroom but without breakfast unless otherwise stated:

€	under €70
€€	€70–€100
€€€	€100–€170
€€€€	over €170

rooms are well-priced for the area and it is a comfortable and convenient base from which to explore the eastern parts of the city.

Kreuzberg and Friedrichshain

Die Fabrik
Schlesische Strasse 18; tel: 611 7116; www.diefabrik.com; €–€€; U1: Schlesisches Tor; map p.139 E4

In a converted red-brick factory building, this hostel is ideal for backpackers, families, groups or individuals on a budget. The quiet rooms are basic but cosy, with wooden floors and rugs. There are shared bathrooms and no lift, televisions or telephones in the rooms. Great value in the heart of the vibrant Kreuzberg district. No credit cards.

Generator
Storkower Strasse 160; tel: 417 2400; www.generatorhostels. com; €–€€; S41, S42, S8, S85: Landsberger Allee

For party-loving teenagers from all over the world, the Generator is the place to be, and it can put up 900 of them at a time. Its futuristic design gives it an edge over most other hostels. The rooms are small and spartan, but safe and clean. Breakfast is plentiful and included. It is a bit of a hike to the more interesting parts of town, but the Generator is well connected. If the nightly in-house parties are not your thing, just join one of the pub crawls offered.

Home-from-Home Hotel & Hostel Friedrichshain
Warschauer Strasse 57; tel: 9700 2030; http://friedrichshain. home-from-home.de; €–€€; S5, S9: Warschauer Strasse

In German, twin beds are *zwei Einzelbetten*. A double bed is a *Doppelbett*.

Interested in staying at a budget place in a neighbourhood with an average age of 21? With kinky shops, bars, nightlife, breakfast until 4pm? Then this is for you: choose from single, twin-bed, triple rooms or dorms with or without private bathroom and TV.

Hotel Sarotti-Höfe
Mehringdamm 57; tel: 6003 1680; www.hotel-sarotti hoefe.de; €–€€; U6: Mehringdamm; map p.138 B4

Very reasonable accommodation in a beautifully converted 19th-century red-brick building in trendy Kreuzberg, populated by a young crowd. The Kreuzberg ethnic restaurants, offbeat shops and nightlife are at hand, while the more traditional sights are just a few metro stops away. Cosy rooms in warm colours and wireless LAN for free throughout the hotel are plus points, as are helpful staff, a €5 buffet breakfast and 10 percent discount if you pay in cash.

Riemers Hofgarten
Yorckstrasse 83; tel: 7809 8800; www.hotel-riehmers hofgarten.de; €€; U6, U7: Mehringdamm; map p.138 B4

A favourite with insiders and gay travellers for many years,

Pension 11. Himmel
Perhaps you never dreamed of staying in an original communist-era prefab. But you've got to give credit to the young people who set up and run this place on the 11th floor (hence the name '11th Heaven') of a high-rise in Marzahn, East Berlin's largest housing development. Their efforts resulted in eclectically decorated rooms with balconies and full bathrooms, offered for incredibly little money. Marzahn is more than a place to sleep: go and see the old windmill and the impressive Gardens of the World, and enjoy your young hosts' company (Pension 11. Himmel, Wittenberger Strasse 85, Marzahn; tel: 937 720 52; www.pension-11himmel.de; S7: Ahrensfelde).

Riemers Hofgarten is a bit out of the way for the main tourist attractions, but located in a charming corner of Kreuzberg not terribly far from Schöneberg. Its affordability and friendly service have won it a devoted clientele, and the elegant 19th-century courtyard after which it is named is a fine piece of bombast. Good restaurant, too.

Below: *zwei Einzelbetten* at the Hotel Bleibtreu *(see p.75)*.

Language

Since most Berliners speak some English, it is generally easy enough to get by. Younger people in particular will enjoy practising their English on you. Learning a few phrases in German is a good idea, however, especially as the German language can be a little tricky. Germans have a habit of joining words together (chances are that you run into '*Schienenersatzverkehr*', literally 'rail replacement traffic', when trains are replaced with buses) or even splitting them (to go out is '*ausgehen*' but '*Ich gehe heute abend aus*' is what you say when you're going out tonight). Happily, at least everything is pronounced the way it is spelt.

The Alphabet

a=ah, ä=ay, b=beh, c=tseh, d=deh, e=eh, f=eff, g=geh, h=hah, i=eeh, j=yot, k=kah, l=ell, m=emm, n=enn, o=oh, ö=oeh, p=peh, q=koo, r=err, s=ess, t=teh, u=ooh, ü=uyuh, v=fow, w=veh, x=iks, y=ypsilon, z=tsett
ä is like the 'e' in 'get'
ö is like the 'er' in 'Bert'
ü as in 'true'
ie as in 'thief'
ei as in 'wine'
ß like 's' in 'sit'

General Words and Phrases

yes *ja*
no *nein*
maybe *vielleicht*
please *bitte*
thank you *danke*
you're welcome *gern geschehen*
hi/hello *Hallo*
Good morning *Guten Morgen*
Good evening *Gute Abend*
Goodbye *Auf Wiedersehen*
see you tomorrow *bis morgen*
I'm looking for... *Ich suche…*
Where is…? *Wo ist…?*
What is…? *Was ist…?*
When is…? *Wann ist…?*

What is your name?
Wie heisst du? (informal)
Wie heissen Sie? (formal)
My name is... *Ich heisse...*
How are you?
Wie geht es Ihnen?
I'm fine, and you?
Mir geht es gut, und Ihnen?
I'm... *Ich bin...*
I don't understand
Ich verstehe nicht
I understand *Ich verstehe*
I don't know *Ich weiss nicht*
Can you repeat?
Können Sie das wieder-holen?
I'm sorry *Es tut mir leid*
Okay *In Ordnung*
Excuse me *Verzeihung*
Where are the toilets?
Wo sind die Toiletten?
Ladies/gentlemen
Damen/Herren
free *kostenlos*
here *hier*
there *dort*
right *rechts*
left *links*
straight on *geradeaus*
upstairs *oben*
downstairs *unten*
near *nah*
far *weit*
opposite *gegenueber*
beside *neben*

today *heute*
tomorrow *morgen*
now *jetzt*
later *später*
open/closed
geöffnet/geschlossen
Help! *Hilfe!*
street *die Strasse*
palace *das Schloss*
church *die Kirche*
art *die Kunst*

On Arrival

How do I get to…?
Wie komme ich zu…?
I want to get off at...
Ich möchte aussteigen...
How far is it?
Wie weit ist es?
departure/arrival
Abfahrt/Ankunft
train station *der Bahnhof*
bus stop *die Bushaltestelle*
train *der Zug*
car *das Auto*
ticket *der Fahrschein*

It should be noted that in Germany, words that feature a double 's' after a long vowel, such as '*Schloss*', may be spelled with the German letter 'ß' and appear as '*Schloß*'. For pronunciation, *see box, left.*

Language

Left: a street sign using the traditional German letters.

How much is it?
Was kostet das?
a different size
eine andere Grösse
Do you take credit cards?
Nehmen Sie Kreditkarten?

Health

doctor *der Arzt*
dentist *der Zahnarzt*
hospital *das Krankenhaus*
pharmacy *die Apotheke*
prescription *Rezept*
I'm sick *Ich bin krank*
It's an emergency
Es ist ein Notfall
police *Polizei*
What is your mobile (phone) number?
Was ist deine Handynummer? (formal)

Numbers

one *eins*
two *zwei*
three *drei*
four *vier*
five *fünf*
six *sechs*
seven *sieben*
eight *acht*
nine *neun*
ten *zehn*
eleven *elf*
twelve *zwölf*
thirteen *dreizehn*
fourteen *vierzehn*
fifteen *fünfzehn*
sixteen *sechzehn*
seventeen *siebzehn*
eighteen *achtzehn*
nineteen *neunzehn*
twenty *zwanzig*
thirty *dreissig*
fifty *fünfzig*
one hundred *einhundert*
one thousand *eintausend*

---

return ticket
die Rückfahrkarte
platform *der Bahnsteig*
city map *der Stadtplan*
I'd like to change
Ich möchte wechseln
money *geld*
I'd like a single-
Ich möchte ein Einzel-
double room
zimmer/Doppelzimmer
with bathroom *mit Bad*
Please show me
Bitte zeigen Sie mir
another room
ein anderes Zimmer
Is breakfast included?
Mit Frühstück?
to book *reservieren*
lift *Fahrstuhl*
key *Schlüssel*

Eating Out

I would like to...
Ich möchte einen Tisch
...reserve a table for four
für vier Personen bestellen
What do you recommend?
Was empfehlen Sie?
breakfast *Frühstück*
lunch *Mittagessen/Lunch*
dinner *Abendessen*
the menu *die Karte*
Do you have vegetarian dishes? *Haben Sie*

vegetarische gerichte?
The bill, please
Die Rechnung, bitte
We'd like separate cheques
Wir möchten getrenn-bezahlen
together *zusammen*
change *Wechselgeld*
SEE ALSO RESTAURANTS, P.119

Shopping

shop *der Laden, das Geschäft*
department store *Kaufhaus*
I'm just browsing
Ich schaue mich nur um
I'd like to buy...
Ich möchte kaufen...
Do you have... *Haben Sie...(formal)*

Below: it is useful to be able to read a few basic German words.

There are three different words for 'the', depending on the gender of the word: *der*, *die*, *das*, *ein* and *eine*. No one minds if you get these wrong, though.

79

Literature

B erlin was a late arrival in the world of literary metropolises. Having only become the German capital in 1871, it had a way to go to catch up with sister capitals Paris and London, long-time national literary hubs. However, in 1929, Expressionist author Alfred Döblin put the city on the literary map with his novel *Berlin Alexanderplatz*, and it has been there ever since. Today, there is a buzzing creative scene, and the annual International Literature Festival Berlin brings together young and acclaimed authors from all over the world, who introduce new works to the public; see www.literaturfestival.com.

Berlin Writers

Bertolt Brecht

Bertolt Brecht (1898–1956) moved to Berlin from provincial Augsburg in the 1920s and matured into a groundbreaking poet and playwright. He fled Nazi Germany in 1933 and returned to post-war East Berlin, where he staged internationally acclaimed productions at the Berliner Ensemble theatre that still shows Brecht plays like *The Threepenny Opera* (1928), *Galileo* (1938) or *The Caucasian Chalk Circle* (1948).

Like many other poets and writers, Bertolt Brecht was buried at the **Dorotheenstädtischer Friedhof** (Chausseestrasse 126; daily in summer 8am–8pm; S1; S2, S25: Nordbahnhof; U6: Zinnowitzer Strasse; map p.134 B4). Famous people interred here include philosophers Hegel and Fichte and authors Heinrich Mann and Anna Seghers. At the entrance to the cemetery is the **Brecht-Weigel-Gedenkstätte**, Bertolt Brecht's house, now a museum and Brecht archive.

Alfred Döblin

Alfred Döblin's (1878–1957) *Berlin Alexanderplatz* (1929) is a powerful depiction of hero Franz Biberkopf's struggle for survival in a tough, frantic Berlin in the years after hyperinflation. The best-selling novel became and still is a source of inspiration for scores of authors, theatre directors and film-makers.

Günter Grass

German-Polish Günter Grass (1927–) set his most famous novel, the magical realist classic *The Tin Drum* (1958) against the backdrop of the Nazi and post-war years. Out-

Below: Bertolt Brecht's grave.

spoken, political and prolific, he continues to be a high-profile figure and was awarded the Nobel Peace Prize in 1999.

Christopher Isherwood

Anglo-American Christopher Isherwood's (1904–86) *Berlin Stories*, including *Mr Norris Changes Trains* (1935) and *Goodbye to Berlin* (1939), are among the best-known Berlin literature, due in large part to their adaptation as the play *I am a Camera* and later, as the popular musical and film *Cabaret* (see Film, p.56). In the 1920s, tolerance of homosexuality in Weimar-era Berlin was what attracted Isherwood. His semi-autobiographical account reflects the years of decadence before the Nazi regime.

Berlin Reading List

FICTION

Thomas Brussig
Heroes Like Us, The Harvill Press (1998)
Christopher Isherwood
The Berlin Stories, New Directions Publishing Corporation (1963)
Erich Kästner Fabian
Fabian: The Story of a Moral-

Left: books about the city for sale in Berlin Story.

and media shop is a popular late-night refuge of book and music lovers. It has a fairly good selection of new English-language paperbacks and hard-cover best-sellers.

Marga Schoeller Bücherstube
Knesebeckstrasse 33, Charlottenburg; tel: 881 1112; www.marga schoeller.de; Mon–Wed 9.30am–7pm, Thur–Fri 9.30am–8pm, Sat 9.30am–6pm; S5, S7, S75, S9: Savignyplatz; map p.133 C1
A Berlin establishment since 1929, Marga Schoeller's was a hub of West Berlin's literary scene during the times of the Wall. It is less of a focal point now but remains a cosy, welcoming place with a superb selection of English titles.

Saint George's English Bookshop
Wörther Strasse 27, Prenzlauer Berg; tel: 8179 8333; www.saint georgesbookshop.com; Mon–Fri 11am–8pm, Sat 11am–7pm; U2: Senefelder Platz, Eberswalder Strasse; map p.135 D4
The quaint shop just off Prenzlauer Allee offers an array of well cared for, mostly second-hand fiction and non-fiction books. Chances are you drop on a comfy leather sofa with a book in hand and forget the world around you for hours.

Below: a local heavyweight.

---

ist, Cyrus Brooks (1993)
Ian McEwan
The Innocent, Vintage (1990)
Peter Schneider
The Wall Jumper, University of Chicago Press (1983)

NON-FICTION
David Clay Large
Berlin, Basic Books (2001)
Anthony Read, David Fisher
Berlin Rising: Biography of a City, W.W. Norton (1994)
Frederick Taylor
The Berlin Wall: 13 August 1961–9 November 1989, Bloomsbury (2007)

Bookshops

Another Country
Riemannstrasse 7, Kreuzberg; tel: 6940 1160; www.another country.de; Tue–Fri 11am–8pm, Sat noon–4pm; U7: Gneisenaustrasse; map p.138 C3
A book lover's home away from home: part bookshop, part library. Another Country has 20,000 volumes on its shelves and also runs film, TV and cooking nights.

Berlin Story
Unter den Linden 26, Mitte; tel: 2045 3842; www.berlinstory.de; daily 10am–8pm; S1, S2, S25,

bus 100, 200: Brandenburger Tor; map p.136 B1
This multilingual bookshop has the best range of Berlin-related books in English, as well as paraphernalia of all kinds. Ask the staff for up-to-date insider tips on the city, as they tend to be well informed. The website is also a good place to browse if you want to do some homework before coming to Berlin.

Books in Berlin
Goethestrasse 69, Charlottenburg; tel: 313 1233; www.books inberlin.de; Mon–Fri noon–8pm, Sat 10am–4pm; S5, S7, S75, S9: Savignyplatz; map p.132 C2
This shop is an excellent source for English and American literature, both new and second-hand. Check the website for occasional lectures and readings.

Dussmann das Kulturkaufhaus
Friedrichstrasse 90, Mitte; tel: 2025 1111; www.kultur kaufhaus.de (German only); Mon–Sat 10am–midnight; S5, S7, S75, S9, U6: Friedrichstrasse, bus 100, 200: Unter den Linden; map p.136 B1
Berlin's largest general book

GÜNTER GAUS
Widersprüche

Monuments and Memorials

B erlin lives with the memory of its past like no other city, and its atonement for the deeds committed in World War II can be seen everywhere, from large-scale projects to the small golden paving stones, *Stolpersteine* (stumbling blocks), hammered by artist Gunter Demnig into the pavements in front of houses where people were taken to concentration camps. You'll also see many other monuments of historical interest in Berlin, marking the conflicts that have shaped the city over the last two centuries.

Cold War Memorials

Checkpoint Charlie
Friedrichstrasse/corner Zimmerstrasse, Mitte/Kreuzberg; U6: Kochstrasse; map p.134 B1
Not much is left of this former border crossing point between East and West Berlin, but some of its history is told in the nearby **Checkpoint Charlie Museum**. As the naming of checkpoints was based on the American spelling code and this one was the third to open, it was given the name Charlie. It was reserved for diplomats, tourists from abroad and military personnel from the Western powers. Today, a 'You are now leaving the American sector' border sign, some sandbags and a copy of a soldier's post commemorate the place where American and Soviet tanks stood face to face during the Cold War. Part-time actors in Soviet and American uniforms pose for photographs.
SEE ALSO MUSEUMS, P.93

Gedenkstätte Berliner Mauer (Berlin Wall Documentation Centre)
Bernauer Strasse 111–9, Wed-

Above: reminders of the Cold War at Checkpoint Charlie (left) and at Gedenkstätte Berliner Mauer (right).

ding; tel: 4679 86666; www.berliner-mauer-dokumentationszentrum.de; Tue–Sun Apr–Oct: 9.30am–7pm, Nov–Mar: 9.30am–6pm; S1, S2, S25: Nordbahnhof; map p.134 B4
There are a number of memorials along the route of the Berlin Wall, many of them clustered on Bernauer Strasse, the 'death strip' on which so many potential escapees were shot, but this small museum and information clearing-house is the place to start if you want to see them. The observation tower gives a good view of

where a long stretch of the Wall stood, and the official city memorial, with its controversial inscription, is right across the street.

Jewish Monuments

Bebelplatz
Mitte; U6: Französische Strasse, bus 100, bus 200: Staatsoper; map p.136 C1
On 10 May 1933, Nazi students from Berlin University (now Humboldt University) across Unter den Linden from this huge square looted the National Library (just west of the University) and piled the books here to burn.

Left: the Holocaust Memorial.

home, which was used as a collection point for Jews being taken to concentration camps. On the right is a group of 13 figures by artist Will Lammert. On the left is a plaque in memory of the 55,000 Jews from Berlin who were deported. (The stones piled atop it are a traditional Jewish gesture of remembrance.) The area behind the monument is the site of the Alter Judischer Friedhof (Old Jewish graveyard), which was desecrated by the Nazis.

Kristallnacht 50th Anniversary Memorial

Koppenplatz, around Alexanderplatz; U8: Weinmeisterstrasse, Rosenthaler Platz; map p.134 C4

Commissioned by the East German government to commemorate the 50th anniversary of the Gestapo rampage against Jewish businesses and synagogues in 1939, this moving sculpture by Karl Biedermann, a table and chairs, one of which has been knocked over, is surrounded by a memorial text by poet Nelly Sachs.

Israeli artist Micha Ullman rose brilliantly to the challenge of memorialising this event with his sunken room of empty white bookcases which can be glimpsed through a window set in the plaza. A plaque nearby quotes Heinrich Heine: 'Where one burns books, it is only a prelude; in the end one also burns people.'

Denkmal für die ermordeten Juden Europas (Memorial to the Murdered Jews of Europe)

Wilhelmstrasse 72–73, Mitte; tel: 2639 4311; www.stiftung-denkmal.de; guided tours and reservations: 2639 4336; Field of Stelae daily 24 hours, Information Centre Tue–Sun Apr–Sept: 10am–8pm, Oct–Mar: 10am–7pm; free; S1, S2, S26: Unter den Linden; U2: Mohrenstrasse; map p.134 B2

Also known as the Holocaust Memorial, this controversial project was first planned in 1988–9 and went through much discussion before Peter Eisenman's design was chosen and realised in 2003. Opened in December 2004, it consists of a 1.9-hectare

(4.7-acre) site covered with a grid of 2,700 concrete stelae, which are blank. Each visitor seems to form his or her own idea of what it means. The Information Centre underground has the names of all known Jewish victims of the Holocaust.

Grosse Hamburger Strasse Memorial

Grosse Hamburger Strasse 24, Around Alexanderplatz; S3, S5, S7, S9: Hackescher Markt; map p.134 C3

This two-part memorial stands on the site of the first Jewish community's old-age

Below: the Grosse Hamburger Strasse Memorial.

Triumphal Monuments

Brandenburger Tor

Pariser Platz, Mitte; www.brandenburgertor.de; bus 100, 200: Brandenburger Tor; S1, S2, S25: Unter den Linden; map p.136 A1

One of the most photographed views in Berlin is that of the Kaiser-Wilhelm-Gedächtnis-kirche *(see p.85)* framed by the 'Berlin Sculpture', which was erected to mark the city's 750th anniversary in 1987. Symbolising the east and west interlocking, but not touching, it is a fitting monument to the division of the pre-reunification years *(see picture, p.2–3).*

83

The Brandenburg Gate, a focal point and iconic symbol of Berlin and German history, is a neoclassical structure built by Carl Gotthard Langhans in 1788–91 as a triumphal arch and city gate on the road to Brandenburg. It was commissioned by King Friedrich Wilhelm as a symbol of peace, and its design was based on the Propylaea, the gateway to the Acropolis in Athens. After the 1806 Prussian defeat, Napoleon took the Quadriga, the statue of a horse-drawn chariot crowning the gate, to Paris where it remained until his defeat in the Battle of Waterloo in 1814. During the Third Reich, the Nazis used the Gate as a backdrop for their torchlight parades. The building of the Wall in 1961 left the Gate in no-man's land between the inner and outer border fortifications. It remained inaccessible to the public until its reopening in December 1989. Ever since, it has served as a symbol of German unity, and provides the location for one of the world's most famous New Year's Eve parties.

Reiterdenkmal Friedrichs des Grossen

Unter den Linden, Mitte; U6: Französische Strasse; S5, S7, S9: Friedrichstrasse; map p.136 C1

This large equestrian statue of Frederick the Great (1786) positioned on the traffic island in the middle of Unter den Linden boulevard was completed in 1851, based on the design by Christian Daniel Rauch, after decades of discussing how best to honour the much-revered monarch. The 13m (44ft) bronze statue of Frederick, known by Berliners as 'Der Alte Fritz' ('The Old Fritz'), on his favourite horse, Conde, is wonderfully ornate, with a pedestal depicting the most outstanding generals of Frederick's army and other leading Germans of the time. Under Frederick the Great, the Forum Fredericianum, the complex of neighbouring buildings including Humboldt University, the former royal library and the opera house, was laid out.

Siegessäule

Grosser Stern/Strasse des 17. Juni, Tiergarten; Apr–Oct: Mon–Fri 9.30am–6.30pm, Sat–Sun 9.30am–7pm, Nov–Mar: daily 10am–6pm; S5, S7, S9: Tiergarten; bus 100: Grosser Stern; map p.133 E2

Shiny 'Goldelse' ('Golden Else'), as the Berliners disrespectfully refer to the 35-tonne gold-covered Goddess of Victory crowning the Vic-

Below: the icon of Berlin: the Brandenburger Tor.

tory Column, can be spotted from almost everywhere in the Tiergarten, as it overlooks a large roundabout in the middle of the park. In Wim Wenders's film *Wings of Desire,* it was the place where angels congregate. The triumphal column, standing 69m (226ft) high, was built in 1864–73 at the request of Kaiser Wilhelm to commemorate the Prussian victories over France, Austria and Denmark. The sandstone blocks the column is made of are decorated with cannon pipes captured from the enemy in the above-mentioned wars. Originally located opposite the Reichstag, the Victory Column was in the way of Hitler's plans for Germania, the grand new 'Capital of the World' that he envisaged, and was moved to its present location in 1939. It can be reached through four tunnels built to plans by Albert Speer in 1941. After a 285-step hike on a spiral staircase, the view from the top is breathtaking.

War Memorials

Kaiser-Wilhelm-Gedächtniskirche

Breitscheidplatz, Charlottenburg; tel: 218 5023; www.gedaechtniskirche-berlin.de; daily 9am–7pm; free; S3, S5, S7, S9, S75, U1, U2, U9: Zoologischer Garten; map p.133 D1
The husk of a neo-Romanesque church that sustained bombing damage in an Allied air raid in 1943 has been preserved as a reminder of the horror of war.
SEE ALSO CHURCHES, SYNAGOGUES AND MOSQUES, P.45

Neue Wache

Eastern end of Unter den Linden, Mitte; bus 100, 200: Deutsche Staatsoper; map p.137 C1
The New Guard House was constructed in neoclassical style in 1816–18 to plans by

Karl Friedrich Schinkel as a memorial to those killed in the Napoleonic Wars. With its portico of Doric columns, the building resembles a Greek temple. From 1818 to 1918, it housed the royal guard. Badly damaged in World War II and rebuilt in the 1950s with an eternal flame burning inside, it served as the GDR's 'Memorial to the Victims of Fascism and Militarism' and saw a grotesque weekly changing of the goose-stepping guard of honour. Re-dedicated once again after the fall of the Wall, it is now officially the 'Central Memorial of the Federal Republic of Germany to the Victims of War and Tyranny'. The centre of the chamber, with its austere and solemn atmosphere, is now occupied by the enlarged *pietà* sculpture by Käthe Kollwitz, *Mother with Her Dead Son.*

Sowjetisches Ehrenmal (Russian War Memorial)

Strasse des 17. Juni, Tiergarten; S1, S2, S26: Unter den Linden; map p.134 A2
Located near the Reichstag, this imposing memorial is constructed out of stone taken from Hitler's Reichs Chancellery and commemorates the Soviet soldiers who died in the battle to take Berlin in 1945. Built almost immediately after the war, it was one of Berlin's biggest headaches for years: the property was owned by the Soviets, yet stood in the British sector, necessitating a British military enclosure guarded by Berlin police to protect the two Russian soldiers whose job it was to be on guard there. Two artillery pieces and two tanks (supposedly the first two into the city, although that is doubtful) flank a monumental statue of a soldier on a column.

Above: the Siegessäule.

Sowjetisches Ehrenmal (Russian War Memorial)

Treptower Park, Treptow; S6, S8, S9, S10: Treptower Park
Erected over a mass grave for soldiers killed in the battle for Berlin, this is the largest Soviet war memorial in Germany. Its central figure is a Russian soldier holding a young girl, a smashed swastika under his feet. Arranged on the periphery of the field which stretches in front of him are 16 coffin-like structures which have scenes of the liberation of Germany by the Russians and cautionary texts in German and Russian in bas-relief. Unparalleled as a powerful piece of Soviet propaganda in Berlin, it is nonetheless a popular picnic spot for people strolling in Treptow Park.
SEE ALSO PARKS AND GARDENS, P.110

Many of the monuments that reveal much about Berlin's history are in fact the city's architecture, such as the surviving neoclassicist constructions of the Nazi era and the monumental GDR projects around Alexanderplatz.
See Architecture, p.28–31.

Museums

Berlin has an extraordinary and vast collection of museums and galleries. It is true that the Dog Museum and the Hairdressing Museum are gone, as is the Gründerzeit Museum of the famed East German transvestite Charlotte von Mahlsdorf, but it is still easy enough to spend a couple of weeks in Berlin doing nothing but soaking up the art and history which has been curated over the years and is displayed here in often striking and audacious ways. Note that most museums close on Mondays but stay open late on Thursday nights. For information on commercial art, *see Galleries, p.60–63.*

Mitte

Alte Nationalgalerie

Bodestrasse 1–3, Museumsinsel; tel: 2090 5801; www.museen-berlin.de; Tue–Sun 10am–6pm, Wed until 10pm; admission charge; S3, S5, S7, S9: Hackescher Markt; bus 100, 200: Lustgarten; map p.137 D2

The Alte Nationalgalerie assembles the Berlin National

Berlin's central collection of museums stretches across what is known as **Museumsinsel** (Museum Island), the skinny island in the Spree river on which the city was founded. Berlin's collection of art was divided during the Allied occupation and is still being sewn back together, a process which is not due to be completed until 2009, but a visit to at least a couple of the ones which are open now is pretty much mandatory for art lovers. A three-day ticket good for a great many Berlin museums is available from the box offices of all participating institutions. Children and youths under 16 have free access to most museums.

Museums' massive collection of 19th-century art under one roof. The third floor displays entirely German painters, including masterpieces by Caspar David Friedrich, as well as architectural renderings by Karl Friedrich Schinkel. On the second floor, a large number of French Impressionists, including Manet, Monet and Renoir, are joined by their German contemporaries, including Feuerbach, Böcklin and Liebermann. The first floor has a display of Adolf Menzel's paintings and an extensive collection of 19th-century German sculpture.

Altes Museum

Am Lustgarten, Museumsinsel; tel: 2090 5577; www.museen-berlin.de; daily 10am–6pm, Wed until 10pm; admission charge; S3, S5, S7, S9: Hackescher Markt; bus 100, 200: Lustgarten; map p.137 D1

The Altes Museum is itself an art treasure, being one of Karl Friedrich Schinkel's masterpieces of neoclassicism. Inside, the central attraction is the bust of Nefertiti, still radiant after 1,750 years, but

there are other Egyptian and classical works on display here as well. In 2009, the Egyptian Museum collection will be transferred to the Neues Museum.

Bode-Museum

Monbijoubrücke, Museumsinsel; tel: 2090 5601; www.museen-berlin.de; daily 10am–6pm, Wed until 10pm; admission charge; S3, S5, S7, S9: Friedrichstrasse; S1, S2, S25: Oranienburger Strasse; map p.137 C2

Housing the Sculpture Museum, the Byzantine Museum and the Numismatic Collection of the city's art treasures, the Bode-Museum was designed in the 19th century to maximise light and display space. Its church-like interior makes it an ideal venue for its medieval and Renaissance sculpture collection, which includes wooden carving masterpieces by Erasmus Grasser and Tilman Riemenschneider. There are also French, Dutch, Spanish and Italian works from this period and sculptures from the Baroque and Romantic periods. The Byzantine collection has many early

Left: sculpture at the Pergamonmuseum.

The German Historical Museum used to be avoided by Western visitors to East Berlin because the East German regime's idea of German history was at such wide variance with that of the West. Today, after a thorough rebuilding of the former Prussian armoury's interior and the addition of a striking annexe in the rear, designed by I.M. Pei, it is one of Berlin's must-see museums. The exhibit starts upstairs with the coming of the Romans and their impact on the Germanic tribes, then quickly moves to the establishment of Christianity and the rise of the German city-states and on through the centuries to World War I. A map or other guide is essential for seeing this in order if you're not already well familiar with the sequence of events. Downstairs, one is plunged into the chaos of the Great War's aftermath, the inflation, rise of Hitler and the Nazis, World War II, the Cold War and the reunification of Germany. This is all presented without flinching, admirably straightforward and sometimes gruesome. The I.M. Pei annexe is used for temporary, more

Christian works, including carved ivory devotional items and an impressive mosaic chapel. Other highlights here are the Basilica, a great hall in which altarpieces from European churches are displayed with paintings appropriate to the period, and the Numismatic Collection, one of the best collections of coins in the world.

Deutsche Guggenheim
Unter den Linden 13–15; tel: 202 0930; www.deutsche-guggenheim-berlin.de; daily 10am–8pm; S1, S2: Unter den Linden; S3, S5, S7, S9, S75: Friedrichstrasse; map p.136 C1

Located on the ground floor of the Deutsche Bank building on Unter den Linden, this tiny space mounts three to four shows a year by important contemporary artists who have often been commissioned to produce works specifically for the show by either the Guggenheim or Deutsche Bank.

Deutsches Historisches Museum (German Historical Museum)
Unter den Linden 2, Museumsinsel; tel: 2030 4444; www.dhm.de; daily 10am–6pm; admission charge; S3, S5, S7, S9: Hackescher Markt; map p.137 C1

Below: the Alte Nationalgalerie wears its treasures on both the inside (left) and the outside (right).

specialised shows amplifying individual aspects of the permanent collection.

Hamburger Bahnhof: Museum für Gegenwart (Museum of Contemporary Art)

Invalidenstrasse 50–51; tel: 3978 3411; www.hamburger bahnhof.de; Tue–Fri 10am–6pm, Sat 11am–8pm, Sun 11am–6pm; admission charge, free Thur 2–6pm; U6: Zinnowitzer Strasse; S3, S5, S7, S9: Hauptbahnhof; S1, S2: Nordbahnhof; map p.134 A4

Located in a building which once housed one of Europe's first train stations (and which later found itself at the Berlin Wall), this space has been provided by the Berlin City Museums as a place for noted private collectors to house their art, as well as for large-scale touring exhibitions curated elsewhere and by the museum staff. The core is built from Erich Marx's collection of late 20th-century works, including many Warhols, Rauschenbergs, Kiefers and Beuys. In 2004, the museum was granted a seven-year loan of the Friedrich Christian Flick Collection, which is housed in the Rieckhallen, a former warehouse. This collection is particularly strong in such contemporary

Below: a Nazi uniform at the Deutsches Historiches Museum.

Above: propaganda displays at the Deutsches Historiches Museum.

European artists as Candida Höfer, Pipilotti Rist, Luc Tuymans and Franz West.

The Kennedys

Pariser Platz 4a; tel: 2065 3570; www.thekennedys.de; daily 10am–6pm; admission charge; S1, S2, S25, bus 100, 200: Unter den Linden; map p.136 A1

This small museum houses the renowned Camera Work collection of photos, documents and memorabilia of the Kennedy family and commemorates JFK's 1963 visit to the divided city, when he made his famous statement, *'Ich bin ein Berliner'.*

Medizinhistorisches Museum an der Charité (Medical History Museum)

Charitéplatz 1; tel: 4505 36156; www.bmm.charite.de; Tue–Sun 10am–5pm, Wed and Sat until 7pm; admission charge, minimum age for admission 16; U6: Zinnowitzer Strasse; S3, S5, S7, S9: Hauptbahnhof; map p.134 B3

Charité Hospital was the site of the development of Robert Koch's germ theory of disease in the 19th century, and the historical buildings on its campus date back further than that. At this museum one can see over 750 preserved wet and dry specimens, collected over the years for display to medical students of pathology, as well as displays showing the evolution of surgery and medicine

over the past four centuries. The entire museum is an outgrowth of the work of Dr Rudolf Virchow, a pioneer in public health and the discoverer of cellular function.

Museum für Naturkunde (Museum of Natural History)

Invalidenstrasse 43; tel: 2093 8591; www.naturkundemuseum-berlin.de; Tue–Fri 9.30am–6pm, Sat–Sun 10am–6pm; admission charge; U6: Zinnowitzer Strasse; S3, S5, S7, S9: Hauptbahnhof; S1, S2: Nordbahnhof; map p.134 B4

If you go to the Museum of Natural History with your kids, it is entirely possible you may get no further than the first hall, with its incredible dinosaur display (including a brachiosaurus which is the largest mounted dinosaur skeleton in the world), much of which was dug up in the early 20th century at Tendaguru, Tanganyika, by scientists from this museum. Video displays have interactive features showing how these remarkable animals lived and moved, and the flat-screen displays bring the skeletons to life. Get past this, though, to find a hall of hoofed mammals, a thorough set of dioramas showing the fauna of Berlin and Brandenburg, minerals galore and Alfred Kieler's famed insect models, including a mosquito at 60 times life-size and a flea at 100 times. Much of the museum is still being renovated and bilingual signage is sporadic, but in most cases the displays are so well done that it is not a problem.

SEE ALSO CHILDREN, P.42

Neues Museum
Bodestrasse, Museumsinsel; tel: 2664 24242; www.neues-museum.de; daily 10am–6pm, Wed until 10pm; map p.137 D2
The impressive Neues Museum, sensitively reconstructed by award-winning English architect David Chipperfield, houses the Egyptian Museum's collection and the Museum for Pre- and Early History. The highlight in this extraordinary array of prehistoric to late-Roman artefacts, is the famous head of Nefertiti as well as items from the excavations of Schliemann at Troy. This is now one of Berlin's top attractions.

Pergamonmuseum
Am Kupfergraben 5, Museumsinsel; tel: 2090 5577; www.museen-berlin.de; daily 10am–6pm, Wed until 10pm; admission charge; S3, S5, S7, S9: Friedrichstrasse, Hackescher Markt; map p.137 C2
With over a million visitors annually, this is one of Germany's most popular

museums, and with good reason: what other museum can boast not only an entire Greek temple complex, but also the approach to the city of Babylon and its fabled Ishtar Gate? The Pergamon temple complex was excavated by Carl Umann in 1864–5 with the cooperation of the Turkish government and moved, stone by stone, to this museum, built especially to house it. The frieze showing a battle between the Greek gods and the Giants is one of Hellenic art's masterpieces. Other pieces of classical sculpture can be seen in the wings off the central temple room. The ancient Near Eastern collection is just as impressive, not only because of the Babylonian walls, but the Desert Palace of Mshatta from Jordan. In addition, the Museum of Islamic Art is upstairs and forms a small but inclusive survey of the subject, including the impressive Aleppo Room from the Syrian city's Christian quarter. Reconstruction of the museum is ongoing so expect sections of it to be closed.

Around Alexanderplatz
DDR Museum
Karl-Liebknecht-Strasse 1; tel: 8471 23731; www.ddr-museum.de; Mon–Sun 10am–8pm, Sat until 10pm; admission charge; S3, S5, S7, S9: Hackescher Markt; bus 100, 200: Lustgarten; map p.137 D1
This small, private museum, below the Radisson SAS DomAquaree Hotel, on the banks of the Spree across from the Berliner Dom, is not nearly the scholarly institution its neighbours are, but it certainly is a lot of fun. With a stated goal of showing everyday life in the former Deutsche Demokratische Republik (East Germany) and with a particular emphasis on East Berlin, it emphasises a hands-on approach, with a Trabant car you can climb into and 'start', a screening room featuring propaganda films and Erich Honecker's private projector, a hidden corner with a Stasi listening-area, and a reconstructed apartment from a Plattenbau apartment building. It does not shrink from the unpleasant aspects of life in the old regime, nor does it edit

Below: the recently revamped Neues Museum.

89

iously filtered natural light and special artificial light to show each of the thousand paintings on the main floor to its best advantage. The art is arranged chronologically in galleries around a central atrium, with the octagonal Rembrandt room, displaying 16 of the master's works, at its apex. Particularly strong in Dutch and Flemish masters, as well as German artists, the collection at the Gemäldegalerie is the result of the painstaking reunion of works from East and West Berlin, as well as ones taken as war booty by the Soviet Union. Downstairs are an additional 400 paintings in a study collection, as well as computers connected to a digital gallery.

out the enjoyable moments. Recommended for teenagers.

Märkisches Museum

Am Köllnischen Park 5; tel: 2400 2162; www.stadtmuseum.de; Tue, Thur–Sun 10am–6pm, Wed noon–8pm; admission charge; U2: Märkisches Museum; S3, S5, S7, S9: Jannowitzbrücke; map p.135 D2

Although small, this recently renovated museum, with its informative displays, gives a fascinating insight into the history of the city. The fragments of Berlin Wall on the outside are worth seeing.

Tiergarten

Bauhaus Archiv Museum of Design

Klingelhöferstrasse 14; tel: 254 0020; www.bauhaus.de; Wed–Mon 10am–5pm; admission charge; U2, U3, U4: Nollendorfplatz; map p.133 E1

The Bauhaus Archive presents the history and impact of the important Bauhaus (1910–33) school of architecture, design and art in the 20th century. Although the Bauhaus movement started in Weimar and moved to Dessau, it ended up in Berlin, and this small museum hosts regular exhibitions of its work along with

interactive terminals which tell its story in German and English. An audioguide is included in the admission.

Deutsche Kinemathek (Museum of Film and Television)

Potsdamer Strasse 2; tel: 3009 0359; www.filmmuseum-berlin.de; Tue–Sun 10am–6pm, Thur until 8pm; admission charge; U2, S1, S2, S25, bus 200: Potsdamer Platz; map p.134 A2

The permanent exhibition on German film history includes gems such as a model of the robot in *Metropolis*, and has compelling stories to tell about early stars like Marlene Dietrich and the making of classics like Fritz Lang's *Caligari*. One room is dedicated to Leni Riefenstahl.

Gemäldegalerie (Picture Gallery)

Matthäikirchplatz 4–6; tel: 2664 23040; www.smb.museum; Tue–Sun 10am–6pm, Thur until 10pm; admission charge; U2, S1, S2, S25: Potsdamer Platz; bus 200: Philharmonie; map p.134 A2

The Prussian royal family's 13th- to 18th-century holdings are displayed at this recently built 7,000-sq m (8,370-sq yd) museum, which uses ingen-

Kupferstichkabinett (Museum of Prints and Drawings)

Matthäikirchplatz 8; tel: 2664 23040; www.smb.museum; Tue–Sun 10am–6pm, Thur until 10pm; admission charge; U2, S1, S2, S25: Potsdamer Platz; bus 200: Philharmonie; map p.134 A2

With half a million prints and 110,000 drawings, watercolours and pastels ranging from Botticelli to Warhol, this

One of the most high-profile names in fashion, Berlin-born photographer Helmut Newton died in 2004, shortly after reaching an agreement with the Prussian Heritage Foundation to donate many of his photographs to a joint foundation venture. The resulting **Museum für Fotografie** (Jebensstrasse 2; tel: 266 2188; www.smb.spk-berlin.de; Tue–Sun 10am–6pm; admission charge; U2: Zoologischer Garten; map p.133 D1) is the largest dedicated photography gallery in the city.

is one of the world's most important collections of works on paper. Illuminated manuscripts, early Italian, Dutch and German masters and 19th-century works are among its strongest points, and a contemporary collection emphasises artists working in Berlin. Owing to the fragile nature of the works, however, only a small part of them are on display at any given time. Scholars can gain access to the entire collection, but visitors are assured of a small but comprehensive central collection and a rotating series of temporary exhibitions.

Musikinstrumenten-museum (Museum of Musical Instruments)
Ben-Gurion-Strasse; tel: 2548 1178; www.sim.spk-berlin.de; Tue–Wed, Fri 10am–5pm, Thur 9am–10pm, Sat–Sun 10am–5pm; admission charge; U2, S1, S2, S25: Potsdamer Platz; bus 200: Philharmonie; map p.134 A2
Tucked away in the complex housing the Philharmonie, the Musical Instrument Museum is a must-see for music fans, spanning the centuries between Stradivarius (not only violins, but also guitars) and synthesisers. CDs at most displays will show you

how an instrument sounds, and occasionally there are live musicians playing them. On Sundays, the huge Wurlitzer theatrical organ is fired up, to the delight of all.

Neue Nationalgalerie
Potsdamer Strasse 50; tel: 2664 23040; www.smb.museum; Tue–Sun 10am–6pm, Thur until 10pm; admission charge; U2, S1, S2, S25: Potsdamer Platz; map p.134 A1
When the Cuban Revolution chased Bacardi Rum out of Havana, Mies van der Rohe wasn't able to build the glass-encased corporate headquarters he had designed for them, but West Berlin needed a modern art museum and the design proved easily adaptable to that purpose. The cornerstone of the Kulturforum near Potsdamer Platz, the Neue Nationalgalerie is best known to Berliners as the venue for blockbuster shows, not only the selection from New York's Museum of Modern Art which broke records a couple of years ago, but also such unexpected hits as 'Art in the DDR'. Mies's design lets in plenty of natural light, so works are shown to great advantage. When travelling shows aren't busy pulling in the crowds, the museum's

own impressive collection of art hangs on the walls, including works by Klee, Munch, Picasso and Kirchner.

Charlottenburg

Bröhan Museum
Schlossstrasse 1a; tel: 3269 0600; www.broehan-museum.de; Tue–Sun 10am–6pm; admission charge; U2: Sophie-Charlotte-Platz; U7: Richard-Wagner-Platz; S8, S45, S46: Westend; map p.132 B3
Located directly across the street from Schloss Charlottenburg, this museum specialises in Art Nouveau, Art Deco and Functionalism, three related movements in fine and applied arts covering the period 1889–1939. Paintings, furniture and objects are arranged in rooms of the same style on the ground floor, a painting gallery is one floor up, and the third floor is reserved for special exhibitions.

Erotik-Museum
Joachimsthaler Strasse 4; tel: 886 0666; www.erotik museum.de (German only); Mon–Sat 9am–midnight, Sun 11am–midnight; admission charge; S5, S7, S9, U2, U9: Zoologischer Garten; map p.133 D1
Formerly the private collection of a Munich scholar of erotica, the contents of the Erotik-Museum were bought

Below: the exterior of the Neue Nationalgalerie, with Henry Moore's bronze *Archer* in front.

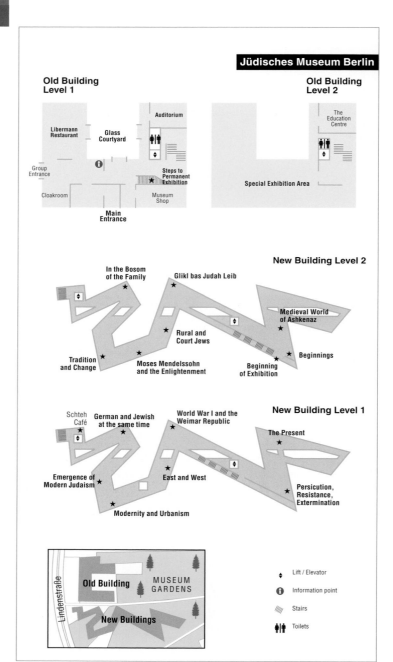

Jüdisches Museum Berlin

Old Building Level 1

Auditorium

Libermann Restaurant

Glass Courtyard

Group Entrance

Cloakroom

Museum Shop

Steps to Permanent Exhibition

Main Entrance

Old Building Level 2

The Education Centre

Special Exhibition Area

New Building Level 2

In the Bosom of the Family

Glikl bas Judah Leib

Medieval World of Ashkenaz

Rural and Court Jews

Tradition and Change

Moses Mendelssohn and the Enlightenment

Beginning of Exhibition

Beginnings

New Building Level 1

Schteh Café

German and Jewish at the same time

World War I and the Weimar Republic

The Present

Emergence of Modern Judaism

East and West

Persicution, Resistance, Extermination

Modernity and Urbanism

Lindenstraße

Old Building

MUSEUM GARDENS

New Buildings

♦ Lift / Elevator

ℹ Information point

///// Stairs

👫 Toilets

Above: the Jewish Museum's striking design makes as much of an impact as the exhibits.

by sex-shop entrepreneur Beate Uhse, who installed it in her flagship store. Artefacts include obsidian dildos from ancient China and depictions of the act in every medium imaginable. The section on the late Beate Uhse, a former Luftwaffe pilot and the mother of the sex industry in post-war Germany, is actually quite interesting. The attached museum shop is a good place for offbeat souvenirs.

Käthe-Kollwitz-Museum and Graphic Collection
Fasanenstrasse 24; tel: 882 5210; www.kaethe-kollwitz.de; daily 11am–6pm; admission charge; U9, U15: Uhlandstrasse or Kurfürstendamm; map p.133 D1
This private museum shows a permanent collection of 200 mainly graphic works and some poignant sculptures by the Expressionist artist and pacifist who spent 50 years of her life in Berlin. An enlarged version of Käthe Kollwitz's famous *Mother with Her Dead Son (pietà)* sculpture can be found in the **Neue Wache** building (New Guard House) on Unter den Linden avenue, now the National Memorial to the Victims of War and Tyranny. SEE ALSO MONUMENTS AND MEMORIALS, P.85

The Story of Berlin
Kurfürstendamm 207–8; tel: 8872 0100; www.story-of-

berlin.de; daily 10am–8pm, admission charge; U1, bus M19, M29, 109: Uhlandstrasse, map p.133 C1
The multimedia exhibition in this modern counterpart to the Märkisches Museum takes visitors through 800 years of Berlin history. The visit to the exhibition includes a guided tour through an original nuclear shelter underneath the Ku'damm-Karree shopping centre, with pretty realistic (and for children, possibly frightening) sound effects.

Kreuzberg and Friedrichshain

Berlinische Galerie
Alte Jakobstrasse 124–8; tel: 7890 2600; www.berlinische galerie.de; Wed–Mon 10am–6pm; admission charge; U1, U6: Hallesches Tor; map p.134 C1
The city museum of modern art, photography and architecture is renowned for staging excellently curated exhibits such as a recent one on German Expressionism. It also has a fine permanent collection, spanning the period from World War I to the 1970s.

Checkpoint Charlie Museum
Friedrichstrasse 43–5; tel: 253 7250; www.mauermuseum.de; daily 9am–10pm; admission charge; U6: Kochstrasse; map p.134 B1
A fascinating exhibition of

attempts to get through the Berlin Wall to West Berlin, including elaborate devices used to hide escapees, marred only by some heavy-handed right-wing polemics.

Jüdisches Museum (Jewish Museum)
Lindenstrasse 9–14; tel: 2599 3300; www.juedisches-museum-berlin.de; Tue–Sun 10am–8pm, Mon 10am–10pm, closed Rosh ha-Shanah, Yom Kippur, Christmas Eve; admission charge; U1, U6: Hallesches Tor; U6: Kochstrasse; map p.134 C1
Controversial in about every way possible, from its much-discussed Daniel Libeskind architecture to the content of its exhibits, Berlin's Jewish Museum makes a provocative supplement to visiting the Deutsches Historisches Museum and is every bit as

Below: erotic art on display at the Erotik-Museum.

Right: Topography of Terror.

much of a must-see. Concentrating as it does on Jewish life in Germany, it tells the story from the earliest Jewish settlements in German cities and towns to renewed Jewish life in the country today through a huge collection of art, artefacts, documents, films and innovative interactive terminals. Jewish contributions to German culture are made plain, and Germany's anti-Semitism is addressed without blinking, as is the Holocaust which resulted from it. Plan an entire day to thread through Libeskind's difficult layout and rest assured that you'll have a lot to talk about after your visit.

Martin-Gropius-Bau
Niederkirchnerstrasse 7, Kreuzberg; tel: 254 860; www.gropiusbau.de; Wed–Mon 10am–8pm; admission charge; S1, S2, U2, bus 200: Potsdamer Platz; map p.134 B1
This huge exhibition hall in an imposing 19th-century red-and-gold neo-Renaissance building plays host to numerous, often excellent, touring collections of archaeological, historical and art exhibitions.

Topography of Terror
Niederkirchnerstrasse 8; tel: 254 5090; www.topographie.de; daily 10am–8pm; free; U2: Mohrenstrasse; map p.134 B1
The remains of the Prinz Albrecht Palais, from which the Gestapo operated, were unearthed during routine excavation here and today house a largely open-air exhibit. A further exhibition on the workings of the Gestapo is housed in a permanent building over the ruins.

Western Districts
Brücke Museum
Bussardsteig 9, Dahlem; tel: 831

2029; www.bruecke-museum.de; Wed–Mon 11am–5pm; admission charge; U3: Oskar-Helene-Heim, then bus 115 to Pücklerstrasse
This private museum is not part of the Dahlem museum complex and is located some way away. It is dedicated to the works of the first group of important German Expressionist artists, who banded together in Dresden under the collective title of 'Die Brücke', the bridge. With over 400 works by Ernst Ludwig Kirchner, Fritz Bleyl, Karl Schmidt-Rottluff, Erich Heckel, Max Pechstein, Emil Nolde and Otto Mueller, it is an essential stop for people interested in 20th-century German art.

Ethnologisches Museum (Ethnological Museum)
Arnimallee 2; tel: 830 1438; www.smb.museum; Tue–Fri 10am–6pm, Sat–Sun 11am–6pm; admission charge; U3: Dahlem-Dorf
The ethnological collections in Dahlem, covering the Americas, the South Seas,

Africa, East Asia and musical ethnology, are an unparalleled resource for those interested in non-European peoples and their cultures. They are displayed with a very contemporary regard for the meanings of the objects, the curators having long ago decided not to show objects which have sacred meaning to the peoples who created them. The American Indian collection, for instance, was largely formed by German explorers in the 19th century, who were taking the scientific study of America's natives seriously at a time when Americans were not; as a result, many items on display are unique. Ritual religious items, however, are only available to recognised scholars, and the stereotyping of Indians by American culture is addressed in a straightforward manner.

The American archaeological rooms show artefacts of the many Central and South American native cultures as they existed up to the time of the arrival of the Spanish, and the South Seas collection not only includes typical buildings and carved and woven items, but entire boats in the huge boat room, which make palpable the immense distances early Polynesian peoples traversed as their culture spread. The East Asian area concentrates on folk art of both China and Japan, while the 'Art from Africa' exhibit, which has won awards, emphasises the link between the sacred and secular in everyday items, thus illuminating the belief-systems of the cultures which created them. In addition to all of this, the Ethnological Museum has a unique treasure in its musical ethnology display: not only are a wide variety of instruments on display, but sound recordings are, too, as an extension of the Berlin Phonogram Archive, which has existed since 1900 to document European and non-European musics, and which was the first project of its type. In its collection are examples of musics which are no longer performed, and it is listed in Unesco's registry Memory of the World.

Museum für Asiatische Kunst (Museum of Asian Art)

Takustrasse 40; tel: 830 1382; www.smb.museum; Tue–Fri 10am–6pm, Sat–Sun 11am–6pm; admission charge; U3: Dahlem-Dorf

This museum is distinct from the East Asian collection at the Ethnological Museum, and collects items from India and East Asia with an eye towards their artistic more than their utilitarian value. Displaying work from

---

> While the city's main museums are described on these pages, this is by no means a comprehensive listing. Berlin is full of small, special interest museums, many in private hands. There's a Sugar Museum, a U-Bahn Museum and a Hemp Museum, among dozens of others.

Afghanistan to Indonesia, the Collection of South, Southeast and Central Asian Art highlights not only India and Tibet, but the varied cultures of Southeast Asia and the Chinese province of Xinjiang. The Collection of East Asian Art has Chinese, Japanese and Korean artworks. Eventually, this museum will be re-housed in the rebuilt Hohenzollern Schloss on Museum Island.

Museum Europäischer Kulturen

Im Winkel 6–8; tel: 2664 26802; www.smb.museum; Tue–Fri 10am–6pm, Sat–Sun 11am–6pm; admission charge; U3: Dahlem-Dorf

The central collection here was created by merging the European part of the Ethnological Museum with the former Museum of Folklore, and shows the commonality and

differences of everyday life on the European continent via traditions and celebrations and the items created for them from the 18th century to the present day.

Treptow and Köpenick

Stasi Museum

Ruschestrasse 103, Haus 1, Lichtenberg; tel: 553 6854; www.stasimuseum.de; Mon–Fri 11am–6pm, Sat–Sun 2–6pm; admission charge; U5: Magdalenenstrasse; S8, S45, S46: Frankfurter Allee

From this grim building the Ministry for State Security, better-known as the Stasi, East Germany's secret police, was directed. Pervading every level of life in East Germany, the Stasi depended on a web of informers and enforcers, collecting vast amounts of information about its citizens. Here, you can visit Erich Mielke's office, from which he directed operations, see spy technology used to gather information and learn about the links with other countries' espionage services. You will also find information about the resistance to the Stasi, which was an important factor in bringing down the East German regime.

Right: remembering the Wall at the Checkpoint Charlie Museum.

Music

From Eastern European street musicians to smoky jazz clubs, *Klezmer* combos, Finnish rock bands and world-class orchestras, Berlin is a crossroads of musical wealth. With two halves of the city sewn back together, Berlin boasts twice the classical music repertoire of most cultural metropolises, alongside a deeply eclectic range of other musical forms. Meanwhile, Berlin's fluid contemporary music scene features influences from all over the world; home-grown talent today covers all genres from techno to electronica to rock to reggae. For listings of more nightclubs that feature live acts, *see Nightlife, p.102–3.*

Classical and Opera

THE SCENE

With several major orchestras, including the Grammy-winning, world-renowned Berlin Philharmoniker, not to mention a number of grand opera houses, visitors to Berlin are spoiled for choice when it comes to classical music. For the chance truly to indulge, visit during September's **MusikFest Berlin** (www.berlinerfestspiele.de), which features several guest ensembles in addition to the local orchestras; the Berlin Philharmoniker tops the bill.

MAJOR VENUES AND ORCHESTRAS

Berliner Philharmonie und Kammermusiksaal
Herbert-von-Karajan-Strasse 1, Tiergarten; ticket hotline tel: 2548 8999; www.berliner-philharmoniker.de; S1, S2, U2: Potsdamer Platz; map p.134 A2
The Berliner Philharmoniker, under the direction of Sir Simon Rattle, is considered by many to be the best symphony philharmonic orchestra in the world, and classical music lovers may

want to plan their trip around their ability to purchase hard-to-get tickets. Even if attending a performance is impossible, the building itself is unique. Completed by Hans Scharoun in 1963, its walls seem to flow like the music that fills them.

Deutsche Oper Berlin
Bismarckstrasse 35, Charlottenburg; tel: 3438 4343; www.deutscheoperberlin.de; advance sales 11am–performance; U2: Deutsche Oper; map p.132 C2
Originally built in 1912, this opera building was destroyed in World War II and not rebuilt until 1961, during the former West Germany's 'economic miracle'. Deutsche Oper is best-known for its innovative interpretations of classic works and for hosting internationally renowned performers.

Komische Oper
Behrenstrasse 55–57, Mitte; tel: 4799 7400; www.komische-oper-berlin.de; advance sales: Unter den Linden 41, Mon–Sat 11am–7pm, Sun 1–4pm; U6:

Französische Strasse, or S1, S2: Unter den Linden; map p.136 B1
This venue is for fans of lighter classical music. The in-house comic opera performs operettas and is well known for extraordinary productions. The orchestra's repertoire also includes symphonies and opera for children.

Konzerthaus Berlin
Gendarmenmarkt, Mitte; ticket hotline tel: 2030 92101; www.konzerthaus.de; advance sales: Mon–Sat noon–7pm, Sun and holidays noon–4pm; U6: Hausvogteiplatz; map p.134 B2

Tickets to classical concerts can be bought at the box office of the relevant concert house, or through *Theaterkassen* (ticket agencies). Note that many will charge a hefty commission on top of the price of the ticket. Alternatively, **Hekticket** is a good bet for last-minute tickets at discounted rates for the same day (Hardenbergstrasse 29D, Charlottenburg or Karl-Liebknecht-Strasse 13, Mitte; tel: 230 9930; www.hek ticket.de; map p.133 D1).

Left: performing in a Mozart opera at the Komische Oper.

noon–7pm; U6, S1, S2, S5, S7: Friedrichstrasse; map p.136 C1
The Staatsoper was built in 1741 for Frederick the Great, by the renowned architect Georg Wenzeslaus von Knobelsdorff. Its repertoire focuses on classical opera and ballet. The opera house was destroyed in World War II, and rebuilt. Located in East Berlin during the Cold War, it is now one of the main attractions in the historic renovation of the palace area on Unter den Linden. It is currently closed for renovation,

Weber's opera *Der Freischütz*, the first major German Romantic opera, had its debut performance here. The Baroque concert house at the elegant Gendarmenmarkt was built by Friedrich Schinkel. After its destruction in the war, it was rebuilt and reopened in 1984. It is home to the Berlin Symphonic Orchestra.

Neuköllner Oper
Karl-Marx-Strasse 131–3, Neukölln; tel: 6889 0777; www.neukoellneroper.de; advance sales Tue–Fri 3–7pm; U7: Karl-Marx-Strasse; map p.139 E2
The influence of this neighbourhood or *kiez theatre*, as the Berliners say, extends well beyond Neukölln. Its 11 productions each year are almost exclusively premières by young authors in genres that range from opera to musicals and musical theatre.

Orangerie Charlottenburg
Schloss Charlottenburg, in the park area, Spandauer Damm 10, Charlottenburg; www.concerts-

berlin.com; S41, 46, 47; U7: Richard-Wagner-Platz; map p.132 B3
This Baroque palace was once the summer residence of Prussian kings, and has been a cultural focal point since its earliest beginnings. The concert series in the Grand Orangerie gives visitors a small taste of Baroque Berlin.

SEE ALSO PALACES AND HOUSES, P.104

**Staatsoper
Unter den Linden**
Unter den Linden 7, Mitte; tel: 2035 4555; www.staatsoper-berlin.org; advance sales daily

**OTHER ORCHESTRAS
Akademie für
Alte Musik in Berlin**
Lübecker Strasse 22; tel: 3230 4440; www.akamus.de; U8: Moritzplatz; map p.135 D1
The academy was founded in East Germany in 1980 and specialises in old music, especially in the baroque period. Outside Berlin, it has performed at New York's Carnegie Hall.

Deutsches Symphonie Orchester (DSO)
Im RBB-Fernsehzentrum, Masurenallee 16–20, Charlottenburg; tel: 20298 7530; www.dso-berlin.de; U2:

Right: the Konzerthaus Berlin in Gendarmenmarkt.

that floats on the Spree river and a sauna with a full-length river-front window. Arena is a popular venue for concerts, festivals and theatre, especially in summer.

Columbiahalle
Columbiadamm 13–21, Kreuzberg; tel: 698 0980; www.columbiahalle.de/main.html; U6: Platz der Luftbrücke; admission charge; map p.138 B3
Together with its smaller sister venue, the Columbia Club, this concert hall has room for 3,500 people and is a popular venue for indie and alternative rock bands as well as other events. Check listings.

Fritz Club im Postbahnhof
Strasse der Pariser Kommune 8, Friedrichshain; tel: 698 1280; www.fritzclub.com; S3, S5, S7, S75, S9: Ostbahnhof; admission charge; map p.135 E2
A large warehouse that has been turned into a popular venue for rock and pop concerts by bands ranging from the almost famous to the internationally acclaimed. Near the East Side Gallery, it has a nice beer garden and popular after-show dance-floor with DJs. Check listings.

Knaack
Greifswalder Strasse 152, Prenzlauer Berg; tel: 442 7060; www.knaack-berlin.de; admission charge; S8, S10, Tram M2: Prenzlauer Allee
On Wednesday nights, the stage belongs to local Berlin bands dreaming of stardom. Weekends rock, swing and groove on four floors with live bands and DJs from around Europe. Fridays offer free student admission.

Theodor-Heuss-Platz; map p.132 A1
Founded in 1946, the Symphonie has performed around the world. As of 2012, the principal conductor and artistic director will be Tugan Sokhiev.

Mahler Chamber Orchestra
Hasenheide 54, Kreuzberg; tel: 417 1790; www.mahler-chamber.de; U7: Südstern; map p.139 C3
The Mahler Chamber Orchestra, founded in 1997 by Claudio Abbado, draws its musicians from all over the world and is led by conductor Daniel Harding.

Contemporary

THE SCENE
Kreuzberg and Neukölln, with their large migrant communities, have produced a new generation of German rap and soul musicians. Meanwhile, rock clubs like Knaack, Lido or Columbiahalle often present new Britpop and US

bands long before they've made it on the world stage, as well as hot German rock bands. Germany's music industry is largely centred in Berlin, and **PopKomm** (www.popkomm.de) in September/October, is Berlin's mega music event, bringing together fans, bands, DJs and the entertainment industry for business and hundreds of house, electro, reggae and rock concerts. On PopKomm club night, €12 buys access to 30 clubs across the city.

VENUES

Arena
Eichenstrasse 4, Treptow; tel: 533 2030; www.arena-berlin.de; U1: Schlesisches Tor; S8, S9, S41, S42: Treptower Park; admission charge
Arena is located in an old bus garage that dates from 1927 and was designed by the architect Franz Ahrens. There are two concert venues, a swimming pool

Lido
Cuvrystrasse 7, Kreuzberg;
tel: 6956 6840; www.lido-
berlin.de; U1, U12, U15:
Schlesiches Tor
One of Berlin's newest live
music bars, this club hosts
young not-yet-famous rock,
soul and pop bands. A long
bar at one end, a stage at the
other, a room full of dancers
in-between.

Max-Schmeling-Halle
Am Falkplatz, Prenzlauer Berg;
tel: 443 0443; www.max-
schmeling-halle.de; admission
charge; U2: Schönhauser Allee;
S8, S41, S42: Schönhauser
Allee
Named after the famous
heavy-weight boxing cham-
pion, this 8500-seat arena
was built in the former no
man's land along a strip of
the Berlin Wall. It hosts sporting events and is home to
professional basketball team
Alba Berlin, as well as being
the venue for many concerts.

Tempodrom
Möckernstrasse 10,
Kreuzberg; tel: 747 370;
www.tempodrom.de; S1, S2:
Anhalter Bahnhof; admission
charge; map p.138 B4
This venue seats 3,500 for
concerts of all sorts, from
rock and pop to musicals.
Check listings for
information about upcoming
concerts.

Velodrom
Paul-Heyse-Strasse 26,
Friedrichshain; tel: 443 045;
www.velodrom.de; S8, S41,
S42: Landsberger Allee; admis-
sion charge
Like the Schmeling-Halle, the
Velodrom was built as part of
Berlin's bid to host the
Olympics. It's a world-class
venue for indoor cycling
competition and also hosts
big-ticket concerts.

Right: Berlin's premier jazz
club, the A Trane.

Jazz
THE SCENE
The avant-garde and experimental continues to thrive in
the local jazz scene. Night
owls might catch local jazz
greats, such as trumpet
player Til Brönner, or rising
star-on-sax Mark Wyand, at
the legendary midnight jam
session at A Trane. Stars like
Wynton Marsalis have been
known to join in and test the
chops of Berlin's young stars.
Major festivals include **Berlin
JazzFest** (www.berlinerfest
spiele.de) in the mid-autumn.

VENUES
Acud Café
Veteranenstrasse 21, Mitte;
tel: 4435 9499; www.acud.de;
U8: Rosenthaler Platz; S1, S2:
Nordbahnhof; map p.134 C4
This venue is a survivor of the
Wild East days that gripped
Mitte after the Wall fell. It's
not a place to hear big
names, but you will catch
young jazz and blues musicians from around the world
passing through Berlin,
searching for their voice.
Concert times and quality
vary.

A Trane
Pestalozzistrasse 105, Charlottenburg; tel: 313 2550; www.
a-trane.de; daily 9pm–2am; S5,
S9, S75: Savignyplatz; admission charge; map p.133 C1

Over the years, Berlin's left-field
and creative reputation has
intrigued legendary musicians,
most notably David Bowie
and Iggy Pop, who lived in
Schöneberg in the 1970s and
recorded some of their most
significant albums here. U2 also
spent time in Berlin, recording
their seminal album, *Achtung
Baby*, which makes many
references to Zoo Bahnhof.

This is Berlin's best and
best known jazz club,
hosting local and inter-
national performers in an
intimate atmosphere.
Reserve seats online.

Aufsturz
Oranienburger Strasse 67,
Mitte; tel: 2804 7407;
www.aufsturz.de; daily 10pm–
2am; U6: Oranienburger Tor;
S1, S2: Oranienburger Strasse;
map p.134 B3
On Fridays and Saturdays,
the Aufsturz features local
and international jazz. The
styles vary from modern to
electronic jazz. During the
week, the club also plays
rock and folk. The club area
measures 150 sq m (180 sq
yds) and has room for 120
grooving people.

Badenscher Hof
Badensche Strasse 29,
Wilmersdorf; tel: 861 0080;
www.badenscher-hof.de;

> The **Karneval der Kulturen** *(see p.54)* is a great place to get a taste of the breadth of Berlin's world music scene, which takes in virtually every crossover of global music imaginable.

Mon–Fri 4pm–late, Sat 6pm–late; U7: Berliner Strasse, Blissestrasse; map p.137 D3
An old West Berlin icon, this is a restaurant and venue for local jazz and blues acts. The crowd is not as young and trendy as you'll find in Mitte or Prenzlauer Berg; it remains more a popular after-work bar for 50-some-things.

b-flat
Rosenthaler Strasse 13, Mitte; tel: 283 3123; www.b-flat-berlin.de; daily 9pm–late; U8: Rosenthaler Platz or Weinmeisterstrasse; admission charge; map p.134 C3
Founded in 1995 by musicians Jannis Zotos and Thanassis Zotos and the actor André Hennecke, b-flat has a great club atmosphere and a long bar, and plays host to a cross-section of European and German bands playing a variety of styles. Be sure to drop in on Wednesday night for Robin's Nest, the jam session hosted by Berlin bass player Robin Draganovich.

Junction Bar
Gneisenaustrasse 18, Kreuzberg; tel: 694 6602; www.junction-bar.de; Sun–Thur concerts 9–11.30pm, DJs 11.30pm–5am, Fri–Sun concerts 10pm–12.30am; U7: Gneisenaustrasse; admission charge; map p.138 C4
A Kreuzberg establishment featuring live jazz, soul, funk and chansons every night of the week.

Kunstfabrik Schlot
Chausseestrasse 18, Mitte; tel:

448 2160; www.kunstfabrik-schlot.de; opening depends on event; U6: Zinnowitzer Strasse; S1, S2, S25: Nordbahnhof; admission charge; map p.134 B4
A somewhat larger and sometimes noisy club, Schlot is still one of the best places to hear local jazz musicians in Berlin. Live music most nights, starting around 9pm. There is a popular jazz brunch on Sunday with a live band.

Quasimodo
Kantstrasse 12a, Charlottenburg; tel: 312 8086; www.quasimodo.de; S3, S5, S7, S9, S75: Savignyplatz; admission charge; map p.133 D1
A cellar bar with stage and dancefloor, Quasimodo is a Berlin institution that hosts live jazz, funk & soul, Latin, blues and rock bands. Check listings and get there a little early for good seats.

Yorckschlösschen
Yorckstrasse 15, Kreuzberg; tel: 215 8070; www.yorck schloesschen.de; U7: Mehring-damm, S1, S2, S25: Yorck-strasse; admission charge; map p.138 B4
This place is proof that West Berlin never died. Located in the heart of Kreuzberg, from breakfast until late at night

Below: instruments are also sold at Musikalienhandlung Hans Riedel.

this venue swings with local disciples of traditional jazz, blues and funk.

Record Shops

Da Capo
Kastanienallee 96, Prenzlauer Berg; tel: 448 1771; www.da-capo-vinyl.de; Tue–Fri 11am–7pm, Sat 11am–4pm; U2: Eberswalder Strasse
A vinyl lover's nirvana, especially if you are looking for old East German rock recordings.

DNS Recordstore
Eberswalder Strasse 30, Prenzlauer Berg; tel: 247 9835; www.recordstore-berlin.de; Mon, Wed–Fri 11am–8pm, Tue, Fri 11am–9pm, Sat 11am–6pm; U2: Eberswalder Strasse
This shop has an amazing selection of club music: anything from techno, minimal, house and drum 'n' bass to electro, electro-pop and ambient. Recordings are on CD or vinyl. They also sell DJ equipment.

Left: the hefty classical music selection at Musikalienhandlung Hans Riedel.

electronic music.

L&P Classics

Welserstrasse 28; tel: 8804 3043; www.lpclassics.de; Mon–Sat 10am–8pm; U2: Uhlandstrasse; S9, S75: Savignyplatz; map p.133 C2

This shop stocks a wide range of CDs and DVDs, focusing on classical music.

Musikalienhandlung Hans Riedel

Uhlandstrasse 38, Wilmersdorf; tel: 882 7395; www.musik-riedel.de; Mon–Fri 9.30am–6.30pm, Sat 10am–3pm; U1: Ulandstrasse; map p.137 C4

Enormous classical music specialist, selling everything from CDs to sheet music to instruments.

Musik unter den Gleisen

Friedrichstrasse 128, Mitte; tel: 285 9144; www.musikdrehscheibe.de; Mon–Fri 11am–7.30pm, Sat 11am–6pm; U6, S1, S2, S5, S7: Friedrichstrasse; map p.134 B2

This store is located under the S-Bahn tracks and has over 20,000 recordings on CD and vinyl, with a focus on alternative rock.

Oye Records

Oderberger Strasse 4, Prenzlauer Berg; tel: 6664 7821; www.oye-records.com; Mon–Fri 1–8pm, Sat noon–6pm; U2: Eberswalder Strasse, Senefelder Platz

Oye has a large selection of techno, house, electro, new rave, funk, soul, disco and new boogie on vinyl and CD, both new releases and used recordings.

Platten Pedro

Tegeler Weg 102, Charlottenburg; tel: 344 1875; www.platten-pedro.de; Mon–Fri 10am–6pm, Sat 10am–1pm; U7: Mierendorffplatz; map p.132 B3

This is the place to come to hunt down rare vinyls. Pedro stocks more than 131,000 vinyl recordings, including hard-to-find Rolling Stones and Beatles singles and other rarities.

Vopo-Records

Danziger Strasse 31, Prenzlauer Berg; tel: 442 8004; www.vopo-records.de; Mon–Fri noon–8pm, Sat noon–4pm; U2: Eberswalder Strasse

They took their name from the nickname for the East German police, 'Volkspolizei', and are into hardcore sounds: punk, metal, garage, hip hop and rock 'n' roll available on CDs, vinyl LPs and singles. They also sell concert tickets.

Freizeitglauben

Petersburger Strasse 81, Friedrichshain; tel: 2904 9151; www.freizeitglauben.com; Mon–Fri noon–8pm, Sat 1–6pm; U5: Frankfurter Tor

Freizeitglauben is an independent label, recording studio and a record shop under one roof, with the main focus on techno, house and electro. It is also a gathering place for local musicians and lovers of the genres they promote. You can also investigate their select choice of CDs, t-shirts and DJ equipment.

Hiphop Vinyl

Grünberger Strasse 54, Friedrichshain; tel: 938 1240; www.hhv.de; Mon–Sat noon–8pm; U5: Frankfurter Tor

The name says it all. HHV has more than 50,000 recordings in its catalogue of hip hop, *Deutschrap* (German-language rap), soul, downbeat, headz, reggae/dancehall and

Below: a listening post at Gelbe Musik.

Nightlife

To survive a night out in Berlin, get some sleep first. The best clubs don't get interesting until well after midnight and keep rocking until after sunrise. Each neighbourhood has its own scene, but you will find the best venues in Mitte, Prenzlauer Berg, Kreuzberg and Friedrichshain. Public transport gets you close to the action and there are late buses, but do not worry about missing the last train home; most U and S lines have an all-night service at the weekend. For information on other places to have a drink or see live music, *see Bars and Cafés, p.32–7, Gay and Lesbian, p.64–7 and Music, p.96–100.*

Mitte

Cookies
Friedrichstrasse 158–164; tel: 2749 2940; www.cookies-berlin.de; Tue, Thur 10.30pm–6am; admission charge; S1, S2, S25, S5, S7, S75, S9, U6: Friedrichstrasse; map p.134 B2
This is Berlin's hippest DJ club, the icon of the Mitte style, laid-back elegance. It can be tough to get in, so show up early. The crowd is young and includes many Berlin celebrities.

Rio
Chausseestrasse 106; tel: 202 50; www.rioberlin.de; Sat

Below: spinning the decks at Watergate.

11.30pm–late; admission charge; map p.134 B4
With a vibe mixing the stylish and the gritty, this club offers an authentic New Berlin experience, with an excellent electro soundtrack that gets everyone dancing.

Around Alexanderplatz

Kaffee Burger
Torstrasse 60; tel: 2804 6495; www.kaffeeburger.de; daily, usually 10/11pm until late; admission charge, some events free; U2: Rosa-Luxemburg-Platz; U2, S5, S7, S75, S9: Alexanderplatz; map p.135 C4
A Mecca for East Berlin intellectuals under communism, this dance bar is now an icon of Ostalgia (nostalgia for the East). Its 'Russian Disco' nights with author and DJ Vladimir Kaminer are legendary. Check local listings.

Sage Club
Köpenicker Strasse 76; tel: 278 9830; www.sage-club.de; admission charge; U8: Heinrich-Heine-Strasse; map p.135 D2
This is the favourite of Berlin's hip hop scene, though rock, electro and

11.30pm–late; admission charge; U6: Zinnowitzer Strasse; map p.134 B4

The main S-Bahn and U-Bahn lines run all night Friday, Saturday and the evening before a holiday, except for the U4, S45 and S85. The rest of the week, night buses are available between 12.30am and 4.30am (Sun until 7am) every 30 minutes along the U-Bahn and S-Bahn lines. Night buses are numbered N1 to N3 and N5 to N9. Taxi service is reliable and can be flagged down on the street or called out by dialling 261 026. *See also Transport, p.129.*

techno also get a look in through the week. Popular with the hip and fashion-conscious.

Tiergarten

40 Seconds
Potsdamer Strasse 58; tel: 8906 4220; www.40seconds.de; Fri–Sat 11pm–late; admission charge; S1, S2, S25, U2: Potsdamer Platz, Nightbus N2; map p.134 A1
A penthouse DJ club for devoted house fans that got its name from the time it takes the lift to reach the

Left: Berlin is renowned as a hardcore party town.

klatt.com; free; U1, U12, U15: Schlesisches Tor; Night bus N65; map p.135 E1

Its laid-back Zen lounge style makes this combination restaurant, bar and DJ club a favourite for refined clubbers. Dinner is taken on lounge chairs with a spectacular view of the Spree river. Later, tables are pushed aside to make room to dance. Reservations recommended.

Watergate Club

Falckensteinstrasse 49; tel: 6128 0396; www.water-gate.de; Wed–Fri 11pm–late, Sat midnight–late, opening times vary in summer; admission charge; U1, U12, U15: Schlesisches Tor; Night bus N65; map p.135 E1

This riverside house and techno club is where the ravers meet. In summer, dance outside on the waterfront patio.

club. The bird's-eye panorama of downtown Berlin is not to miss.

Prenzlauer Berg

Club 23

Kulturbrauerei; Schönhauser Allee 36; tel: 4431 5155; www.soda-berlin.de; Fri–Sat from 11pm; admission charge; U2: Eberswalder Strasse; map p.135 D4

The best dance club at the Kulturbrauerei, an old brewery transformed into a cultural factory with no fewer than eight clubs. Friday and Saturday offer ladies' admission free, with drinks free until 1am.

Magnet

Falckensteinstrasse 48; www.magnet-club.de; admission charge; S8, S10, Tram M4, M10, N54: Greifswalder Strasse; map p.135 D4

This is the heart of Berlin's Indie and Britpop scene. Popular with students, who hop between the club's two rooms, one for live bands and the other a dancefloor with DJ.

White Trash Fast Food

Schönhauser Allee 6–7; tel:

5034 8668; www.whitetrash fastfood.com; daily 6pm–late; admission charge; U2: Senefelder Platz, Rosa-Luxemburg-Platz; map p.135 C4

If Russ Meyer and Jim Morrison were looking for a place to hang, this would be it. A trash roadhouse in a former Chinese restaurant, it has two bars, the best burgers in Berlin, its own tattoo parlour and diverse live music on offer, from Finnish punk to jazz to Japanese new wave.

Kreuzberg and Friedrichshain

Matrix

Warschauer Platz 18, Gewölbe 3; tel: 2936 9990; www.matrix-berlin.de; admission charge; S3, S5, S6, S7, U1, U12, U15: Warschauer Strasse

This popular dance club is built into the vaulted roofs of a railway overpass. As the trains roll by overhead, dance the night away on four floors and six cocktail bars. Or dip in the indoor pool.

Spindler & Klatt

Köpenicker Strasse 16–17; tel: 3198 81860; www.spindler

There are all-night *Döner kebap* stands throughout the city, but word on the street is that the **Grill und Schlemmerbuffet** at Rosenthaler Platz in Mitte makes the best *Döner* in Berlin. Other popular late or all-night *Döner* and *Currywurst (see Food and Drink, p.58)* stands include: **Döneria Fantasia** (Brückenstrasse 2; 24 hours; U8: Heinrich-Heine-Strasse), **Currywurst** (Kantstrasse, under S-Bahn bridge; until 3am or later; S3, S5, S7, S9, S75: Zoologischer Garten), **Bagdad** (Schlesische Strasse 2; 24 hours; U1, U12, U15: Schlesisches Tor), **Döner-Imbiss**, Corner of Boxhagener Strasse-Münzstrasse; until late; U5: Frankfurter Tor or Samariterstrasse), **Max & Moritz** (Bötzowstrasse 51; until 5am; tram M4: Hufelandstrasse)

Palaces and Houses

G iven the amount of bombing damage Berlin suffered in World War II, it is quite remarkable that any old buildings at all remain in the city. Because of that and the fact that Berlin is, on the whole, a very young city by European standards, there is little to see here in terms of magnificent relics of the past. However, those such as Schloss Charlottenburg and Schloss Köpenick, which remain or have been restored, offer fine examples of how the royal and wealthy lived in bygone days.

Palaces

Schloss Charlottenburg

Spandauer Damm 10–22, Charlottenburg; tel: 320 910; www.spsg.de; (Old Palace) Tue–Sun, Apr–Oct 10am–6pm, Nov–Mar 10am–5pm, (New Wing) Wed–Mon, Apr–Oct 10am–6pm, Nov–Mar 10am–5pm; admission charge; U2: Sophie-Charlotte-Platz; S45, S46: Jungfernheide; map p.132 B3

Easily the most spectacular building in Berlin, this magnificent structure was built by the Elector Frederick III (later known as Kaiser Frederick I of Prussia) as a summer palace for his wife, Sophie-Charlotte, in 1699 so that she could escape the unhealthy air around the Stadtschloss. She did not enjoy many summers there, dying in 1705, but the property was used by many subsequent Hohenzollerns, who added bits and pieces as they went along. The Old Palace consists of over 20 rooms furnished in high 18th-century style, with exhibits of royal porcelain and silver. The New Wing was built by Frederick the Great and contains his state apartments, as well

Berlin is historically a working-class city, with fewer grand homes but some interesting worker-housing solutions, such as Le Corbusier's *Unités d'Habitation (see Architecture, p.30)*.

as the winter quarters of Wilhelm III, his successor. A large number of Frederick the Great's collection of French paintings is on view here, including some masterpieces. As notable as the palace are the formal gardens, which contain an 18th-century teahouse, a Neapolitan-style villa (the New Pavilion), and the mausoleum of Queen Luise. SEE ALSO PARKS AND GARDENS, P.108

Schloss Friedrichsfelde

Am Tierpark 125 (Lichtenberg Tierpark Zoo), Lichtenberg; tel: 666 35035; www.stadtmuseum.de; Tue–Sun tours hourly 11am–2pm; Zoo admission charge; U5: Tierpark

This 18th-century palace was home to Princess Anna Charlotta Dorothea, as well as various minor nobility. Period paintings and tapestries are displayed along with metal-

work, including a fine selection of pieces from the Royal Ironworks. Note that admission to the Schloss is only available with a tour, and that you will also have to buy a ticket for the Lichtenberg Zoo (called Tierpark Berlin). SEE ALSO PARKS AND GARDENS, P.111

Schloss Köpenick

Kunstgewerbemuseum, Schlossinsel; tel: 6566 1749; www.smb.spk-berlin.de; Tue–Sun 10am–6pm; admission charge; S3: Köpenick; Tram 60, 61, 62, 68: Schlossplatz Köpenick

Divided from the old town by wooden bridge and located right on the water is Schloss Köpenick, the Köpenick palace (1677–82), a significant example of 17th-century Baroque architecture that has been wonderfully restored. The Hohenzollerns used it as a summer palace and hunting lodge and, occasionally, as a court room. In 1730, King Frederick I put his son Frederick II (later 'the Great') on trial here for desertion. The heir to the throne narrowly escaped the death sentence. Today, the palace houses the

Left: Schloss Charlottenburg.

Berlin's finest, although Ephraim himself was despised for having devalued Prussia's currency in order to help the Kaiser finance the Seven Years War. The current structure is a thorough re-creation of the house which had been torn down in 1935 so that Mühlenstrasse could be widened. The facade was carefully dismantled and stored and in 1989, placed back on a new structure erected for Berlin's 750th anniversary. Today, temporary art exhibitions are held inside.

Knoblauch-Haus
Poststrasse 23, Mitte; tel: 2400 2162; www.stadtmuseum.de; Tue, Thur–Sun 10am–6pm, Wed noon–8pm; free; U2: Klosterstrasse; map p.135 C2
Johann Christian Knoblauch built this delightful house for his family between 1759 and 1761. For many years the family lived there, sharing the space with the silk-ribbon business which provided them with their fortune. Its original Baroque facade was replaced in 1806 by a more classical one which remains today. Inside is a small museum dedicated to the family, housed in rooms decorated in typical Biedermeier style.

Museum of Decorative Arts (Kunstgewerbemuseum), showing Baroque and Renaissance furniture and other objects. A nice alternative way to reach the palace is by boat from Treptower Hafen.

Stadtschloss
Karl-Liebknecht-Strasse opposite Lustgarten and Altes Museum, Mitte; map p.137 D1
The castle complex of the Hohenzollern dynasty was heavily damaged during World War II bombing, and its remains destroyed by the East German regime in 1952. One part remains, integrated into the former Council of State building on Werderscher Markt and plainly standing out from its functional architecture. From the topmost balcony, Karl Liebknecht announced the Socialist Republic of Germany in 1918 after the Kaiser had fled. This event made it worth preserving by the GDR. The rest of the land facing onto Karl-Liebknecht-Strasse has been earmarked by the city for a complete restoration of the Stadtschloss from the original plans, which still exist. Upon its completion, the city

will move the Dahlem collections of non-European art into it. In order to reconstruct the Stadtschloss, the Palast der Republik, the central administrative building of the GDR, had to be destroyed, a move which angered many in the Eastern part of the city. Its remains, facing onto the river, can still be seen, although they will eventually be totally obliterated. Funds for the construction of the Stadtschloss are still uncertain, so a date for completion is not yet set.

Houses

Ephraim Palais
Poststrasse 16, Mitte; tel: 2400 2162; www.ephraim-palais.de; Tue, Thur–Sun 10am–6pm, Wed noon–8pm; admission charge; U2: Klosterstrasse; map p.135 C2
Veitel Heine Ephraim was a 'court Jew', a position which allowed him to trade loans and financial advice to the Kaiser in return for protection, and he was made court jeweller to Frederick the Great in 1745. This house, originally built in 1765, was considered

Right: Schloss Köpenick.

105

Pampering

Berlin is rich in options to relax, detox and be pampered; you can lose your sense of time in a floatation tank or enjoy a Balinese temple massage, though for the most local forms of relaxation, opt for one the city's fantastic saunas or a traditional hamam. Berlin boasts some unusual venues for unwinding, particularly with the options for swimming in special floating constructions on the Spree river. Meanwhile, even if a stay at one of the smartest hotels in town is financially out of reach, day passes at their luxurious in-house spas are often available.

Saunas

Liquidrom
Möckernstrasse 10, Kreuzberg; tel: 2580 07820; www.liquidrom-berlin.de (German only); daily 10am–midnight, Fri–Sat til 1am; S1, S2, S25, bus 29, M41: Anhalter Bahnhof; map p.138 B4
A contemporary art spa: minimalist architecture, quality materials and 'liquid sound', an experience for all senses that combines bathing in warm Dead Sea waters with sound and light therapy. While you float in the pool, listen to whale sounds or new age music from the underwater speakers. The use of the sauna and steam bath is included in the admission charge. Back rubs, hot stone or Balinese herbal massages should be reserved in advance.

Sauna auf dem Badeschiff
Eichenstrasse 4, Treptow; tel: 01789 500 163; www. badeschiff.de; opening hours subject to change; robes, towels, slippers for hire; S41, S42, S8, S85, S9: Treptower Park
For a unique Berlin experience, rub shoulders with a hip crowd in the floating sauna on the Spree. Throughout the cold months, the Badeschiff floating swimming pool on the river is converted into a futuristic-looking sauna-ship. Fantastic view of illuminated Oberbaumbrücke bridge. Open daily, but check times.
SEE ALSO SPORTS, P.125

Thermen am Europa-Center
Nürnberger Strasse 7, Charlottenburg; tel: 257 5760; www. thermen-berlin.de; Mon–Sat 10am–midnight, Sun 10am–9pm; U1, U2: Wittenbergplatz; S5, S7, S75, S9: Zoologischer Garten; map p.133 D1
The Thermen is a 1970s retro-style Berlin classic. You can indulge in head-to-toe pampering (facials, body-wraps, depilation, thalasso treatments, massages) or detox in what is still Berlin's largest sauna landscape, complete with 32-degree indoor and outdoor rooftop thermal-water swimming pool and terrace overlooking the city. The Thermen is mixed; clothing is optional in the pools but not allowed in the saunas.

Left: glamorous natural beauty products at Belladonna.

Left: the pool at Thermen am Europa-Center.

shop, which specialises in natural products. Also a great place to buy make-up and essential oils.

Float-store am Gendarmenmarkt
Kronenstrasse 55–8, Mitte; tel: 3229 8617; www.float-store.de (German only); Mon–Sat 10am–8pm; U2, U6: Stadtmitte; map p.134 B2

Classy anti-ageing oasis. Float in an egg-shaped saltwater tank, inhale pure oxygen or enjoy a classic anti-cellulite or Ayurvedic massage.

Hamams

Hamam
Mariannenstrasse 6, Kreuzberg; tel: 615 1414; www.hamam berlin.de; Mon 3–11pm, Tue–Sun noon–11pm, children can be taken on Thur; map p.135 D1

A Turkish bath for women only, offering traditional Turkish soap massage, exfoliation, depilation and various treatments. Excellent massage therapists on staff. Bring your own towels and slippers or rent them.

Sultan Hamam
Bülowstrasse 57, Schöneberg; tel: 2175 3375; www.sultan-hamam.de; daily noon–11pm, Mon men only, Tue–Sat women only, Sundays mixed; U2: Bülowstrasse; U7, S1, S2, S25: Yorckstrasse; map p.138 A4

An authentic oriental steam bath, complete with a lounge offering shishas and oriental snacks. There are steam and exfoliation rooms, as well as a bio-sauna with coloured light therapy. Treatments for both men and women include waxing, massages and facials, all at very reasonable prices. Try the Sultan Package. It can be tricky to find the backyard entrance in the dark, so come early.

Hotel Spas

Adlon Day Spa
Behrenstrasse 72; tel: 3011 17200; www.adlon-day-spa.de; Sun–Mon 9am–8pm, Tue–Sat 9am–10pm; U1, U2, U25, bus 100: Unter den Linden; map p.136 A1

The Adlon Day Spa, open to non-guests, allows you to luxuriate in style. A spacious pool, water shiatsu and treatments of all kinds, from the 'True Romance Package' for two to 'Executive De-stress', will help you regenerate in no time and in a private atmosphere: no mixed saunas here.

Day Spa Berlin
Friedrichstrasse 106, Mitte; tel: 2849 0407; www.day-spa-berlin.de; daily 10am–11pm; S5, S7, S75, S9, U6: Friedrichstrasse; map p.136 B2

This impressive, nicely decorated new day spa is part of the Artist Riverside Hotel. Open to everyone, it provides everything you might need – dressing gowns, towels, slippers – and offers a wellness trip around the world. You can choose from Hawaiian, Balinese, Egyptian, Tibetan and more treatments and baths,

> Going to the sauna is very much part of the German lifestyle. Be aware that public saunas are usually co-ed and the dress code is birthday suits. Large hotels tend to have separate saunas.

have a hot chocolate massage, float in a saltwater tank or just enjoy the view over the Spree from one of the saunas.

Beauty

Aveda Lifestyle Salon and Spa
Kurfürstendamm 26a, Charlottenburg; tel: 8870 8790; www.aveda.de; Mon–Fri 10am–8pm, Sat 9am–6pm; U1, bus M46, 110, 249: Kurfürstendamm; map p.133 D1

Come for a facial, a body-wrap, a new hairstyle or make-over. By appointment only; services for both women and men. All products for sale.

Belladonna
Bergmannstrasse 101, Kreuzberg; tel: 694 3731; www.bella-donna.de; Mon–Fri 10am–7pm, Sat 10am–6pm; U7: Gneisenaustrasse; map p.138 B3

Beauty heaven at this pretty

107

Parks and Gardens

Berlin has a lot to offer in terms of leafy respites from hectic urban life. Enjoy the scenery in the sprawling Tiergarten and the variety of plant life and solitude in the Botanical Garden, or get off the beaten path and discover a mix of fine horticulture and active recreation in Britzer Garten in Neukölln. Apart from providing viewpoints, garden art and occasional concerts, all the green spaces are great for people-watching: Berliners love their gardens and tend to live life outside in the short summers.

Tiergarten

Tiergarten

Free; U2, U9, S5, S7, S75, S9: Zoologischer Garten; S5, S7, S75, S9: Tiergarten, Bellevue; S1, S2, S25: Unter den Linden, Potsdamer Platz; bus 100: Grosser Stern, Schloss Bellevue; map p.133 E2/134 A2

Berlin's largest park, the Tiergarten ('Animal Garden') was originally laid out as a game reserve for the Hohenzollern kings. The 252-hectare (630-acre) expanse of woods and gardens stretches from the Brandenburg Gate in the East to the Zoological Garden in the West, bordering on Potsdamer Platz and the Reichstag. It is best to explore by bicycle or Velotaxi. Pedal along waterways and ponds,

Cycle rickshaws for leisurely tours of the Tiergarten can be found at the Brandenburg Gate. The red-and-silver Deutsche Bahn rental bikes parked in strategic locations all over the city can be unlocked by mobile phone. You need to register so that your credit card can be debited.

past islands, statues and vintage gas lamps from all over Europe, and take a break in the rose garden or the beer garden at Café am Neuen See, on the western edge of the park, where you can rent a boat and row across the lake. Sights in the park include the Siegessäule and the **Sowjetisches Ehrenmal** (Soviet War Memorial). At least equally impressive, albeit only in May and June, are the multicoloured rhododendron woods. At weekends, Tiergarten turns into a heavy-duty recreation park shared by joggers, walkers, cyclists, t'ai chi

aficionados, sunbathers and Turkish barbecue lovers.
SEE ALSO MONUMENTS AND MEMORIALS, P.84

Charlottenburg

Schlossgarten Charlottenhof

Geschwister-Scholl-Strasse 34a; May–Oct daily 6am–10pm; admission charge; S41, S42, S46: Westend; bus M45: Schloss Charlottenburg; map p.132 B3

Also known as the Schlosspark, this Baroque garden and English-style park has been restored to its 18th- and 19th-century glory. In addition to the Charlotten-

Below: cycling in the Tiergarten.

Left: relaxing in the idyllic surrounds of the Schlossgarten Charlottenburg.

stage uses the idyllic setting as a welcome backdrop for films and performances.

Western Districts

Botanischer Garten

Unter den Eichen 5–10; tel: 8385 0100; www.botanischer-garten-berlin.de; daily Nov–Jan 9am–4pm, Feb until 5pm, Mar and Oct until 6pm, Apr and Aug until 8pm, May–July until 9pm, Sept until 7pm; admission charge; S1, bus M48: Botanischer Garten

The beautifully landscaped 50-hectare (126-acre) botanic garden is home to 22,000 different species of plants, offering a botanical journey around the world in one day. Best to enjoy the serene surroundings

Below: the varied features of Volkspark Friedrichshain.

There is even a vineyard on one of the slopes of the Kreuzberg. The Kreuz-Neroberger is grown here, one of Europe's northernmost wines.

---

burg palace and the manicured greenery, points of interest here include a carp pond, a mausoleum for Queen Luise and the Belvedere, a former teahouse and outlook point that now houses a collection of porcelain. There is a landing for boats to Potsdam nearby, at Schlossbrücke.
SEE ALSO PALACES AND HOUSES, P.104

Kreuzberg and Friedrichshain

Viktoriapark

Kreuzbergstrasse/Katzbachstrasse; free; U6: Platz der Luftbrücke; map p.138 B3

With its winding trails, rocky areas and a deep waterfall, Viktoriapark is not your average urban park. Located on the Kreuzberg ('Cross Mountain'), it is a great vantage point offering interesting views from the national mon-

ument crowning the steep hill. It was built by great Karl Friedrich Schinkel to commemorate the Napoleonic Wars. Great people-watching here, and the park reflects Kreuzberg's diversity.

Volkspark Friedrichshain

Am Friedrichshain/Landsberger Allee; free; tram M4: Platz der Vereinten Nationen; bus 200: Am Friedrichshain; map p.135 E3/4

The Friedrichshain Public Park is Berlin's oldest park. One popular attraction for children is the beautiful fountain adorned with fairytale characters, the Märchenbrunnen (Fairytale Fountain). However, this park has something for everyone: large, well-kept playgrounds, the shade of old trees overlooking a pond, a hike up the 78m (256ft) high Grosser Bunkerberg, or 'Mont Klamott' ('Rubble Mountain'), as it was made from debris after World War II, as well as a picnic and a ball game on the heavily used lawn at the northern corner of the park. With its well-lit, versatile pathways, it is also a popular running spot. After dark, an open-air during the week, when you have the garden almost to yourself. It is a wonderful retreat from the city, not too central to be packed out but still easy to reach from Alexanderplatz or Potsdamer Platz. Once a month, the local registry performs marriage ceremonies in the Mediterranean greenhouse.

Liebermann Villa at Lake Wannsee

Colomierstrasse 3; tel: 8058 5900; www.max-liebermann.de; Wed–Mon 10am–6pm, Thur until 8pm; admission charge; S1, S7: Wannsee, then bus 114: Colomierstrasse

After many years of being used by a diving club, the Lake Wannsee residence of famous Berlin painter Max Liebermann was painstakingly restored, including the grounds, which are complete with the floral opulence and diversity in his garden that inspired many of his paintings. They can now be viewed where they where created and compared with the subjects Liebermann depicted.

Pfaueninsel (Peacock Island)

Pfaueninselchausee 1, Zehlendorf; www.pfaueninsel.info; free; May–Aug 8am–9pm, shorter hours in winter; bus 218: Pfaueninsel, then ferry

King Friedrich Wilhelm II bought this island in the middle of Havel river in 1793 and

Directly across Invalidenstrasse from the Hauptbahnhof is a brick wall, behind which is one of Berlin's newest and least-known parks, **Moabit Prison Historical Park**. The prison which once stood here housed Wilhelm Voigt, the notorious 'Captain of Köpenick' *(see Treptow and Köpenick, p.22–3)*, as well as poet Albrecht Haushofer, who wrote the *Moabit Sonnets* there. Today it is a large, grassy park with some enigmatic monuments.

conceived it as a park. He and his successor Friedrich Wilhelm III turned it into a world of its own, filled with artificial ruins, exotic plants and free-range peacocks. The winding pathways offer changing views of the natural beauties and picturesque buildings, some of them designed by Karl Friedrich Schinkel. A romantic, magical place, it can only be reached by ferry.

Treptow and Köpenick

Treptower Park

Between Puschkinallee and Am Treptower Park; free; S4, S6, S8, S9, S85: Treptower Park, Plänterwald

Leafy Treptower Park is located on the banks of the Spree in the East of Berlin, not far from the impressive red-brick Oberbaumbrücke bridge and the huge 'Molecule Man' sculpture in the middle of the river. Archenhold Observatory, the oldest of its kind, is located here, complete with the world's largest refractor telescope. Don't miss the imposing **Sowjetisches Ehrenmal** (Soviet War Memorial) at the entrance from Puschkinallee avenue, dedicated to the 5,000 Soviet soldiers who were killed in the Battle of

Below: catching a boat is the only way of getting to Pfaueninsel (Peacock Island); once there, it is a lovely spot for relaxing.

Left: explore gardens of the world at the tranquil Marzahner Erholungspark.

Apr–Sept until 8pm; admission charge; S7, bus 195: Marzahn
The Marzahn Recreational Park, Britzer Garten's twin in the East, is also worth a trip. Here, the 'Gardens of the World' are the main attraction. Chinese, Japanese, Korean, Balinese and Islamic theme gardens represent the very distinct fine garden art of the respective region, including authentic plants and materials. The Chinese 'Garden of the Reclaimed Moon', complete with a teahouse and water-scape, is particularly notewor-thy and the largest of its kind in Europe. Other park features include a Renaissance-style hedged maze, a rhododen-dron grove, a herbal garden and several playgrounds.

Tierpark Berlin
Am Tierpark 125, Lichtenberg; tel: 515 310; www.tierpark-berlin.de; daily 9am–7pm; admission charge; U5: Tierpark
If you want to experience 10,000 animals in more nat-ural habitats than in the crowded Zoologischer Garten and you enjoy walking around beautiful gardens, try the sprawling Tierpark in the East, Europe's largest land-scape zoo. It is renowned for its elephant-breeding pro-gramme, the concerts in **Schloss Friedrichsfelde** palace and the fine flower and shrubbery displays.
SEE ALSO PALACES AND HOUSES, P.104

Berlin and buried here. The grand layout includes grave-stones carrying Stalin quotes and a huge monument of Soviet soldier crushing a swastika and carrying a German child. With its grand layout, the memorial is well worth visiting. Elsewhere in Treptower Park, locals picnic on the lawn along the river, hang out at the old 'Zenner' beer garden, rent a rowing boat or cross over to 'Insel der Jugend' island.
SEE ALSO MONUMENTS AND MEMORIALS, P.85

Further Out
Britzer Garten
Sangerhauser Weg 1, Neukölln; tel: 700 9060; www.gruen-berlin.de; daily Nov–Feb 9am–4pm, Mar and Oct until 6pm, Apr–Sept until 8pm; admission

charge; U6: Alt-Mariendorf, then bus: 179, or taxi from station
This park, landscaped in 1985 as a national garden show venue and maintained for Berliners, who were at that time cut off from the surrounding countryside by the Wall, is now a beautifully grown-in garden well worth the longish trip. On an area of 90 hectares (225 acres) are hills, lawns with free deckchairs, big lakes, play-grounds, modern sculp-tures, theme gardens and animal enclosures. A great family outing for next to nothing. Dogs and bicycles are not allowed.

Garten der Welt
Eisenacher Strasse, Marzahn; tel: 700 9060; www.gruen-berlin.de; daily Nov–Feb 9am–4pm, Mar and Oct until 6pm,

Every spring in Britzer Garten, 'Tulipan', a spectacular tulip show, attracts thousands of flower-lovers and photogra-phers, just like the 'Dahlia Fire' exhibit in autumn.

Restaurants

Berlin has never been known as a restaurant town, due to a combination of the austere local cooking and the city's overwhelmingly working-class nature, but in the past decade, there's been a notable change. As more Germans have started taking holidays out of the country and Berlin's status as the country's capital has swung into action, the quality of food available in its restaurants has improved remarkably, with increasing numbers of cheap ethnic eateries and an ever-growing array of Michelin-starred fine dining establishments. For more information about Berlinese food, *see Food and Drink, p.58–9*.

Mitte

GERMAN

Guy Restaurant

Jägerstrasse 59–60; tel: 2094 2600; www.guy-restaurant.de; €€€€; Mon–Fri noon–3pm, 6pm–1am, Sat 6pm–1am; U6: Französische Strasse; map p.134 B2

In the courtyard of a converted mansion which also houses Berlin's Rolls-Royce dealership, half-German, half-French chef Hartmut Guy presents virtuoso cuisine in a remarkably relaxing atmosphere. Of particular note is the seasonal menu, which takes advantage of the best that farmers from the surrounding region have to offer. The business lunch is a particular bargain, given its quality. The sommelier has some wonderful surprises, and the service is top-notch.

Approximate prices per person for a three-course meal with a glass of house wine:

€	under €20
€€	€20–€35
€€€	€35–€50
€€€€	over €50

Restaurant Vau

Jägerstrasse 54–55; tel: 2029 730; www.vau-berlin.de; €€€€; Mon–Sat noon–2.30pm, 7–10.30pm; U6: Französische Strasse; map p.134 B2

Where the renowned Jewish intellectual Rachel Varnhagen had her salon in the late 18th century, chef Kolja Kleeberg now presides over a different kind of forum. The prix-fixe €110 menu is filled with variations on traditional themes given a fascinating twist by Kleeberg's philosophy of no more than three ingredients on a plate. The €14-per-plate lunch menu even has intriguing offerings for vegetarians.

AUSTRIAN

Kellerrestaurant im Brecht-Haus

Chausseestrasse 125; tel: 282 3843; €€; daily from 6pm; U6: Oranienburger Tor; map p.134 B4

Photographs of Bertolt Brecht, the great playwright and poet, show him gaining weight after moving back to Berlin after World War II, but you don't have to be a liter-

You will sit at your table all night and day waiting for the server to volunteer the bill. Germans signal they are finished eating by placing their napkin on the plate.

ary critic to find out why: many of the dishes on the menu here in the restaurant beneath the house he lived in are from a notebook kept by his wife, Helene Weigel. Her Bohemian roots show in the *fleischlabberln* (ground-meat patties) and the *paradiessuppe* (tomato soup), among other dishes. In the summer, you can dine outdoors in the garden, if you can ignore the fact that Berti and Helene are buried just over the wall. If there's a lecture at the Literaturforum upstairs when you plan to dine, make reservations.

Lutter & Wegner

Charlottenstrasse 56; tel: 2029 5410; €€–€€€; daily 11am–2am, kitchen open until midnight; U2, U6: Stadtmitte; map p.134 B2

Lutter & Wegner were wine merchants who opened a

Left: preparing for a smart dinner at the Lorenz Adlon.

Madagascan vanilla and Italian beef. The hotel's stature also attracts special events, with star chefs and vintners showing off their skills.

Margaux

Unter den Linden 78 (entrance on Wilhelmstrasse); tel: 2265 2611; www.margaux-berlin.de; €€€€; Mon–Sat 7–10.30pm; S1, S2, bus 100, 200: Unter den Linden; map p.136 A1

Chef Michael Hoffmann calls his style 'classic avant-garde', which describes it perfectly: a combination of roast pork or steamed fish with molecular gastronomy. It works most of the time, especially when he's dealing with seafood, but stumbles do occur. The interior is a bit austere, but the service is friendly and the wine list is extraordinary.

Around Alexanderplatz

GERMAN

Honigmond

Borsigstrasse 28; tel: 2844 5512; www.honigmond-berlin.de; €–€€; Mon–Fri noon–2am, Sat–Sun 9am–2am; S1, S2, S25: Nordbahnhof, Oranienburger Strasse; map p.134 B4

A neighbourhood gem, this place is so successful that it

restaurant in 1811, where the Regent Hotel stands today at Charlottenstrasse 49. Famed for their *sekt* (sparkling white wine), their gastronomy took second place. Today it is the other way around: with an Austrian-based menu, including what is probably Berlin's best *wiener schnitzel*, Lutter & Wegner's Gendarmenmarkt location makes it a top destination. Strictly traditional, strictly high-quality ingredients and a wine list which reminds you of their original business.

FRENCH

Gourmet Restaurant Lorenz Adlon

Hotel Adlon, Unter den Linden 77; tel: 2261 1960; www.kempinski.com; €€€€; Tue–Sat 7–10.30pm; U1, U2, U25: Unter den Linden; map p.136 A1

A luxury hotel has to have a luxury restaurant, and this spot, named after the hotel's founder, certainly fits the bill. Chef Thomas Neeser's impeccably French cuisine makes use of ingredients from around the world, including Iranian caviar,

Below: for those who like literary interest with their dinner, the Kellerrestaurant im Brecht-Haus.

when there is, like a shrimp-and-strawberry salad with balsamic dressing, it's still good. Appetisers (the caponata is legendary), pastas (squid-ink pasta with truffles) and main courses (stew of organic lamb) are all excellent and served on handmade plates. There is a superb wine selection, which the sommelier will guide you through. Menus are in Italian only, which forces the server to translate, which can be a problem for large parties.

SOUTHEAST ASIAN
Monsieur Vuong
Alte Schönhauser Strasse 46; tel: 9929 6924; www.monsieur vuong.de; €–€€; Mon–Sun noon–midnight; U8: Weinmeisterstrasse; map p.135 C3

There really is a Monsieur Vuong, although he's not the handsome devil with the rolled sleeves in the big photo here (that's his father). A decade ago, he and his German partner started providing Berlin with authentic Vietnamese soups and noodle dishes, and, although the current location is five times the size of the one they started with, it is still impossible to get a seat quickly, but worth it to wait as reservations cannot be made. Nice touches include a slice of grapefruit in the mineral water.

Tiergarten

GERMAN
First Floor
Budapester Strasse 45 (at Palace Hotel, Europacenter;

has spawned two hotels. And no wonder: Berlin specialities like *königsberger klopse*, an unbeatable beef stew with fried slices of dumpling and vegetarian *maultaschen* (a Swabian speciality which resembles oversized ravioli) are regulars on the menu here. The real treasures are on the weekly selection, which is seasonal and in German only. Soups are creative, and only the rare forays into Chinese-like food do not live up to the restaurant's otherwise impeccable quality. Even the bread is addictive.

EAST ASIAN
Makoto
Alte Schönhauser Strasse 13; tel: 9789 3857; €; Mon–Sat noon–4pm, 6–11.30pm; U8: Weinmeisterstrasse; map p.135 C3

Where do homesick, impoverished Japanese students and artists go for a taste of home? This welcoming little noodle joint. Specialising in ramen in countless variations, with both soy and miso broth, it also does udon and soba dishes and a few rice-bowls. Japanese beer, sake and a full range of shochu cocktails add to the authenticity.

ITALIAN
Al Contadino sotto le Stelle
Auguststrasse 34–6; tel: 281 9023; www.alcontadino.com; €€–€€€; daily 6pm–midnight; U8: Weinmeisterstrasse; map p.134 C3

The Mutagnola family from southern Italy have become a force to be reckoned with in Berlin's Italian restaurant scene. This is their high-end restaurant; there is also a trattoria on Fuggerstrasse in Schöneberg and a superb pizzeria in Monbijou Park. There is not much messing with tradition here, although tel: 2502 1182; www.palace.de; €€€; Mon–Fri noon–3pm, 6.30–11pm, Sat–Sun 6.30–11pm; S5, S7, S75, S9, U2; Zoologischer Garten; bus 100, 200: Breitscheidplatz; map p.133 D1

Reopened in 2007 under master chef Matthias Buchholz, the Michelin-rated First Floor offers haute cuisine in a salon-like classical ambience. Go with the recommended food and wine pairings as they are excellent. The sommelier is in command of an outstanding collection of 12,000 bottles.

Charlottenburg

GERMAN
Florian
Grolmanstrasse 52; tel: 313 9184; www.restaurant-florian.de; €€; daily 6pm–3am; S3, S5, S7, S9: Savignyplatz; map p.133 C1

Owned by two sisters from Swabia, armed with one of Germany's best culinary traditions, this gathering place for stars of stage and screen and the media who report on them is also welcoming to non-celebrities. Hearty portions of rigorously traditional Swabian dishes at fair prices make it one of the neighbourhood's best bargains, and there are a few outdoor tables during the summer for unparalleled people-watching on one of central Berlin's most upscale streets.

Marjellchen
Mommsenstrasse 9; tel: 883 2676; www.marjellchen-berlin.de; €€; daily 5pm–midnight; S3, S5, S7, S9: Savignyplatz; map p.132 C1

No-nonsense Prussian, Silesian and Pomeranian food served in a welcoming atmosphere. Recommended dishes include *schlesisches himmel-*

reich (smoked meats stewed with dried fruit, served with a yeast dumpling), *mecklenburger kümmelfleisch* (leg of lamb stewed with root vegetables and caraway seed) and *falscher gänsebraten* (pork chops stuffed with apples, plums and dark bread). They also know their German wines here, so ask for a recommendation.

FRENCH
Paris Bar
Kantstrasse 152; tel: 313 8052; www.parisbar.de; €€; daily noon–2am; S3, S5, S7, S9: Zoologischer Garten; map p.133 D1

The Paris Bar is famous, and if you are, too, you'll enjoy the food and service. If you are not, you may find the service less than friendly. However, this remains one of Berlin's iconic restaurants. The walls are adorned with art traded for meals, and there are pictures of various German celebrities around, as well as, on occasion, the celebrities themselves. If you are with one of them, you will be in luck.

ITALIAN
12 Apostel
Bleibtreustrasse 49; tel: 312 1433; www.12-apostel.de; €–€€; daily from 7am; S3, S5, S7, S9: Savignyplatz; map p.133 C1

It's not often that all night restaurants are this good, or even that pizza in Berlin is this good, although conceptually it is a bit of a shame they've added to the original 12, each named for an Apostle: 'Judas' features spicy salami and chilli pepper. Pasta, salads and a few meat and fish dishes round out the menu. Also at: Georgenstrasse 49, Mitte; tel: 201 0222; www.12-apostel.de; S3, S5, S7, S9: Friedrichstrasse; map p.136 C2.

Grünfisch
Willibald-Alexis-Strasse 27; tel: 6162 1252; www.gruenfisch.de; €€–€€€; daily 6pm–midnight; U3: Spichernstrasse; map p.137 D4

Finely prepared Sicilian food is the draw at this elegant, award-winning place, which focuses on modern and traditional seafood preparations seasoned with mint, fennel and oranges. The original location is in Kreuzberg and proved so popular that the owners added this more central one. An exclusive wine list includes Nero d'Avola vin-

Right: Marjellchen.

Below: gourmet dining at Die Quadriga.

tages from little-known but high-quality producers. Reservations essential.

MODERN EUROPEAN
Die Quadriga
Eislebener Strasse 14; tel: 2140 5650; www.brandenburger-hof.com; €€€€; Tue–Sat from 7pm; U3: Augsburger Strasse; map p.133 D1
High temple of gourmet cuisine inside the Hotel Brandenburger Hof, where Michelin-starred chef Bobby Bräuer creates exquisite, seasonal dishes with international influences. There is also a cellar of 850 excellent German wines at its disposal to go alongside the food. This very upscale restaurant is intimate, only capable of seating a small number per sitting, so be sure to book in advance.

Prenzlauer Berg

ALSATIAN
Gugelhof
Ecke Knaackstrasse 37; tel: 442 2929; www.gugelhof.com; €€–€€€; Mon–Fri 4pm–1am, Sat–Sun 10am–1am; U2: Senefelder Platz; map p.135 D4
Berlin's most famous Alsatian restaurant offers excellent versions of *tarte flambée* (melted cheese over bits of meat on a crackery crust), *bäckeoffe* (the Alsatian answer to *pot-au-feu*) and *choucroute garni*, along with ever-changing weekly specials. The wine list has a fine selection of German and Alsatian wines, particularly rieslings, and the after-meal selection of *eaux de vie* is the best in town. Weekends see the entire neighbourhood arriving for breakfast or lunch, and reservations are mandatory.

AMERICAN
The Bird
Am Falkplatz 5; tel: 5105 3283; www.thebirdinberlin.com; €€–€€€; Mon–Thur 6–11pm, Fri 5pm–midnight, Sat noon–midnight, Sun noon–11pm; U2, S45, S46: Schönhauser Allee
Despite its name, The Bird is about red meat, specifically, that hard-to-find commodity in Berlin, beef. Burgers and cut-to-order steaks are just about all that's on the menu (although there are incredibly hot chicken wings available as appetisers), served with hand-cut french fries. It is an authentic piece of American Germany (the owners are from New York) and always packed with homesick Americans and Americanophilic Germans, to the point where a reservation is almost always a must.

CHINESE
Ostwind
Husemannstrasse 13; tel: 441 5951; €–€€; Mon–Sat 6pm–1am, Sun 10am–1am; U2: Eberswalde Strasse
Given that most 'Chinese' restaurants in Berlin serve up a caricature of the cuisine, it is a pleasure to come across this basement restaurant which is as dedicated to Chinese culture generally as it is to good Chinese cuisine. Eschewing MSG, it strives for freshness and authenticity. Service can be slow and some dishes are oddly bland, but a careful perusal of the menu can result in a fine meal.

Approximate prices per person for a three-course meal with a glass of house wine:

€	under €20
€€	€20–€35
€€€	€35–€50
€€€€	over €50

EAST ASIAN
Omoni
Kopenhagener Strasse 14; tel: 361 9244; €–€€€; daily 5pm–midnight; U2, S45, S46: Schönhauser Allee
This understated Korean-Japanese restaurant not only offers some of the best sushi in town from a huge menu, but some of the only authentic Korean cuisine, epitomised by bibimbap, a huge, heated bowl of rice dressed with raw egg, vegetables and Korean pickles, which you then mix up with the spoon provided. Organic produce when available, friendly service and reservations essential.

ITALIAN
Due Forni
Schönhauser Allee 12; tel: 440 17 333; €; open daily noon–midnight; U2: Senefelder Platz; map p.135 D4
This once elegant building housed the Polish Consulate back in communist times and now plays host to a frantic bunch of yelling, gesticulating waiters scurrying from the two ovens that give the place its name, to the customers, who will tuck into one of the bewildering number of pizzas on offer. There is also a blackboard full of pasta dishes and salads, but clearly pizza's the star. Good, inexpensive carafe wine, too.
Trattoria Paparazzi
Husemannstrasse 35; tel: 440 7333; €–€€; daily 6pm–1am; U2: Eberswalder Strasse
Ignore the name and book a table for some remarkable southern Italian food at this long-time neighbourhood favourite, run by a German woman who returned from holiday fired with enthusiasm for what she had been eating and went to culinary school in Italy to learn the tricks.

If, in some of the lower-end establishments, your server seems a bit snarly, don't worry: it's Berliner Schnauze, best translated as 'attitude'. The locals find it charming, visitors usually less so.

Yes, they do pizza, but look beyond that to the malfatti (rolled, stuffed pasta) and strangolapreti (hand-cut pasta with cheese, spinach, and ham). Check for daily specials, which are often dishes found nowhere else in town.

RUSSIAN
Restaurant Pasternak
Knaackstrasse 22–24; tel: 441 3399; www.restaurant-pasternak.de; €–€€; Mon–Sat 9am–midnight, Sun 10am–midnight; U2: Senefelder Platz; map p.135 D4
Comrades! Collectively endeavour to avail yourself of the traditional specialties of the Russian people! Don't let the somewhat silly retro-communist trappings of the menu put you off of some excellent Russian cuisine. Be it tea and blinis or a full meal of herring, borscht and shashlik, this place delivers the goods. Of particular note are the Jewish specialities: latkes, kreplach and more, cooked just as authentically as the rest of the menu. Incredibly popular, so booking is essential.

Schöneberg
GERMAN
Renger-Patzsch
Wartburstrasse 54; tel: 784 2059; www.renger-patzsch.com; €–€€; daily 6–11.30pm; U7: Eisenacher Strasse; map p.137 E3
This Alsatian-German restaurant is set in a fabulous old dining hall with wooden

117

panels and elegant bentwood chairs. The food is very tasty indeed and the portions are more than generous. The menu concentrates on a few classic dishes such as sauerkraut and pork but a particular speciality are the *Flammkuchen,* pizza-like flatbreads with a variety of toppings. They have a wide range of well-priced wines by the glass and the daily specials are well worth looking out for.

INDIAN
India Haus
Feurigstrasse 21; tel: 213 8826; www.india-haus.de; €; daily noon–midnight; U4: Innsbrucker Platz; map p.137 E3

Maybe it is due to the fact that it is located just behind the Odeon, Berlin's oldest English-language cinema, but this veteran Indian restaurant is one of the very few recommendable ones in the city. It could be that British visitors who know korma from kofta have allowed the owners to make a profit on traditionally prepared and seasoned dishes. As with most British restaurants, it is all from the northern Indian tradition, so while there are no surprises, there are no let-downs, either. They will make it properly spicy if you ask.

ITALIAN
Café Aroma
Hochkirchstrasse 8; tel: 782 5821; www.cafe-aroma.de; €€; Mon–Fri 6pm–1am, Sat 2pm–2am, Sun 11am–1am; S1, S2, S25, U7: Yorckstrasse; map p.138 A4

Café Aroma has been Berlin's top northern Italian restaurant for years and has a large and devoted clientele, much of it made up of Italians living in Berlin. The gathering place for the local 'Slow Food'

Above: an authentically Italian cappuccino at Café Aroma.

movement, it is also something of an embassy for Italian culture in general, with language classes often being offered. There is always something unusual on the blackboard and classics on the printed menu. The atmosphere is loud and somewhat chaotic, and the service is friendly.

Kreuzberg and Friedrichshain
GERMAN
Altes Zollhaus
Carl-Herz-Ufer 30; tel: 692 3300; www.altes-zollhaus-berlin.de; €€–€€€; Tue–Sat 6pm–midnight; U1: Prinzenstrasse; map p.139 D4

It is hard to believe you are in Berlin while dining at this canalside, half-timbered cottage, which served as a customs depot in the 19th century. Rather, it is until you see the menu, on which the produce of the surrounding Brandenburg countryside is subjected to chef Günter Beyer's alchemy. Duck is a speciality, but seasonal spe-

cials change week by week as fruit and vegetable crops come and go. There's a range of choices from traditional to slightly avant-garde, and the restaurant has its own exclusive winery making wines to complement the cuisine.

Henne
Leuschnerdamm 25; tel: 614 7730; www.henne-berlin.de; €; Tue–Sat 7pm–midnight, Sun 5pm–midnight; U8: Moritzplatz; map p.135 D1

Does it seem absurd to have to make a reservation for a bar that serves a roasted half-chicken for €6.50 and pretty much nothing else? Not after you've tasted the chicken, an organic, milk-marinated one from Bavaria raised by the owner's brother. Add another €3 for a portion of potato or cabbage salad and a couple more for a draught beer, and you have a quintessential Berlin dining experience. You will feel sorry for John F. Kennedy, who wrote them a letter (displayed above the bar) expressing his disappointment that he couldn't come for dinner after his *'Ich bin ein Berliner'* speech.

Jolesch
Muskauer Strasse 1; tel: 612 3581; www.jolesch.de; €–€€; Mon–Fri 11.30am–midnight, Sat–Sun 10am–midnight; U1:

Approximate prices per person for a three-course meal with a glass of house wine:

€	under €20
€€	€20–€35
€€€	€35–€50
€€€€	over €50

118

Görlitzer Bahnhof or Schlesisches Tor; map p.135 E1

A wonderful neighbourhood restaurant, Jolesch offers a wide selection of German and Austrian dishes, from the very basic to almost fancy. The locals gather for breakfast, lunch (a particular bargain, with a three-course meal for €7.90) and dinner, or hang out at the bar in the front. Unpretentious, friendly and affordable.

FRENCH
Le Cochon Bourgeois
Fichtestrasse 24; tel: 693 0101; www.lecochon.de; €€–€€€; Tue–Sat 6pm–midnight; U7: Südstern; map p.139 D3

Given Kreuzberg's political leanings, it is hardly surprising that its best French restaurant should be known as the 'bourgeois pig', but the irony stops at the name. In a city with few top-notch, authentic French places, this is a magnet for the city's French population, as chef Benjamin Stoeckel prepares a crisp salad with warm cheese, adds Moroccan accents to the fish and has assembled a wine list of some distinction.

SPANISH
Sol Y Sombra
Oranienplatz 5; tel: 6953 3887; www.solysombra-berlin.de; €; daily 5pm–late; U8: Moritzplatz; map p.135 D1

Your typical neighbourhood tapas bar, frequented mostly by a local Kreuzberg crowd. Pick from a wide selection of Andalusian goodies on display. All the staples of Spanish cuisine, including a delicious gazpacho.

TURKISH
Hasir
Adalbertstrasse 10; tel: 614 2373; www.hasir.de; €–€€; daily 24 hours; U1, U8: Kottbusser Tor; map p.135 D1

There are actually six Hasirs: one next door to this and others in Wilmersdorf, Schöneberg, Spandau and Mitte, the latter featuring a liveried doorman. This is the one where it all started, though, from the invention of the döner kebap to the idea that Germans might want to eat Turkish cuisine. From a light soup to heartier appetisers to the grilled meat specialities which put the place on the map originally, through the traditional closing rice pudding, it's dead-on authentic and tasty. Note that only this location is open day and night; check their website for other locations' addresses and opening hours.

Eating Out Vocabulary
Vorspeise **appetiser**
Hauptgericht **main course**
Beilage **side dish**
Fleisch **meat**
Gemüse **vegetable**
Salat **salad** (also lettuce)
Getränke **drinks**
Schweinefleisch **pork**
Rindfleisch **beef**
Hänchen **chicken**
Kalbsfleisch **veal**
Pute, Truthahn **turkey**
Ente **duck**
Gans **goose**
Wildschwein **wild boar**
Kaninchen **rabbit**
Wurst **sausage**
Schinken **ham**
Lachs **salmon**
Kabeljau **cod**
Hering **herring**
Zander **pike-perch**
Barsch **perch**
Thunfisch **tuna**
Krabben **small shrimps**
Garnelen **prawns**
Kohl **cabbage**
Rotkohl **red cabbage**
Blumenkohl **cauliflower**
Rosenkohl **Brussels sprouts**
Gurke **cucumber** (also pickle)
Kartoffel **potato**
Bohnen **beans**
Erbsen **peas**
Tomate **tomato**
Champignon **mushroom**
Knoblauch **garlic**
Zwiebel **onion**
Wasser **water**
Mineralwasser **mineral water**
mit/ohne Kohlensäure **with/without gas**
Milch **milk**
Saft **juice**
e.g. Orangensaft **orange juice**
Tee **tea**
Kaffee **coffee**
Bier **beer**
helles/dunkles **light/dark**
Weissbier **wheat beer**
Wein **wine**
Rotwein **red wine**
Weisswein **white wine**
Schnaps **spirits/liquor**
See also Language, p.79.

Below: the dining scene is becoming ever more lively and stylish.

119

Shopping

While you will have no trouble hunting down the big names in Berlin, there is a considerable amount of idiosyncratic shopping to be done here, in offbeat boutique stores and the myriad markets; when looking for distinctive purchases, you will notice that nostalgia for East Germany (ostalgia) is a big theme. Germany liberalised its once restrictive shop opening hours a while back and Berlin, typically, scrapped just about all restrictions. Shopping for basic needs is possible at just about any time, but generally department stores and most shops open at 10am and close at 8pm or 10pm, with many still closing on Sundays.

Department Stores

F95
Frankfurter Allee 95–97; tel: 4208 3358; www.f95store.com; Mon–Fri noon–8pm, Sat 11am–6pm; S4, S10, U5: Frankfurter Allee
A self-described lifestyle concept store, this shop even transforms the arrangement of its products into art installations. Goods are arranged on wooden pallets; jeans hang from the ceiling as if floating in space. Berlin's young, trendy clientele love it.

Galeries Lafayette
Friedrichstrasse 76–78; tel: 209 480; www.galeries-lafayette.de; Mon–Sat 10am–8pm; U2: Stadtmitte or Französische Strasse; map p.134 B2
A short walk from Unter den Linden, this is the Berlin branch of the famous Parisian department store and the stunning, glass centrepiece of a new shopping district in central Berlin. Be sure to visit the French delicatessen and exquisite collection of wines in the basement.

KaDeWe
Tauentzienstrasse 21–24; tel: 21 210; www.kadewe-berlin.de; Mon–Thur 10am–8pm, Fri 10am–9pm, Sat 9.30am–8pm; U1, U2: Wittenbergplatz; map p.133 D1
Opened in 1907 by the Jewish merchant Adolf Jandorf, it belongs today to Karstadt Quelle. For a full century, its concept has remained the same: to rival London's Harrods with a massive display of luxury and everyday goods and name brands, as well as eating extravagance at its 30 gourmet bars. The luxury food hall takes up the whole sixth floor. A Berlin institution and a must-see.
SEE ALSO FOOD AND DRINK, P.59

Below: shopping at the Galeries Lafayette.

Left: quirky bargains at the Berliner Antik and Flohmarkt.

shaped chairs to buttons with images from East German stamps, lighting, chairs, dishes and leather jackets worn by the East German police. They also have trendy bags in contemporary designs.

Flea Markets

Antique Market at Ostbahnhof
Erich-Steinfurth-Strasse; tel: 2900 2010; Sun 9am–3pm; S3, S5, S7, S9, S75: Ostbahnhof; map p.135 E2
This market near East Berlin's former central station has had its ups and downs, but is now experiencing a healthy revival. Come early to find the best antiques before professional shop dealers scoop up the bargains.

Berliner Antik und Flohmarkt
Georgenstrasse; Wed–Mon 11am–6pm; S3, S5, S9, S75, S25, U6: Friedrichstrasse; map p.136 B1
Follow the S-Bahn away from the Friedrichstrasse station down Georgenstrasse and you will find this and other antique shops under the arches of the S-Bahn. Everything from antique jewellery and vintage furniture to Jugendstil lamps.

Berliner Kunst-und Nostalgiemarkt
Am Kupfergraben; Sat–Sun 11am–5pm; U2, S5, S7, S75, S9: Alexanderplatz; map p.137 C2
This is a pretty flea market along the banks of the Spree river on the way to Pergamonmuseum. Visitors can find stalls full of books and clothes, antiques, souvenirs and sundry items. Popular with tourists; bargain hard to pare down inflated prices.

Shopping Malls

Alexa
Grunerstrasse 120; tel: 269 3400; www.alexacentre.com; Mon–Sat 10am–9pm; S3, S5, S7, S9, S75, U2, U5, U8: Alexanderplatz; map p.135 D3
Alexanderplatz has been a Berlin crossroads and meeting place for over a century. Alexa is the latest addition, a massive shopping mall in neo-Art Deco design with 180 shops offering everything from food and fashion to computers and music.

Stilwerk Berlin
Kantstrasse 17; tel: 315 150; www.stilwerk.de; Mon–Sat 10am–7pm; S9, S75, S5, S3: Zoologischer Garten, or U15: Uhlandstrasse, map p.133 D1
This is a distinctive shopping mall concept, with boutiques and sales outlets offering high-quality luxury and lifestyle accessories for the home, from furniture by international designers to lighting, kitchenware and fine textiles.

Second-Hand and Retro Stores

Colours
Bergmannstrasse 102; tel: 694

Being Continental Europe's largest department store, the KaDeWe is not much fun to explore with kids in tow. You can, however, park them in the nice childcare facility on the third floor, right next to the toys. Exclusive kidswear and a children's hair designer are also available here.

3348; www.kleidermarkt.de; Mon–Fri 11am–7pm, Sat noon–8pm; U7: Mehringdamm; map p.138 B3
At this popular shop in the heart of Kreuzberg you can buy retro clothing priced by the kilogram. It is a quick walk from the Mehringdamm station. Combine a trip here with a visit to the Turkish open-air market on Bergmannstrasse.

Waahnsinn Berlin
Rosenthaler Strasse 17; tel: 282 0029; http://waahnsinn-berlin.blogspot.com; Mon–Sat noon–8pm; U8: Weinmeister Strasse; map p.135 C3
This is the place to go for 'ostalgia'-infleunced retro. They have got everything from 1968 East German egg-

Flea Market at Arkonaplatz

Arkonaplatz; tel: 786 9764; www.troedelmarkt-arkona platz.de; Sun 10am–4pm, closed in winter; U8: Bernauer Strasse

Located on one of the most beautiful neighbourhood squares in Mitte, this market caters to those hunting down artefacts from daily life in the old East Germany. But you can also find antique books and second-hand clothing, linen and other odds and ends. After shopping, relax in one of the cafés on the square.

Flea Market at Boxhagener Platz

Boxhagener Platz; tel: 0174 946 7557; Sun 10am–6pm; U5: Frankfurter Tor, Samariter Strasse

This is a bargain-hunter's paradise and a favourite of students or anyone on a low budget looking for cheap treasures in the cardboard boxes and on the tables of the merchants. After shopping, visit the many local art galleries and cafés.

Flea Market at John-F.-Kennedy-Platz

John-F.-Kennedy-Platz; tel: 332 224 6723; Sat–Sun 8am–4pm; U4: Rathaus Schöneberg; map p.137 E3

This is a popular local market on the square in front of the Rathaus Schöneberg. Reflecting its neighbourhood character, this market lacks the 'scene' feel of markets in Mitte and Prenzlauer Berg, but is more intimate and relaxed for it.

Flea Market at Mauerpark

Bernauer Strasse 63–64; tel: 0176 2925 0021; Sun 8am–6pm; U8: Bernauer Strasse; U2: Eberswalderstrasse

> Cash is king. With few exceptions, German retailers loathe credit cards. Many restaurants and clothing stores will not take them. The upside is that you can often request 'Skonto', a discount of 3 percent or more if you agree to pay in cash, especially for big items like furniture. Maestro debit cards are accepted almost everywhere.

Perhaps Berlin's most bohemian market, it takes its name from the Berlin Wall. The park is located on a stretch of land where the Wall once stood, and the market occupies land that was once mined and guarded with lethal force. It's a great place to look for old vinyl albums, CDs and East German paraphernalia. Be sure to take time to kick back in one of the beach bars, with real sand, house music DJs and cool drinks. Note, though, that the annual left-wing May Day riots are often launched from Mauerpark.

Flea Market at Strasse des 17. Juni

Strasse des 17. Juni; tel: 2655 0096; Sat 11am–5pm, Sun 10am–5pm, S3, S5, S7, S9, S75; Tiergarten; map p.133 D2

Russian military paraphernalia, Art Deco lamps, Biedermeier furniture, handmade clothing, CDs, doorknobs and other hardware, it's all here at one of Berlin's most popular flea markets. Popular among tourists, but it's also a favourite of locals. One tip: barter hard to push down inflated prices.

Gift and Specialist Shops

Ach Berlin

Markgrafenstrasse 39; 9212 6880; www.achberlin.de;

Left: browsing records at the Berliner Antik und Flohmarkt.

Mon–Sat 11am–7pm; U2, U6: Stadtmitte; U2: Hausvogteiplatz; map p.134 C2

It took Berlin a long time to adopt the self-confidence of New York's 'I Love NY' campaign. But the city is changing, and Ach Berlin is a sign of that change, a collection of gifts from coffee mugs to shoe brushes with every imaginable Berlin motif: the Berlin bear, the TV Tower, Brandenburg Gate. All that's missing is the slogan, 'I Love Berlin'.

Ampelmann Shops
Potsdamer Platz Arcaden; tel: 2592 5691; www.ampelmann.de; Mon–Sat 9am–9pm, Sun 1–7pm; S1, S2, S25, U2: Potsdamer Platz; map p.134 B1

A fierce battle erupted between East and West Berliners when after unification the Westerners tried to remove the East's 'traffic light man', a green striding figure for go and a standing red figure for wait. The East won, and the *'Ampelmann'* became an icon, adorning T-shirts, bags, sweets, lamps

Above: 'ostalgic' gifts at Mondos Art.

Below: book-shopping at the Kunst- und Nostalgiemarkt.

and many other objects. (Also at: Karl-Liebknecht-Strasse 1; tel: 2758 3238; Mon–Sat 10am–9pm, Sun 11am–8pm; S1, S2, S25: Unter den Linden; map p.137 D1; and Rosenthaler Strasse 40–41; Hackesche Höfe, Hof 5; tel: 4404 8801; Mon–Sat 10am–10pm, Sun 11am–7pm; S/Tram Hackescher Markt; map p.135 C3)

Herrlich Männergeschenke
Bergmannstrasse 2; tel: 784 5395; www.herrlich-online.de; Mon–Sat 10am–8pm; U7: Gneisenaustrasse; map p.138 B3

Everything a man needs: kitchen stuff, compasses, camping knives, pens and warm blankets. This gift shop specialises in presents for boyfriends, husbands, fathers and grandfathers. Forget the tie and socks this year.

Misses & Marbles
Raumerstrasse 36; tel: 4978

6282; www.misses-marbles.de; Mon–Sat 10am–7pm, Sun 11am–6pm; U2: Eberswalder Strasse

A cosy hole-in-the-wall shop that exemplifies a Berlin trend: the combination coffee bar, gift and newspaper shop. Souvenirs on sale are largely from Berlin designers and include blankets, kids' T-shirts and odd accessories, purses made out of used sail cloth and much more.

Mondos Art
Schreiner Strasse 6; tel: 4201 0778; www.mondosarts.de; Mon–Fri 10am–7pm, Sat 11am–4pm; U5 Samariterstrasse

East German retro, this shop carries it all, from DVDs of old East German Defa film studio movies to board games, East German passports and a beer called Red October.

Sports

The 2006 World Cup inspired a new lease of life for Berlin's sporting world, not least the iconic Olympiastadion, which benefited from an extensive renovation. Yet with the Berlin Marathon attracting tens of thousands of runners every year, Berlin was already known for its participatory activites. It has a lot on offer in addition to the traditional sports: water activities on Grosser Wannsee, ice-skating on Unter den Linden and cycling just about everywhere. For the less active, spectator events like watching local football side Hertha BSC or the Six-Day Cycling Race are reasonably priced and accessible.

Participant Activities

CYCLING

Berlin is flat, green and laced with a network of cycle paths. In fact, cycling is so much a part of the local culture and city infrastructure that renting a bike for a day is easy, and a great way to sightsee. Start by biking around the Reichstag, through the Brandenburger Tor, then follow the Spree, or cut through the Tiergarten. With its many back roads and quiet neighbourhoods, Berlin is a great city to explore by bike. If you can, start on a Sunday morning, when you have the city almost to yourself. Most streets have bike lanes, and drivers tend to be careful. If you feel more comfortable in a group, choose from a variety of organised English-language sightseeing tours by bicycle, such as www.berlinonbike.de.
SEE ALSO TRANSPORT, P.129

INDOOR CLIMBING
Magic Mountain
Böttgerstrasse 20–26, Wedding; tel: 88715 7900; www.magic

mountain.de (German only); admission charge; Mon–Fri noon–midnight, Thur from 10am, Sat–Sun 10am–10pm; U8, S1, S2, S25, S41, S42: Gesundbrunnen
With the nearest mountains hundreds of miles away, this spacious facility offers the opportunity to experience the thrill of climbing in the heart of the city. Magic Mountain has 200-plus climbing routes that challenge everyone from novices to veterans. You can also work out in the gym or relax in the sauna after you are done. Children six and older welcome.

Below: rental bicycles.

INLINE SKATING
For everyday inline skating, join the Berliners on Kronprinzessinnenweg along the Grunewald forest or start at Brandenburger Tor and go west on wide pavements on Strasse des 17. Juni, past the Siegessäule, cutting through the Tiergarten park.
Skate by Night Berlin
http://berlin.skatebynight.de
Skaters used to have the run of the city every summer Sunday night (bringing traffic to a standstill), but now skate nights are confined to just a few nights a year. Check for dates and courses.

RUNNING AND WALKING
Banks of the Landwehrkanal
U1: Prinzenstrasse
A flat and picturesque route following the treelined Landwehr Canal that winds through the city. Get to know leafy, upmarket parts of the Kreuzberg district, with stately old buildings and shady trees. A cycle path follows the 10km route which is also perfect for a leisurely stroll. The path is

Left: at the Olympiastadion.

Strandbad Wannsee
Wannseebadweg 25, Zehlendorf; www.strandbad wannsee.de; Apr daily 10am–6pm, May–July Mon–Fri 10am–7pm, Sat–Sun 8am–8pm, July–Aug Mon–Fri 9am–8pm, Sat–Sun 8am–9pm, Aug–Sept daily 10am–7pm; admission charge; S1, S7: Nikolassee
Have a swim in the clear water of Lake Wannsee, go windsurfing or rent a boat at this long, sandy beach.

Berliner Bäder
www.berlinerbaederbetriebe.de
You're never far from a swimming pool in Berlin. This website has a list of all the public pools in the the city.

Spectator Sports

CYCLING

Berlin Six Day Race
Velodrom, Paul-Heyse-Str. 29, Prenzlauer Berg; tel: 9710 4204; www.sechstagerennen-berlin.de (German only); admission charge; every January; S41, S42, S8, S85: Landsberger Allee
A major sporting event, that has been running for almost a century, bringing together thousands of cycling enthusiasts to watch the skills, speed and stamina of cyclists from around the world being challenged.

FOOTBALL

Olympiastadion
Olympischer Platz 3, Charlottenburg; tel: 3068 8100; www.olympiastadion-berlin.de; U2, S75, S9: Olympiastadion
The Olympiastadion, a city landmark refurbished for the World Cup finals in 2006 and capable of seating almost 75,000, is home to 'Berlin's old lady', Hertha BSC, the capital's principal football team. Games run from August until May.

dotted with cafés and illuminated in the evening.

Berlin Marathon
Start at Brandenburger Tor, Mitte; tel: 301 28 810; www.real-berlin-marathon.com; annually in September; registration charge
The flat and fast course takes you past all the major sights, while enthusiastic crowds and mostly pleasant temperatures make it one of the world's most popular marathons, always good for a world or personal record. It attracts up to 40,000 runners, skaters and wheelchair athletes. Register early if you want to take part.

Tiergarten
S5, S7, S75, S9: Tiergarten, Bellevue or Zoologischer Garten; S1, S2, S25: Unter den Linden; map p.133 E2/134 A2
Berlin's 'Central Park' is flat, safe and pleasant to run or walk in. You can jog on wide avenues or narrow paths along the ponds and waterways and take in blooming rhododendrons or colourful foliage. The adjoining government district with the Reichstag and Kanzleramt is easy

Ice-rinks are set up in attractive locations during the winter season – one on Unter den Linden avenue, more at Potsdamer Platz and Alexanderplatz. Skates can be rented for little money – go with the flow and enjoy Berlin's skyline.

to include. Wider paths are partly illuminated at night.

WATER SPORTS AND SWIMMING

Badeschiff (Swimming Ship)
Eichenstrasse 4, Treptow; tel: 01789 500 163; www.arena berlin.de; from May, opening hours subject to change; admission charge; robes, towels, slippers for hire; S41, S42, S8, S85, S9: Treptower Park
A floating swimming pool anchored on the Spree river, part of the Arena venue and complete with an artificial beach and beach bar. Mix with a hip young crowd and float in the illuminated pool. The Badeschiff is converted into a sauna landscape with heated pool in the winter.
SEE ALSO PAMPERING, P.106

Theatre and Dance

G erman theatre has always been political, and you can journey through the city's many theatres and plays to encounter the country's turbulent past. Major playwrights such as Bertolt Brecht, Ferdinand Bruckner, Gerhard Hauptmann and Heiner Müller have lived and worked in Berlin, and the city retains its reputation as a fertile ground for innovative forms of theatre. Similarly, the local classical and contemporary dance scenes are thriving, and modern productions often overlap with theatre, music and other art forms.

Theatre

MAJOR THEATRES

Berliner Ensemble
Bertold-Brecht-Platz 1; tel: 2840 8155; www.berliner-ensemble.de; S3, S5, S7, S9, S75, U6, Tram M1, 12: Friedrichstrasse; map p.136 B2
This is the house that Brecht built. His famous *Threepenny Opera* had its première here, and after the war he was the theatre's director. For years after his death, the BE saw itself as the guardian of Brecht's legacy. More recently, playwright Heiner Müller has found a home here, and today performances cover a broad range of German playwrights.

Deutsches Theatre
Schumannstrasse 13a; tel: 2844 1225; www.deutsches-theater.de; S3, S5, S7, S9, S75: Friedrichstrasse; map p.134 B3
This is considered the most conservative of Berlin's main theatres. It focuses on classic German theatre.

Maxim Gorki Theatre
Am Festungsgraben 2; tel: 202 210; www.gorki.de; U6, S3, S5, S7, S9, S75, S9: Friedrichstrasse; S1, S2: Unter den Linden; map p.137 C1

This is not a Russian theatre, but a venue for contemporary pieces and classics from German and international theatre.

Schaubühne
Kurfürstendamm 153; tel: 890 023; www.schaubuehne.de; U7: Adenauerplatz; S5, S7, S9: Charlottenburg; map p.136 B4
Founded in 1962, The Schaubühne has always been edgy, with a focus on political and social themes. It is also known for providing a venue for new international dramatists and avant-garde dance.

Volksbühne
Linienstrasse 227; tel: 240 655; www.volksbuehne-berlin.de; U2: Rosa-Luxemburg-Platz; S5, S75, S9: Alexanderplatz; map p.135 D3
The visually interesting Volksbühne makes a habit out of its total disregard for political correctness. It is provocative and willing to take risks.

FRINGE THEATRES

English Theatre Berlin
Fidicinstrasse 41; tel: 693 5692; www.etberlin.de; U6: Luftbrücke; map p.138 B3
More than a venue for expats, the ETB has earned a

solid reputation in Berlin for its English-language performances, which include American and British classics and new writers.

Grips-Theater
Altonaer Strasse 22; tel: 3974 7477; www.grips-theater.de; U9: Hansaplatz; map p.133 D3
Grips, which is German slang for being clever, is theatre for children and young adults. It is best-known for its award-winning play *Linie 1*, which takes place on Berlin's U1 and has been running since 1986.

Hebbel-Theater
Hau 1: Stresemannstrasse 29, Hau 2: Hallesches Ufer 32, Hau 3: Tempelhofer Ufer 10; tel: 259 0040; www.hebbel-am-ufer.de; Hau 1: S1, S2, S25: Anhalter Bahnhof; Hau 2, 3: U1, U6: Hallesches Tor; Hau 1: map p.134 B1; Hau 2,3: map p.138 B4
This ensemble of three

> A line from Brecht's *Die Dreigroschenoper (The Threepenny Opera)*, a smash hit in Berlin in the 1920s, is still quoted today when Germans debate social justice: 'First the grub, then the morality.'

Left: the ornate lobby of the Deutsches Theatre.

140 performances a year. Get tickets early; performances are often sold out.

Staatsballett Berlin
Deutsche Oper, Bismarckstrasse 35; tel: 3438 4343; www.deutscheoperberlin.de; advance sales 11am–performance; U2: Deutsche Oper; U7: Bismarckstrasse; map p.132 C2
Berlin's dance tradition goes back to 1794, when the first independent ballet company was founded. In 2004, the dance companies of the city's three opera houses merged to create the Staatsballett. The programme is a mix of modern dance and classical ballet.

FESTIVALS
Tanz im August – Internationales Tanzfest Berlin
www.tanzimaugust.de; different venues
Germany's biggest dance festival, this four-week programme is the highlight of Berlin's dance community. It is organised by Hebbel-Theatre and Tanzwerkstatt Berlin. Performers include dancers such as Tanztheater Wuppertal or the Jirí Kyliáns Nederlands Dans Theater, as well as newcomers.

Below: Jasmin Wagner in *Cassandra/Elektra.*

Heiner Müller (1929–95), widely considered the most significant German dramatist of the 20th century after Brecht, wrote and staged many provocative plays in Berlin, such as *Die Umsiedlerin,* until the communist authorities censored him and prevented most of his works from being performed in East Germany.

---

theatres in close proximity to each other provides a venue for contemporary German and international theatre, dance and performance art.

Kleines Theater
Südwestkorso 64; tel: 821 2021; www.kleines-theater.de; U9: Friedrich-Wilhelm-Platz; U3: Rüdesheimer Platz
In this small theatre, with just 99 seats, a small troupe of actors perform drama by local authors as well as musical pieces and comedy.

Dance

COMPANIES
Minako Seki
Venues vary; tel: 618 5211; www.minakoseki.com
Minako Seki, born in Japan, has been dancing in Berlin since 1986. A third generation butoh dancer, she co-founded the 'Tatobea: Théâtre Danse Grotesque', the first German-Japanese butoh ensemble. She performs her own pieces in Berlin and internationally.

MS Schrittmacher
Zossener Strasse 52; tel: 6981 4344; www.msschrittmacher.de; U6, U7: Mehringdamm; map p.138 C4
This is a growing independent dance company. Founded by choreographer Martin Stiefermann in 1998, Schrittmacher uses dance to confront issues such as suicide, the loss of balance, trust and the failure of human relationships.

Sasha Waltz & Guests
Sophienstrasse 3; tel: 246 2800; www.sashawaltz.de; U8: Weinmeisterstrasse; map p.134 C3
This is the most innovative and popular dance company in Berlin. Waltz founded the company together with Jochen Sanding in 1993 and from 1999 to 2004 was artistic manager of the Schaubühne. Now, as an independent company, Waltz puts on more than

Transport

Getting to Berlin is straightforward, with several scheduled daily international flights and a historic role as a European rail hub. Given that Berlin sprawls over a vast area, getting around the city is surprisingly easy, too. The city's public transport, made up of underground trains, light rail and buses and sewn back together following the fall of the Wall, penetrate every corner of the city and its near suburbs. Tickets can even be used on a couple of boats. Note that the Berlin Public Transit Authority (BVG) website (www.bvg.de) is a useful resource for all public transport information.

Getting To Berlin

BY RAIL

As the halfway point between Paris and Moscow and also Stockholm and Rome, Berlin has been a European rail hub since train travel started; the Hamburger Bahnhof (now an art museum, see p.88) is one of the oldest stations in Europe. Today, the gleaming new **Hauptbahnhof** on the banks of the Spree river near the Reichstag is where most passengers disembark from one of Deutsche Bahn's trains. It is easily connected to all of Berlin's public transport, and if you can get to your destination via S-Bahn, your train ticket will cover you for this portion of your journey, too.

BY AIR

Most international flights on regular carriers continue to arrive at **Tegel** in the north, and travellers can connect to either the TXL express bus, serving central Berlin, or buses 109 and 128 to less central destinations. Budget airlines are served by **Schönefeld**, in the south-

> The round-trip flight from London to Berlin will set back your carbon balance by 0.45 tonnes. To feel better, you can buy a carbon offset certificate from www.myclimate.org, www.climatecare.org or www.terrapass.com.

east, which is preparing to become Berlin's main airport. The city centre is about 30 minutes away by Airport Express Regionalbahn, or 50 minutes on the S-Bahn.

Getting Around Berlin

A single ticket is good for two hours' travel in one direction on the **U-Bahn** (Untergrundbahn) and **S-Bahn** (Schnellbahn) lines, **trams**, **buses** and **ferries** within **A–B zones**. Single tickets, good for one-way travel for two hours, are €2.10. Day tickets, valid for travel until 3am, are €6.10. Week tickets, valid until midnight a week later, cost €26.20 and also allow travel with another adult and up to three children aged 6–13 after 8pm.

BY U-BAHN AND S-BAHN

The U-Bahn often runs above ground, and the S-Bahn below. The system is fast, and the map is clear; many U-Bahn stations display maps showing the time taken between stations. Note that Berlin tradition has the crowd on the platform charge the doors the second they open, meaning that sometimes passengers have to push their way out.

Some lines run 24 hours a day; if you're going to be out late it pays to check for the last train before leaving the station. Most have extended operating hours at weekends and holidays. Most central U-Bahn and S-Bahn stations are safe, although you may be approached by beggars or drug-dealers at some of the seamier ones, as well as those looking to sell used tickets.

BY BUS AND TRAM

Berlin has an extensive bus network which connects U-Bahn and S-Bahn stations with the city's smaller streets, particularly in outlying areas. Maps are available at all BVG kiosks, located in

Left: a U-Bahn train.

doubling as bike lanes, Berlin is easy to traverse by bicycle. Find bike rental addresses at www.fahrradstation.de (German only) or get one of the red-and-silver Deutsche Bahn rental bikes parked in strategic locations all over town (Apr–Nov). You can register by mobile phone and unlock the bike with a code that is texted to you. Currently, the fare is 7 cents a minute, charged to your credit card.

If you prefer some guidance, call **Berlin On Bike** (tel: 4373 9999; www.berlinonbike.de) and book one of their many guided bike tours leaving from Kulturbrauerei in Prenzlauer Berg, to explore major sights or hidden places, or go along the former death strip. Guides speak English.

Guided tours with American-owned **www.fattire biketours.com** leave from Alexanderplatz (Panoramastrasse 1a, at the foot of the TV Tower) or Zoologischer Garten station. Rental rates get cheaper if you rent for more than one day (tel: 2404 7991).

It is possible to take bicycles on U-Bahn and S-Bahn trains, but you need to buy an extra *Fahradkarte* (discounted ticket).
SEE ALSO SPORTS, P.124

Below: a guided bike tour.

major stations. Bus stops are identified by a green H in a green-and-yellow circle. There is a reduced service at night, with night lines taking different routes and identified by the N suffix.

Eastern Berlin is largely served by a network of modern, Swiss-built trams, whose stops are marked the same way. They usually stop running around midnight.

BY BOAT
Treptower Hafen
Puschkinallee 15; tel: 536 3600; www.sternundkreis.de; Mar–Oct daily; S3, S41, 42 (ring train), S6, S8, S9: Treptower Park
Berlin's port and marina is the place to board boat tours on Berlin waters or all the way up to Poland.
SEE ALSO CHILDREN, P.43

BY TAXI
In crowded areas, you can normally hail a taxi. If you are out of luck, call one of the major taxi companies:
City-Funk: 210 202
Funk-Taxi Berlin: 261 026
TaxiFunk Berlin: 0800 443 322 (freecall)

> All single, day and week tickets must be validated at time of purchase by cancelling them in the machine next to the vending machine. Exceptions are tickets bought on trams or buses, which are pre-validated.

Taxi-Ruf Würfelfunk: 0800 222 2255 (freecall)
Taxis are beige in Berlin, have meters and are safe. Taxis in Berlin tend to be cheap, and taxi ranks are everywhere. Hailing a taxi in the street is not a problem, unless you are in a very deserted part of town. In that case, go to a café or bar and ask the bartender to call a taxi. The *Kurzstrecke* is a €3 fare for a ride of less than 2km (1¼ miles) if you hail the taxi in the street and tell the driver you want a *Kurzstrecke*. Taxis can also be arranged to get you from bus stops at night. Ask your driver or staff at the station.

BY BICYCLE
Do as the locals do and get a bike. With its many kilometres of bike paths and bus lanes

Atlas

The following streetplan of
Berlin makes it easy to find the
attractions listed in the A–Z section.
A selective index to streets and sights
will help you find other locations
throughout the city

Map Legend

	Autopista		Railway
	Dual carriageway	**U**	U-Bahn Station
	Main road	**S**	S-Bahn Station
	Minor road		Bus station
	Footpath		Airport
	Pedestrian area	ℹ	Tourist information
	Notable building	★	Sight of interest
	Park		Cathedral / church
	Hotel	☾	Mosque
	Urban area	✡	Synagogue
	Non urban area	🚹	Statue / monument
✝ ✝	Cemetery		Hospital

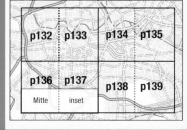

p132	p133	p134	p135
p136	p137	p138	p139
Mitte	inset		

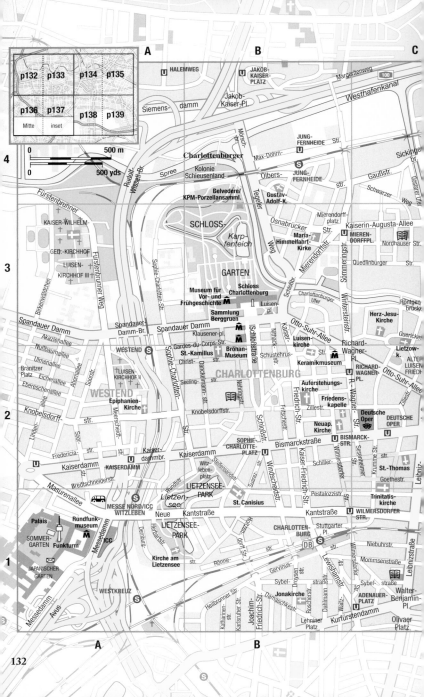

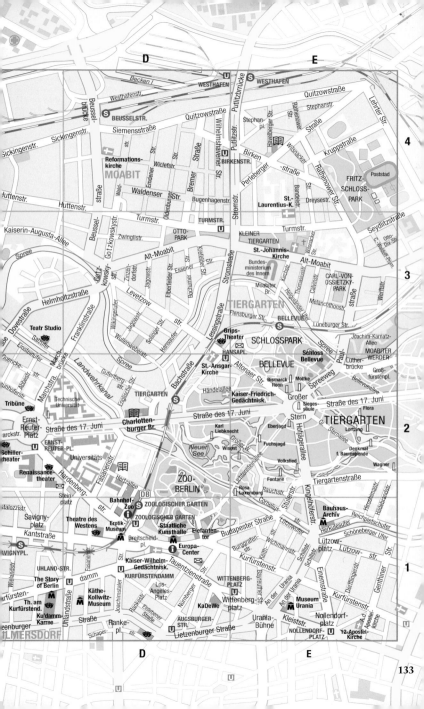

A   B   C

4

PARK AM NORDBAHNHOF
Dokumentationszentr. Berliner Mauer
KIRCHHOF VON ST.-ELISABETH
FRIEDHOF DER SOPHIENKIRCH-GEMEINDE
Anklamer Str.
Brunnenstraße
Nord-hafen
Heidestraße
Berlin-Spandauer-Schifffahrtskanal
Scharnhorststr.
Boyenstr.
SCHWARTZKOPFF-STR.
Chausseestraße
Schwartzkopffstr.
Gartenstr.
Bergstr.
NORDBAHNHOF
Invalidenstraße
Elisabethk.
Pappel-platz
VOLKSPARK WEINBERG
Rosenth
Lehrter Str.
Poststad
0   500 m
0   500 yds
96
FRITZ-SCHLOSS-PARK
GESCHICHTS-PARK
Minna-Cauer-Str.
Lärter Str. Schifffahrtskanal
Hamburger Bahnhof Mus. für Gegenwartskunst
INVALIDEN-FRIEDHOF
INVALIDEN-PARK
Museum für Naturkunde
ZINNOWITZER STR.
Zinnowitzer
Museum
Zoologisches Museum
Platz vor dem Neuen Tor
Invalidenstraße
Tieckstr.
Schlegelstr.
Golgatha-Kirk
H.-ZILLE-PARK
ROSENTHALER PLATZ
Koppen-pl.
Linienstr.
Augustr.
Kunst-Werke
Invalidenstraße
Robert-Koch-Platz
DOROTHEEN-STADT. & FRANZ.
Torstraße
St.-Joh. K.
Neue Synagoge
Sophien-kirche
Hackesch
3
Europa-platz
Seydlitzstraße
Jugend-gästeh
C.-Waldoff-Prom.
Invalidenstraße
HAUPTBAHNHOF
Humboldt-hafen
G.-Heinemann-Brücke
Washington-platz
Hugo-Preuß-Brücke
Universitäts-klinikum
Luisenstr.
Kammer-spiele Deutsches Th.
Hannoversche Str.
ORANIEN-BURGER TOR
Friedrichstadt-palast
ORANIEN-BURGER STR.
Ziegelstr.
Sophie

SEE PAGES 136-137

Alt-Moabit
Spree
Moltke-brücke
SPREEBOGEN-PARK
Kronprinzen-brücke
Reinhardt str.
Karlpl.
Marienstr.
Am Weidendamm
FRIEDRICHSTR.
Bode-Museum
Museums-insel
Alte Natio
Neues
Neue
Pergamon museum
MONBIJOU-PARK
KANZLER-GARTEN
Bundeskanzler-amt
Paul-Löbe-Allee
Joachim-Karnatz-Allee
Haus der Kulturen der Welt
Tipi-Das Zelt
REICHSTAG
Platz der Republik
Reichstags-gebäude Deutscher Bundestag
Luisenstr.
Robert-Koch-Mus.
Georgenstr.
Dorotheenstr.
Am Weidendamm
Deutsches Historisches Museum
MITTE
Altes Mus
LUST GARTEN

MOABITER WERDER
John-Foster-Dulles-Allee
Kurfürsten-platz
Groß-fürstenpl.
Carillon
Scheidemannstr.
Pariser Platz
Platz des 18. März
UNTER DEN LINDEN
Komische Oper
Märk
2
Flora
Herkules mit der Lyra
Straße des 17. Juni
Bremer Weg
Bellevueallee
Amazone
TIERGARTEN
Tiergartentunnel
Musiker-denkmal
Goethe
Lessing
Sowjetisches Ehrenmal
Brandenburger Tor (Brandenburg Gate)
Löwen-denkmal
Behren-
Akademie d. Künste
Denkmal für die ermordeten Juden Europas
Ebert-
Wilhelm
Unter   den   Linden
UNTER DEN LINDEN
FRANZÖSISCHE STR.
Französische Str.
Französischer Dom
Jägerstr.
Schjaupiel-haus
STADT-MITTE
Mauerstr.
Taubenstr.
Deutscher Dom
Friedrichswerdersche (Schinkelmuseum)
HAUS VOGTEI-PLATZ
Hausvogtei-platz

Großer Weg
Königin Luise
Friedrich-Wilhelm III.
Wilhelm I.
Musikinstr.-mus.
Beisheim-Center
Sony Center
Deutsche Kinemathek
IMAX
Voßstr.
POTSDAMER PLATZ
Leipziger Pl.
MOHRENSTR.
Kronenstr.
Kronenstr.
Leipziger Straße
Friedrichstr.
Krausenstr.
Spit

Wagner
Österre
Kunstgewerbe-museum
Gemälde-galerie
Kulturforum
Matthäi-kirchpl.
St.-Matthäus-Kirche
Neue National-galerie
Phil-harmonie
Musical-Th.
Potsdamer Pl.
Potsdamer Platz
POTSDAMER PL.
Potsdamer-Platz-Arkaden
Martin-Gropius-Bau
Museum für Kommunikation
Haus am Checkpoint Charlie Mauermuseum
Checkpoint Charlie
Zimmerstr.
Rudi-Dutschke-Str.
Axel-Springer-Str.

1
Reichpietschufer
Schöneberger Ufer
Hildebrandtstr.
Stauffenbergstr.
TILLA-DURIEUX-PARK
St. Lukas-K.
Bernburger Str.
Stresemannstr.
Topographie des Terrors
Zimmerstr.
KOCHSTR.
Kochstraße
Charlotten
Markgra
Lützow-
Wintergarten
Apostelk.
A.d. Apostel-kirche
Kurfürstenstr.
Potsdamer Straße
Pohlstr.
KURFÜRSTEN-STR.
GLEIS-DREIECK
Köthener Str.
Kleinstr.
Karlsbad
MENDELSSOHN-BARTHOLDY-PARK
MENDELSSOHN-BARTHOLDY-PARK
Askanischer Platz
ANHALTER BAHNHOF
Tempodrom
Stresemannstr.
Schöneberger Str.
Hallesches-Ufer
Möckernstr.
Hallesche Str.
Willy-Brandt-Pl.
Postbank
Hebbel-theater
Dreifaltigkeits-kirche
St-Clemens Kirche
E.-T.-A.-Hoffmann-Promenade
Franz-Klühs-Str.
Jüdisches Museum Berlin
Mehring-platz
Fr. Stampfer-str.
Friedenssäule
Am Berlin-Museum
Alte Jacob
Lindenstr.
Neuenburger Str.
St.-Agne Kirch

A   B

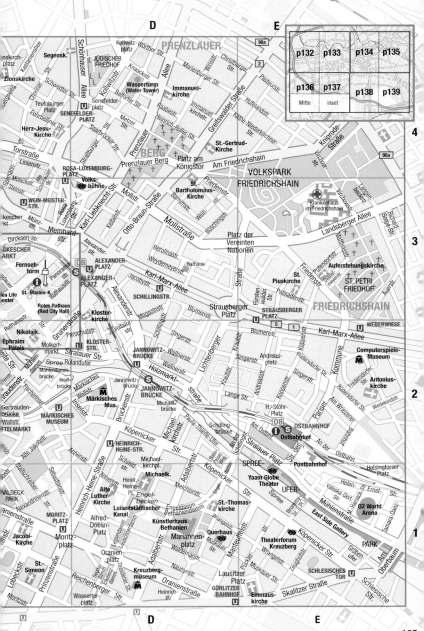

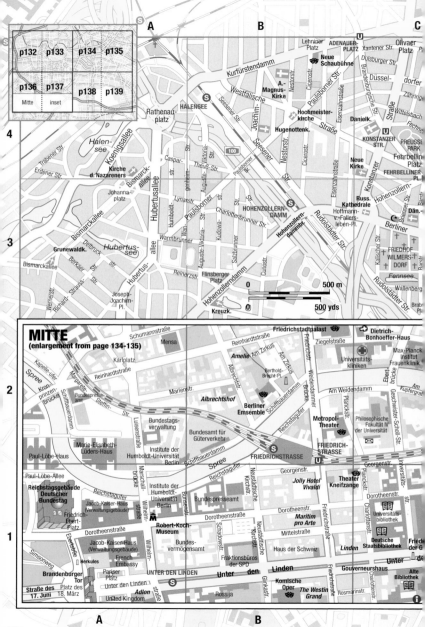

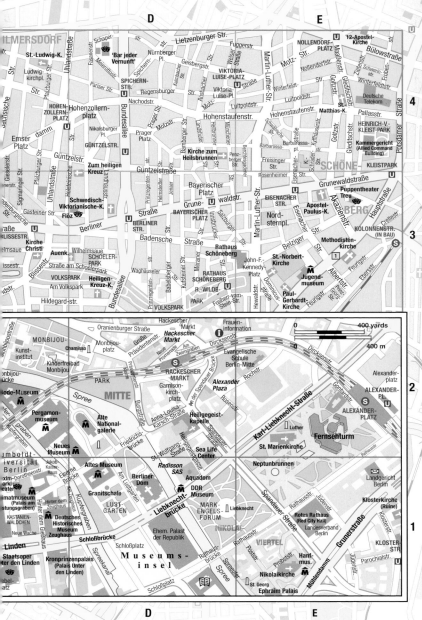

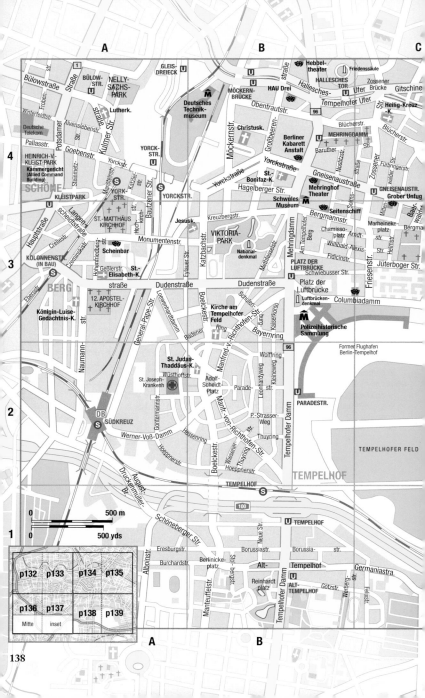

D   E

Moritzstr.
Wasserstr.
Wassertor-platz
Emmaus-kirche
Spreewald-platz
Schlesische Str.
PRINZENSTR.
Skalitzer Straße
Kohlfurter Str.
Admiralstr.
Mariannenstr.
Lausitzer Str.
Liebauer Str.
Sorauer Str.
Falckensteinstr.
Wiener Straße
Marienkirche
Tabor-kirche
BÖCKLER-PARK
Stadthaus
Böcklerpark
GÖRLITZER PARK
Görlitzer Str.
4
Baerwaldstr.
Urbanhafen
brücke
Tau
Traenkelufer
Kottbusser Brücke
Paul-Linke-Ufer
Ölberg-kirche
Maybachufer
Reichenberger Str.
Onkeler Str.
Forster Str.
Lenaustr.
Glogauer Str.
Ratiborstr.
Wiener Brücke
Karl-Kunger-Str.
Tzinnstr.
Wilmsstr.
Planufer
Admiral-brücke
179
Schinkelstr.
Hobrecht-brücke
Paul-Linke-Ufer
Martha-kirche
Lohmühlenstr.
Heidelberger Str.
ostelk.
Melanchthon-kirche
Planufer
Böcklstr.
SCHÖNLEINSTR.
Bürknerstr.
Sander-str.
Friedelstr.
Liberdastr.
Maybachufer
Manitusstr.
Grabow.
Crabow. Str.
Schmoller.
EUZBERG
Krankenhaus Am Urban
Dieffenbachstr.
Müllenhoff-str.
Christus-kirche
Boppstr.
Pflügerstr.
Thielen-brücke
Lohmüllen-brücke
Harzer Str.
Bouchéstr.
Urbanstraße

Kirche am Südstern
SÜDSTERN
Körtestr.
Graefestr.
Fichtestr.
Werner-Düttmann-Pl.
Urbanstr.
Hobrechtstr.
Friedelstr.
Reuterstr.
Reuter-platz
Nicodemus-kirche
Pflügerstr.
Nansenstr.
Pannier-str.
Weichsel-platz
Ossastr.
Weichselstr.
Weigandufer
Wildenbruch-straße
3
Fontanestr.
Freiligrathstr.
Hasenheide
Herrmann-platz
Sonnenallee
Weserstr.
Donaustr.
Fuldastr.
Weserstraße
Schan-dauer Str.
Wildenbruch-platz
Weserstraße
therstr.
Lilienthalstr.
St.-Johannes-Basilika
VOLKSPARK HASENHEIDE
HERMANN-PLATZ
Wissmannstr.
Karl-Marx-Str.
Jensstr.
Elbestr.
Laubestr.
Rosinen-bomber
Rixdorfer Teich
Columbiadamm
Naturdenkmal Jahneiche
Neuapostolische Kirche
Biebricher str.
Braunschweiger str.
RATHAUS NEUKÖLLN
Schönstedtstr.
Erkstr.
Sonnenallee
ISLAMISCHER FRIEDHOF
Flughafenstraße
Mahlower Str.
Selchower Str.
Weisestr.
BODDIN-STR.
Mainzer Str.
Boddin-Pl.
Boddinstr.
Neckarstr.
Rollbergstr.
Anzengruber Str.
Ganghoferstr.
Heimatmus. Neuköln
2
GARNISON-FRIEDHOF
Genezarethkirche
Herrfurth-platz
Herrfurth-str.
Schierker Promenade
Lichtenrader Str.
Oderstr.
Kienitzer Str.
Allerstr.
Okerstr.
Werbellinstr.
Falkstr.
Kopfstr.
Morusstr.
St-Clara-Kirche
LESSING-HÖHE
Leinestr.
Mittelweg
Thomas-Höhe
KARL-MARX-STR.
Uthmannstr.
Bernstorffstr.
Karl-Marx-Straße
Puppentheater-Museum
Karl-Marx-Pl.
Richardplatz

TEMPELHOFER FELD
LEINESTR.
Leinestr.
ST.-THOMAS-KIRCHHOF
Leykestr.
ST.-MICHAEL-KIRCHHOF
ST.-THOMAS-KIRCHHOF
Thomasstr.
NEUKÖLLN
Kirchhofstr.
Schöne-weider Str.
ST.-THOMAS-KIRCHHOF
KIRCHHOF JERUSALEM U. NEUE KIRCHE V
Warthe-platz
Warthestr.
Warthestr.
Jonas-str.
Schierker Str.
Nogatstr.
Emser str.
Isestr.
Selkestr.
KÖRNER-PARK
179
NEUKÖLLN
Kranoldstr.
Saalestr.
1
Oderstr.
Nettelstr.
ST.-JACOBI-KIRCHHOF II
HERMANNSTR.
Hermannstraße
HERMANNSTR.
E.-Müller-Platz
Ringbahnstr.
Silbersteinstr.
Werbellinstr.
NEUKÖLLN
Lahnstr.
OBERLANDSTR.
Oderstraßen-brücke
Emser Str.
Siegfriedstr.
Oberlandstr.
Silbersteinstr.
Herta-str.
Ph. Melanchthon-K.
Delbrück-str.
Kranold-platz
Bendastr.
Vivantes Klinikum
Britzer Damm
GRENZALLEE

D   E

139

Index

Insight Smart Guide: Berlin
Text by: Claudia Himmelreich, Ed Ward, William Boston
Updated by: Maria Lord
Proofread and indexed by: Neil Titman
Edited by: Sarah Sweeney/Cathy Muscat
All photos by: John Santa-Cruz/APA; Except: Action Press/Rex Features 54/55; Adenis/Laif 67; Debbie Bragg/Every night images 102; Geoffrey M. R. Hammond/istock photo 39BL; Claudia Himmelreich 111; Katja Hoffmann/Laif 102/103; JazzSign/Lebrecht 98; Naki Kouyioumtzis/ Axiom 114; Monika Rittershaus/ Lebrecht 96/97; Flikr Olivier Bruchez 89; Corrie Wingate/ APA 118; World Pictures/Photoshot 112/113; www.visitBerlin.de 54/64/65/119/124/125/130/131
Maps: James Macdonald and Mapping Ideas Ltd

Design Manager: **Steven Lawrence**
Art Editor: **Richard Cooke**
Series Editor: **Sarah Sweeney**

Second Edition 2011; First Edition 2008
©2011 Apa Publications (UK) Limited
Printed by CTPS-China
Worldwide distribution enquiries:
APA Publications GmbH & Co Verlag KG (Singapore branch); 7030 Ang Mo Kio Ave 5, 08-65 Northstar @ AMK, Singapore 569880; email: apasin@singnet.com.sg
Distributed in the UK and Ireland by:
GeoCenter International Ltd; Meridian House, Churchill Way West, Basingstoke, Hampshire, RG21 6YR; email: sales@geocenter.co.uk
Distributed in the United States by:
Ingram Publisher Services
One Ingram Blvd, PO Box 3006, La Vergne, TN 37086-1986; email: customer. service@ingrampublisherservices.com

Distributed in Australia by:
Universal Publishers; PO Box 307, St. Leonards, NSW 1590; email: sales@universalpublishers.com.au
Contacting the Editors
We would appreciate it if readers would alert us to errors or outdated information by writing to: Apa Publications, PO Box 7910, London SE1 1WE, UK; fax: (44 20) 7403 0290; email: insight@apaguide.co.uk

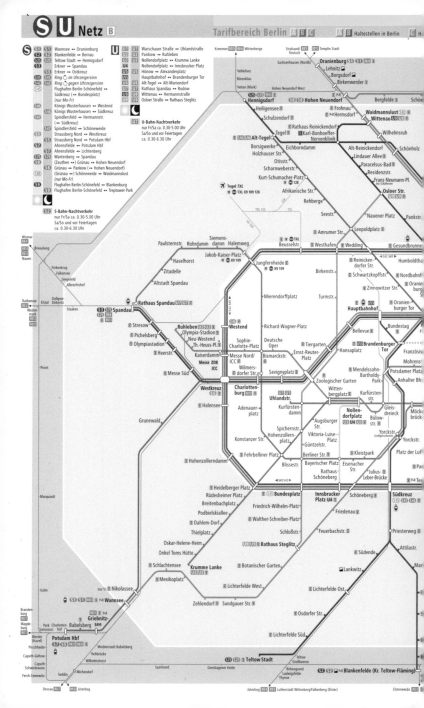

S U Netz B

Tarifbereich Berlin A B C   A B Haltestellen in Berlin   C H.

S-Bahn

- S1 Wannsee ↔ Oranienburg
- S2 Blankenfelde ↔ Bernau
- S25 Teltow Stadt ↔ Hennigsdorf
- S3 Erkner ↔ Spandau
- S5 Erkner ↔ Ostkreuz
- S41 Ring ↻ im Uhrzeigersinn
- S42 Ring ↺ gegen Uhrzeigersinn
- S45 Flughafen Berlin-Schönefeld ↔ Südkreuz (↔ Bundesplatz) (nur Mo-Fr)
- S46 Königs Wusterhausen ↔ Westend
- S47 Königs Wusterhausen ↔ Südkreuz (↔ Südkreuz)
- S5 Spindlersfeld ↔ Hermannstr. (↔ Südkreuz)
- S5 Spindlersfeld ↔ Schöneweide
- S5 Strausberg Nord ↔ Westkreuz
- S7 Ahrensfelde ↔ Potsdam Hbf
- S75 Ahrensfelde ↔ Lichtenberg
- S8 Wartenberg ↔ Spandau (Zeuthen ↔) Grünau ↔ Hohen Neuendorf
- S85 (Grünau ↔) Pankow (↔ Hohen Neuendorf) (Grünau ↔) Schöneweide ↔ Waidmannslust (nur Mo-Fr)
- S9 Flughafen Berlin-Schönefeld ↔ Blankenburg
- S9 Flughafen Berlin-Schönefeld ↔ Treptower Park

☾ **S-Bahn-Nachtverkehr** nur Fr/Sa ca. 0.30-5.00 Uhr Sa/So und vor Feiertagen ca. 0.30-6.30 Uhr

U-Bahn

- U1 Warschauer Straße ↔ Uhlandstraße
- U2 Pankow ↔ Ruhleben
- U3 Nollendorfplatz ↔ Krumme Lanke
- U4 Nollendorfplatz ↔ Innsbrucker Platz
- U5 Hönow ↔ Alexanderplatz
- U55 Hauptbahnhof ↔ Brandenburger Tor
- U6 Alt-Mariendorf ↔ Alt-Tegel
- U7 Rathaus Spandau ↔ Rudow
- U8 Wittenau ↔ Hermannstraße
- U9 Osloer Straße ↔ Rathaus Steglitz

☾ **U-Bahn-Nachtverkehr** nur Fr/Sa ca. 0.30-5.00 Uhr Sa/So und vor Feiertagen ca. 0.30-6.30 Uhr